CHRISTIANITY
in the
People's Republic
of
CHINA

G. Thompson Brown

. . . unless a grain of wheat falls into
the earth and dies, it remains alone;
but if it dies, it bears much fruit.
(John 12:24)

John Knox Press
ATLANTA

This book is dedicated to
Mardia whom I first met in Asia
and to
Mary, George, William, Charlotte, and Bruce
who added much to our years there

Library of Congress Cataloging in Publication Data

Brown, G. Thompson (George Thompson), 1921-
Christianity in the People's Republic of China.

Bibliography: p.
Includes index.
1. China—Church history—20th century.   I. Title.
BR1288.B76   1983   275.1'082   82-49018
ISBN 0-8042-1484-0

© copyright John Knox Press 1983
10 9 8 7 6 5 4 3 2 1
Printed in the United States of America
John Knox Press
Atlanta, Georgia 30365

PREFACE

Appreciation is expressed to the following friends without whose help this book could not have been written:

To Robert Burns, Chairperson, and to members of the Division of International Mission, General Assembly Mission Board, Presbyterian Church in the U.S., who assigned to me the task of writing a study book on China and provided me with the time to do so.

To Clifton Kirkpatrick, Director, and to the staff of the Division of International Mission for their encouragement, support, and advice.

To the many friends who supported the "Mission Possible Book Project."

To Paul Lauby, Executive Director of the United Board for Christian Higher Education in Asia, for providing the opportunity to return to China in 1980 where the idea of such a book originated.

To Charles West of Princeton Theological Seminary; Donald MacInnis of the Maryknoll Fathers and Brothers China Project; Arthur Glasser of Fuller Theological Seminary; Newton Thurber of the Program Agency of the United Presbyterian Church; and to my daughter Mary Brown Bullock of the National Academy of Science's Committee on Scholarly Communication with the People's Republic of China for reading the manuscript, suggesting numerous corrections and changes and advice.

To Franklin Woo, Director of the China Program of the National Council of Churches in the U.S.A., for *China Notes* and other resources published by his office.

To Raymond Fung of the World Council of Churches for permission to quote extensively from his "Case Studies from China" which appeared first in the *International Review of Mission*, April 1981, and has since been published under the title *Households of God on China's Soil*, Geneva, World Council of Churches, 1982.

To Joan Crawford and other staff members of the John Knox Press for putting it all together.

To Nancy Hardesty for copyediting the manuscript.

To Jeannette Scholes for patiently typing the several manuscript versions.

66707

To Columbia Theological Seminary for providing space and library resources.

*****

A word of explanation must be said about the complex problem of spelling Chinese names and places. The traditional way of rendering the Chinese characters into English is known as the Wade-Giles system and is the spelling that has become familiar to Western readers. A new system, known as *Pinyin,* has recently been adopted by the Chinese government and is used in all their official documents. In this book the *Pinyin* system is used as it is the form which now appears in most newspapers, maps, and current literature. Exceptions to this rule are certain cases where the older spelling has become firmly fixed in the English language, such as: Canton, Hong Kong, Chiang Kai-shek, and Sun Yat-sen. The first time a word is used and at times where there might be some confusion for the reader, the Wade-Giles spelling is put in parentheses.

CONTENTS

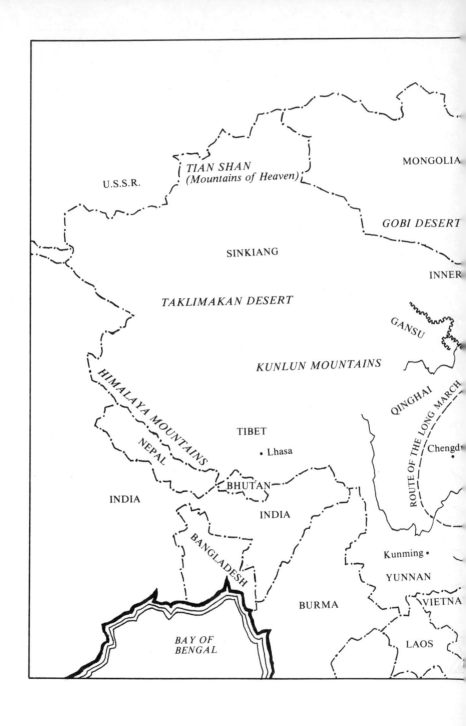

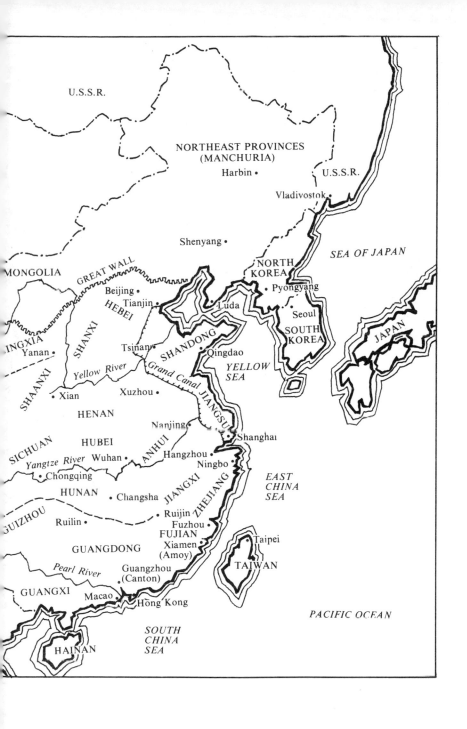

A BRIEF CHRONOLOGY
Christianity and Chinese History

Dynasties/Dates	Events
SHANG (1766–1122 B.C.)	PREHISTORY Mythical rulers. Beginning writing. Silk culture.
CHOU (1122–400)	GOLDEN AGE OF ANTIQUITY Confucius. Lao-tzu. Taoism.
WARRING STATES (400–246)	CIVIL STRIFE Mencius.
CH'IN (246–206)	UNIFICATION OF ALL CHINA Great Wall begun. Burning of Confucian classics.
HAN (206 B.C.–A.D.220)	FIRST CHINESE EMPIRE Triumph of Confucianism. Porcelain. Paper. Foreign trade. Literature. Empire extended.
THREE KINGDOMS (220–617) 400	FEUDALISM Nomadic invasions. Strife. Romantic literature. Introduction of Buddhism.

T'ANG
(617–907)
    635
    841
    900
	EMPIRE EXTENDED
	Buddhism flourishes. Trade with the West.
	Nestorian missionaries come to China.
	Buddhism persecuted. Confucianism resurgent.
	By end of the T'ang Dynasty traces of Christianity have all but disappeared.

FIVE DYNASTIES (907–960)	BARBARIAN ENCROACHMENTS Civil Strife.

SUNG
(960–1270)
    1206
    1227
	GOLDEN AGE OF CULTURE
	First printed book. Painting. Foreign trade. Abacus.
	Footbinding introduced.
	Genghis Khan unifies Mongol tribes.
	Genghis Khan dies after having defeated the Chin.

YUAN (MONGOL)
(1271–1368)
    1260–1294
    1271–1292
    1294
 	
    1368
	CHINA CONQUERED BY MONGOLS
	China culture prevails. Trade with the West. Paper money. Religious toleration.
	Kublai Khan.
	Marco Polo visits China.
	John of Montecorvino and Franciscans begin missionary work in Beijing (Peking).
	All traces of Christianity disappear from China.

MING		MONGOLS EXPELLED
(1368–1644)		Orderly government. Social stability. Examination system. Gentry class.
	1601	*Matteo Ricci and Jesuits arrive in Beijing.*
CH'ING (MANCHU)		CHINA CONQUERED BY MANCHUS
(1644-1911)		Confucianism supreme. Rapid rise in population.
	1645–1742	*The "Rites Controversy." Jesuit influence declines. Persecutions.*
	1807	*Robert Morrison, first Protestant missionary, arrives in Canton.*
	1839–60	"Opium Wars." "Unequal Treaties."
	1844	*Beginning of American Presbyterian mission work in Ningbo.*
	1850–64	Dynastic decline. Taiping Rebellion.
	1866	*Hudson Taylor founds China Inland Mission.*
	1867	*Begining of Presybterian, U.S. mission work in Hangzhou (Hangchow).*
	1883–85	Sino-French War. French take Indo-China.
	1894–1895	First Sino-Japanese War. Taiwan ceded to Japan. China loses Korea.
	1900	*The "Boxer Year." Thirty-thousand Chinese Christians, 235 missionaries lost their lives.*
REPUBLIC		NATIONALISM
(1911–49)		Modernization. Wars and civil strife. Economic woes.
	1911	Sun Yat-sen establishes the Republic.
	1912–27	Period of the warlords.
	1919	May Fourth student antiforcign riots.
	1921	Organization of the Chinese Communist party (CCP).
	1927	*First General Assembly of the Church of Christ in China—eleven synods, 120,000 communicants.* Break between Kuomintang (KMT) and Communists. Chiang Kai-shek begins northern campaign against warlords to unite country.
	1931–32	Japan occupies Manchuria.
	1934–35	Mao Zedong (Mao Tse-tung) begins "The Long March" to Yanan (Yenan).
	1937	Outbreak of Sino-Japanese War
	1941	Japanese bomb Pearl Harbor. *Most missionaries in China interned, evacuated.*
	1945	Japan surrenders.
	1946	*Missionaries return and resume work.*
	1946–49	Civil war. Inflation, chaos, corruption.

PEOPLE'S REPUBLIC (1949–/)		REVOLUTION

PEOPLE'S
REPUBLIC
(1949–/)

REVOLUTION

Social reform. Marxist ideology. Self-reliance.

1949	October 1—proclamation of the establishment of the People's Republic of China (PRC) by Mao Zedong.
1950	*Beginning of the Three-Self Patriotic Movement. Accusation meetings. Missionaries begin to leave.* The Korean conflict.
1952	*Last PCUS missionaries, Dr. and Mrs. Frank W. Price, leave China.*
1956–57	"Let a hundred flowers bloom" followed by antirightist campaign.
1958–60	Great Leap Forward.
1960	China and Russia break relationships.
1966–76	The Great Proletarian Cultural Revolution.
1971	Beginning of "thaw" in U.S.–China relations. PRC seated at the U.N. "Ping-pong diplomacy."
1972	U.S. President Richard Nixon visits China. Shanghai Communique.
1975	Chiang Kai-shek dies.
1976	January: Zhou Enlai (Chou En-lai) dies. September: Mao Zedong dies. Hua Guofeng (Kuo-feng) appointed chairman and premier. October: "Gang of Four" arrested.
1977	Deng Xiaoping (Teng Hsiao-ping) reappointed as vice-premier. The Four Modernizations.
1978	"Billboard Democracy." U.S. President Jimmy Carter announces recognition of PRC.
1979	*Mo En Church reopens. First public worship service in Shanghai in thirteen years. Churches across China begin to open. Bishop K. H. Ting leads first delegation of Christian leaders from PRC to visit U.S.*
1980	*Formation of the Chinese Christian Council. Reopening of Nanjing Theological Seminary.* Hu Yaobang appointed Mao's successor.
1981	*NCC delegation from U.S. invited to China in first official visit.*
1982	Twelfth Party Congress adopts new constitution.

INTRODUCTION

The personal reasons why a book is written may not be important. A book ought to be able to stand, for better or worse, on its own merits. Yet a reader has the right to know the perspective and the inevitable bias of the one who writes, the reasons which motivated the author to give time and energy to writing the book. Especially is this true for another book on China. China is so vast a country that we each experience it in our own individual way. The way this author has come to his knowledge of China undoubtedly colors and influences what he has felt and what he has written.

My China experience began at birth for I was born in 1921 at the mountain resort town of Yushan (Kuling) in the Yangtze River valley. My parents, the Rev. Frank A. and Charlotte Brown, were Presbyterian Church, U.S., missionaries and served there for most of the time between 1910 and 1949. These four decades spanned the tumultuous years from the fall of the Manchu Dynasty to the first days of the People's Republic. We lived in the city of Xuzhou (Suchow), a railroad junction in northern Jiangsu (Kiangsu) Province. Because of its strategic location it was fought over by the revolutionaries of 1911 and the nationalists in 1927. The Japanese bombed the city and besieged it in 1938, and a decisive battle between the armies of Mao Zedong (Mao Tse-tung) and Chiang Kai-shek was fought there in 1948. In his memoirs my father mentions ten revolutions, battles, and looting episodes which he experienced in our city up to the year 1934. Then he lost count! The China I knew as a boy was a land of warlords, bandits, crowded troop trains, refugees, evacuations, famines, and Yellow River floods. But those years are also filled with happy memories of family, boyhood Chinese friends, life in the dormitory at the Shanghai American School, summers at Qingdao (Tsingtao), visits to country villages in the old Model T Ford, and travel down the Grand Canal by Chinese junk.

My second China experience came in 1945 when I returned as a lieutenant in the United States Army and was assigned to the China Theater Headquarters in Shanghai. I was able to do some sightseeing in Beijing (Peking) and to visit our old home in Xuzhou where my parents had just resumed their missionary service. My army assignment involved verifying the deaths and locating the graves of United States personnel who died during the war, and it was of great interest to find the grave of Captain John Birch, for whom the society was named, on the hill overlooking our home! I observed the abortive efforts of General George Marshall's peace teams who were attempting to work out agreements between the People's Liberation Army (PLA) and Kuomintang (KMT). The China I remember from 1945 was a war-wasted, war-weary land of civil strife, corruption, and terrible inflation.

My next China experience came when I received an invitation from the United Board for Christian Higher Education in Asia to accompany their delegation to China in June 1980. What would it be like to return to the land of one's birth after thirty-four years and a revolution? Can one really ever go home again? I accepted the invitation with strange mixed feelings of excitement and apprehension.

We arrived in Beijing on June 4, 1980. There were twenty-three in our delegation headed by Dr. Nathan Pusey, former president of Harvard University and chairman of the United Board. His reputation and that of Harvard gave us a receptive hearing and the red carpet treatment.

We visited universities in Beijing, Nanjing (Nanking), Shanghai, Chengdu (Chengtu), and Guangzhou (Canton). We were especially interested in the campuses of the former Christian colleges—such as Yenching, Ginling, St. John's, West China Union—all of which had been incorporated into the state university system. We talked freely with faculty and students. They told us that the massive concrete statues of Mao which dominated their campus were an embarrassment, but there was nowhere else to put them! We met with officials of the Ministry of Education and on one memorable evening were invited to the Great Hall of the People for an audience with Hu Qiaomu, chief ideologist and influential member of the Communist party secretariat. The *People's Daily* reported our visit, and we were glad they included the name "Christian" in the name of our delegation. We were given a reception and briefing at the United States Embassy by Stapleton Roy, deputy chief of mission, whose father, a retired United Presbyterian China missionary, was a member of our group.

Although not always on the itinerary, we were able to meet with

Christian leaders in every city we visited. Some of us spent a morning with the pastors of the Protestant Church in Beijing and discussed the present state of religion in China with Zhao Fusan of the Institute for the Study of World Religions. In Nanjing we met with Bishop K. H. Ting (Ding Guangxun), leader in the Three-Self Movement and one of the most articulate representatives for Christianity in China. We met with pastors in Chengdu and worshiped in the newly opened church there. In Shanghai we visited the Mo En Church. It was on a weekday, and the church was being used by a middle school. Two large pictures of Helmsman Mao and Chairman Hua hung over the pulpit. Apparently they were taken down or covered when the sanctuary is used for worship.

I returned to China again in the spring of 1981 with a small delegation representing the Presbyterian Church in the United States. The purpose of our trip was twofold: to establish personal relationships with leaders of the Christian Church in China, and to follow up on some possible projects. Dr. Paul S. Crane, surgeon from Nashville and chairperson of the Division of International Mission's Asia Committee, was the head of the delegation. We visited Hong Kong, Beijing, Xuzhou, Nanjing, Suzhou (Soochow), and Shanghai. In each city we visited with Christian leaders and pastors although often these events were not on the itinerary and had to be squeezed into a busy day of sightseeing. In Hong Kong we were privileged to meet with Bishop K. H. Ting and a delegation of Chinese church leaders attending a conference sponsored by the Christian Council of Asia. In Beijing we were briefed on the current religious situation by Zhao Fusan. In Nanjing we were thrilled to meet with the faculty and students of the newly opened Union Seminary and to visit a church full of scaffolding which was being repaired for a grand reopening on Easter Sunday. In Suzhou we were moved to tears by the gracious hospitality and radiant faith of a group of pastors who entertained us with tea and led us in an informal worship service in a small attic room. In Shanghai we visited the offices of the national committee of the Chinese Christian Three-Self Movement and heard an explanation of why the churches had to emphasize their own self-reliance and make a clean break with the past.

Fascination with China took me back in June 1982. This time my wife, Mardia Hopper, and I accompanied a tour group of church people. We visited for the first time Xian (Sian) and Guilin (Kweilin) and talked with friends made on previous trips in other cities.

Perhaps the one most lasting impression of these trips was the friendliness of the Chinese people—particularly our Christian brothers and sisters. We had every reason to believe that this was genuine and sincere. They made it clear that the self-reliance of the Christian community and its freedom from dependence on Western organizations, structures, and money was a high priority. But they also were emphatic in saying that they wanted to renew their relationships with Christians and churches outside China as long as these relationships are formed on the basis of mutual respect.

For me the most moving experience took place on the railroad platform of my home town of Xuzhou on June 8, 1980. Our train was to pass through Xuzhou at eight o'clock Sunday morning and be at the station for fifteen minutes. I had tried in vain to get permission from the travel service to leave the group there, visit with friends, and rejoin the party in Nanjing later that evening. To no avail! It was all blamed on "travel formalities." This was a bitter disappointment. But while in Beijing I had sent two telegrams to people whom I had known long years before. I gave the time of the train's arrival and said I would like to see them even for a brief visit on the station platform. Our guides had promised to do what they could to permit me to meet my friends, but I think they doubted whether anyone would show up. As the train came closer to the station, I became more apprehensive. I had talked so much about my home town and my friends that it would have been a great loss of "face" if nobody appeared. Maybe my friends were busy. Maybe they would not remember who I was or would not want to see me. After all it had been thirty-four years since I had been there, and then I had been wearing the uniform of the United States Army.

As the train pulled into the station, I jumped out on the platform and was overwhelmed with joy to see Pastor Dai, eighty-one years old and on crutches, and my boyhood friend James Wang. They were smiling, bowing, welcoming! For fifteen minutes we had a wonderful time of fellowship and renewal. Their English was much better than I had expected. Then I asked, somewhat guardedly for a large crowd had gathered around to see what was happening, the one question on my mind: "Are there any groups of Christians meeting in Xuzhou?" The response was shouted back: "Six house congregations are meeting regularly! Soon we hope to move back into the West Gate Church which is being rehabilitated with government aid!"

The train was about to leave. Pastor Dai presented me with a book of water-colored landscape paintings he had drawn. I gave my friends the book I had brought for this occasion—the Good News Bible in English.

On my return to China in 1981 our group was able to spend two days in Xuzhou. I visited the old mission compound and saw the house where I had lived as a boy. It was in a terrible state of disrepair but still being used by local cadres, local party functionaries.

Three of our delegation were permitted to visit the old mission hospital which had been started by Dr. Nettie Donaldson Grier in 1907. For seventy-three years it had given more or less uninterrupted service ministering to the sick, the lame, and the blind! It was crowded with patients as it always had been in the past. In "Aunt Nettie's" day, the hospital had thirty beds. Today it has four hundred. Each year two hundred students graduate from the attached medical school. A much newer reinforced concrete structure towers beside the original old gray brick missionary building. We were served tea in what must have been an upper bedroom of "Aunt Nettie's" house. A few older members of the hospital staff had been there during the time of the missionaries. The superintendent said that the reputation of the hospital for good medicine and service extended far and wide and that this was based on the tradition they had inherited as a mission hospital.

Saturday afternoon we visited the old West Gate Presbyterian Church, which I had attended as a boy. It had been open for about six months. The interior was freshly painted and there were new benches purchased from funds received from the government as partial payment for the years they had used it. We were enthusiastically invited to the church services the next morning. But our guide said that it could not be arranged. Off limits! Another disappointment. We argued with them about their decision but did not want to do anything to embarrass our Christian friends. In the end something of a compromise was reached. One of our number, Dr. Insik Kim, was taken alone to the service and permitted to observe from an open doorway what was going on. He is a

Korean-American, and would not stand out like a sore thumb in the crowd! Dr. Kim reported the church was filled to capacity with an overflowing and enthusiastic congregation!

In the evening a group of four Christian leaders came to the guest house for some conversations with three of us. We were alone, for the guides had taken the rest of the delegation to a Chinese opera. Dr. David Chu, Chinese-born Presbyterian missionary to Korea and a member of our delegation, was our interpreter when we needed one. We talked late into the evening about the Old China and the New China, about friends in China and friends in the United States and friends in heaven. Most of all we talked about the church of Jesus Christ. How had it gone? What had happened to the little congregations in the country which had been started by my father? Almost all of the older Christians had died or moved away. But there were new believers! How they had heard the gospel was difficult to say because there had been no one to preach or teach. "God works in strange ways," they said.

The church of Jesus Christ was alive and well! In spite of all the dire predictions and prophecies of failure, the Christian community had endured one of the darkest periods of church history and was indeed flourishing. This is the single most important fact coming out of China today.

The China I knew as a boy is gone. The once familiar street signs and places—Bubbling Well Road, the Race Track, the Shanghai American School on Avenue Petain, the Shanghai Hong Kong Banking Corporation on the Bund, Legation Street in Peking—have disappeared. The United States Asiatic Fleet, the British Fusiliers, and the Japanese Marines have long since departed.

The missionary era has also come to an end. Perhaps it had to die in order that its mission could be accomplished.

> . . . unless a grain of wheat falls into the earth and dies, it remains alone; but if it dies, it bears much fruit. (John 12:24)

1

Who Would Have Believed It?

Then the LORD said to his people, "Keep watching the
nations around you, and you will be astonished at what you
see. I am going to do something that you will not believe
when you hear about it."

(Habakkuk 1:5 TEV)

No one could have predicted it! It was beyond the wildest im-
agination of the "China watchers." "Old China hands" did not think
it possible. It came as a shock to theologians both within and outside
China. But in God's own time it happened.

That time was September 2, 1979. The place was the Mo En
Church (formerly Moore Memorial Methodist Church) in Shanghai.
Two American eyewitnesses were there for the historic event and this is
what they reported:

> As we were gently hurried down the right aisle, Dr. [Paul] Lauby and
> I could see that we were the only non-Chinese in attendance. We
> quickly discovered that over a thousand people had more than filled
> the main floor and balcony. An extra wooden bench was placed next
> to one of the already filled pews by a middle-aged man who insisted
> on sitting behind a pillar so that I could see the platform. Behind me
> a young man who spoke a little English identified the four men in
> their seventies sitting on the platform. He indicated the denomination
> with which each participant had been affiliated: the Methodist minis-
> ter offered the welcome and benediction, the Presbyterian pastor read
> the scriptural lesson, the clergyman from The Little Flock (an indige-
> nous Chinese Church) gave the pastoral prayer, and a Baptist pastor
> preached the sermon.

> On the left of the platform a man in his late twenties played an an-
> cient upright piano. The congregation was predominantly over 55
> years of age, but many young married couples were also in attend-
> ance. As in any church around the world, teenagers and young adults
> had found their way to the balcony. To my left, above the balcony,

were three large gothic windows. Rocks had smashed huge holes
· through each of them.

For the congregation the most fervent part of the service was the
opening prayer. To my right, my benchmate swayed, his head tilted
back, weeping, occasionally joining others in responding aloud. I
still remained the sympathetic observer. But when the congregation
swept into "Holy, Holy, Holy" and "Joyful, Joyful, We Adore
Thee," I became a fellow worshiper, sharing the congregation's
emotion and tears. It was easy to believe in that moment that even
if the Christian minority played an obscure role in public events,
Christianity could never be eradicated from the fabric of Chinese
life.[1]

What had taken place at Mo En was Shanghai's first public worship
service in thirteen years, and it set off a chain reaction. Churches which
had been used for decades as warehouses, factories, and schools began
to reopen for Christian worship across the length and breadth of China's vast land. Many pastors were released from work camps and
sought out to lead these congregations. Perhaps even more amazingly,
when these churches were opened, they were filled with overflow
crowds. A church that many observers thought had died was alive and
well!

How did it happen? What does it mean for China and for us? These
are questions which lay behind the writing of this book, for surely this
must be one of the most amazing survival stories of our time.

But it is more than that. The opening of the churches was part of a
larger picture of other profound changes taking place in China following the death of Mao. These events have dramatically changed the relationships between our two countries. American Presidents Richard
Nixon, Gerald Ford, and Jimmy Carter have been toasted in the Great
Hall of the People opposite the mausoleum where Mao has been laid to
rest. China's strong man Deng Xiaoping was *Time* magazine's Man of
the Year for 1978 and has triumphantly toured the United States from
shore to shore. Bob Hope has done his act on the Great Wall. Coca-
Cola is now being bottled in Beijing. Pierre Cardin has enthralled a
perplexed proletarian audience with a fashion show near the place
where Mao exhorted the Red Guards to beware of the evils of decadent
western culture. Texaco and DuPont commercials adorn the landscape
not far from the once "Forbidden City." Americans are no longer the

"running dogs" and "paper tigers" but honored "foreign guests" and "experts"!

To Change China

Events in the Middle Kingdom have had a strange fascination for Americans ever since the China clipper ships "discovered" China during the latter part of the eighteenth century. Some have called it "the American itch to change China." Merchants, educators, adventurers, missionaries, philanthropists, reformers, generals, and diplomats have all taken their turn. There was John Hay and the "Open Door Policy," Frederick Townsend Ward and his "Ever Victorious Army," Herbert Hoover and his engineers, John D. Rockefeller, Jr., and the Peking Union Medical College, J. Leighton Stuart and Yenching University, General Joseph W. Stilwell and the Burma Road, Colonel C. L. Chennault and the Flying Tigers, George C. Marshall and his "Peace Teams." All were Americans who made valiant efforts to change China on China's behalf. All at one point or another were frustrated in the attempt.

Part of the American fascination and frustration over China has been that it simply did not want to change. Through the centuries it has seemed that we in the West have been more interested in China, than China has been in us. In response to overtures for trade and commerce from British King George III's ambassador to Beijing in 1793, the emperor of the Celestial Kingdom replied: "We possess all things. I set no value on things strange and ingenious and have no use for your country's manufactures."[2]

America's relationships with China have had as many "ups" and "downs" as a ride on a roller coaster. When China was at the zenith of its empire, there was *admiration* for China's ancient history and culture. The very name "China" conjures up thoughts of fine porcelain, brocaded silk, cloisonné, jade, Ming vases, rugs, and bronze images. As China's empire began to disintegrate under the later Ch'ing emperors, admiration became *contempt* for its perceived backwardness, superstition, and corruption. This changed to *compassion* expressed through mission programs and philanthropy. Massive efforts were made to establish hospitals, schools, and orphanages and to engage in famine relief. For a while there was *fear* of being overwhelmed by

China's millions, and in response to the "Yellow Peril" the United States' Congress adopted restrictive immigration laws. When there was a common enemy to fight, *admiration* returned for China's heroic and sacrificial defense against the Japanese invaders. This changed quickly to *disenchantment* when, at the end of World War II, China turned from Western liberalism to Russian Marxism. Disenchantment deepened to open *hostility* as our armies clashed in the mountains of Korea. When the fighting ended, there was a period of *disengagement* when we lost all contact with each other. With the very recent normalization of relationships and the fall of the "Gang of Four," we now seem to vacillate between *euphoria* and *skepticism*, unable to make up our minds as to what to believe about the flood of reports pouring out of the Middle Kingdom.

For the Christian, China has had an even deeper fascination. This was the "mission field" par excellence. First the Nestorians came in A.D. 635 and flourished under the T'ang Dynasty. But by the end of that dynasty (A.D. 900), virtually all traces of Nestorian Christianity had disappeared except for one stone monument in Xian. The Franciscans had their turn in the fourteenth century under the Mongols. But at the end of the Mongol era all traces of Christianity had disappeared. Matteo Ricci and the Jesuits arrived at the Mongol court in 1601. They taught astronomy and mathematics and brought a new faith which they called "the religion of the Heavenly Lord." Robert Morrison, the first Protestant missionary, arrived from England in 1807 and after seven years baptized his first convert. In its heyday China was the largest "mission field" in the world. In 1926, 8,000 Protestant missionaries were serving in that land.

And then, suddenly, all was changed. Four years from the time Mao Zedong proclaimed the establishment of the People's Republic on October 1, 1949, all missionaries had either left China, were in jail, or were under house arrest. Within sixteen years not a single Christian church was open in that vast land. It had all come to an end. Or had it?

Some Unanswered Questions

Our interest in China is more than just a fascination with a people on the other side of the globe who have behaved quite differently from our expectations. Recent events there have raised some perplexing questions of considerable significance for our understanding of the Christian faith and our view of the church's mission.

There is, first, a *theological problem*. Mao's revolution, at least in its early years, was a great success. All the pests were destroyed. Prostitutes and beggars disappeared from the streets. Gambling and opium smoking were ended. The basic minimum requirements of life—food, clothing, health care, primary education—were provided for most of China's millions. All these good things, to which every Christian would say a hearty "Amen," have been accomplished. The China that resisted change for its Western advisors has undergone a radical transformation. This has happened, not in the name of Jesus Christ in accordance with the Scriptures, but in the name of Mao Zedong and his little red book!

A high price was paid for these changes. An evaluation of any revolution must reckon with the cost in human lives and the loss of personal freedom. How do we as Christians understand Mao's revolution—perhaps the most momentous event to date in the second half of the twentieth century? Theologians and "China watchers" have held widely differing viewpoints on this issue. Some have seen in it the coming of the kingdom of God on earth. Others have called it the work of the devil.

During the Cultural Revolution (1966–76) Christian visitors to China spoke in euphoric terms about the creation of a "new man" who was disciplined and self-sacrificing, kind and generous. Yet today the assessment given this period of history by the Chinese themselves is that, far from being idyllic, it was a catastrophe. How shall we then understand Mao's attempt to create a new breed of humanity?

Then there is a *missiological problem*. Over the years the Roman Catholic and Protestant churches of Europe and North America had made a massive commitment of people, funds, and energies toward the conversion of China. The church was there for one hundred and fifty years through revolutions, floods, famines, antiforeign riots, and civil war. The effort was not without great sacrifice. In 1900 the "Boxer Year," more than two hundred missionaries gave their lives. Between 1874 and 1926 forty small children of Presbyterian Church, U.S., missionary parents died and were buried there.[3]

Yet after all these efforts and sacrifices, less than one-half of one percent of the Chinese people ever accepted the gospel the missionaries preached. What went wrong? The question must be raised as to the relationship between the missionary movement and the colonial system of the times, with which it was so closely identified. On the other hand, what went right? The survival of a church at all, after what has happened during the long years since 1949, is witness to the fact that some things must have been done well. What lessons can we learn from the China experience that might help us in mission to other parts of the world—and in the United States of America?

Then there is an *ecclesiastical question*. With the reopening of the Mo En Church in Shanghai, Christianity became visible again. But the church that has emerged from the shadows is not the same as before. The same God is worshiped. The same Bible is read. The same hymns are sung. But something is different. The old forms and structures have disappeared. A postdenominational era has begun. Surely we need to listen to, understand, and learn from this church and these Christians!

China is of interest, not just to the Sinologist, but to every Christian who has a serious concern for the mission of the church of Jesus Christ in the revolutionary world of today.

Interpreting the China Experience

Because of the relevance of these questions for Christian faith and responsibility, Roman Catholic and Protestant mission boards and agencies have given high priority to the study, evaluation, and interpretation of what might be called the "China experience." Since the 1950s the Division of Overseas Ministries of the National Council of Churches has been engaged in a China Program and in the publication of the quarterly *China Notes*. In Louvain, Belgium, the Lutheran World Federation and Pro Mundi Vita, a Roman Catholic information and research center, sponsored an ecumenical colloquium entitled "Christian Faith and the Chinese Experience," in September 1974 with more than one hundred Roman Catholic and Protestant scholars taking part.

The Maryknoll Fathers have recently initiated a major research project which will prepare a critical history of the society's work in China. The United Board for Christian Higher Education in Asia sent a

delegation to China in June 1980 and is now in the process of implementing various exchange and research projects. Churches in Great
Britain now cooperate in the China Study Project which publishes a
documentation quarterly *Religion in The People's Republic of China*.
The Canadian Council of Churches' China Programme held an international conference on China in October 1981 on the general theme
"God's Call to a New Beginning." This conference was significant in
that ten Roman Catholic and Protestant church leaders from China participated in the discussions along with more than one hundred fifty representatives of churches from around the world.

A number of China research and study centers have opened in Hong
Kong. The United Methodists have a China Liaison Office there which
publishes the newsletter *China Talk*. The Christian Study Centre at Tao
Fong Shan in Kowloon, originally established for Christian-Buddhist
dialogue, is now giving more and more emphasis to China study and
interpretation. The Chinese Church Research Center, representative of
independent church groups, publishes the quarterly *China and the
Church Today*. Such is the interest and excitement of the worldwide
Christian church in China studies and interpretation today!

Presbyterians have been no exception to this enthusiasm to learn
from our new relationship with China and the Christians there. The
1979 General Assemblies of the United Presbyterian Church
(UPCUSA) and the Presbyterian Church in the United States (PCUS)
adopted joint statements which called for

> . . . the development of ecumenical contacts with Christian commu-
> nities in China so that we can learn from each others' experience and
> share our faith, concerns and commitments. . . .

> . . . becoming better acquainted with Chinese culture, history, reli-
> gion, and politics through the study of materials which have been
> prepared for this purpose and through contacts with persons who
> have informed interest of experience in China. . . .

> . . . the welcoming of visiting Chinese scholars, students and guests
> into our homes, churches, communities and places of work . . . spe-
> cial sensitivity for mutual learning and sharing. . . .[4]

A joint Presbyterian China Conference was sponsored by the two
churches and held in Richmond, Va., in May 1980 to give guidance to

the Program Agency (UPCUSA) and General Assembly Mission Board (PCUS) in the development of a China program. A joint theological statement entitled "Theological Foundations for Ecumenical Cooperation" was adopted by the conference and later ratified by the two denominations. Two newsletters, *China Update* (UPCUSA) and *China News* (PCUS), are now mailed to interested subscribers.

The response from the churches to all this China study and interpretation has been one of great enthusiasm and perplexity. There has been enthusiasm because of the widespread fascination with China's size, age, mystique, and culture on the part of the American public; the interest of Christian people in the extensive missionary commitment in that land prior to 1949; and the reemergence of the Christian church in that land, which must be one of the most inspiring episodes in the history of Christianity. There has also been perplexity because of the widespread ignorance of the events which have taken place during the past thirty years; the varied interpretations of China's Marxist revolution which have swung from one extreme to the other; and the flood of new information, much of it contradictory, which has come out of China since the normalization of relationships between our two countries.

The people of China—one fourth of the world's population—need to be understood. The Christians of China—a tiny, growing, vital minority with an amazing record of endurance—also need understanding. It is our hope that in this process of understanding China, the mission of the church of Jesus Christ in our revolutionary times will become more clear. To understand that church and those people, we must seek to examine the events through which they have passed.

2

Wise Men from the West

Listen to me, my people,
  listen to what I say:
I give my teaching to the nations;
  my laws will bring them light.
I will come quickly and save them;
  the time of my victory is near.
I myself will rule over the nations.
  Distant lands wait for me to come;
  they wait with hope for me to save them.
          (Isaiah 51:4–5 TEV)

Early Christian Beginnings (635–1700)

The Nestorians.   When did Christianity first come to China? The event is chiseled into the stone of the remarkable Nestorian Monument of Xian (Sian), erected in 781 but not unearthed for nearly a thousand years. The monument tells of the arrival of the monk A-lo-pên at the capital city of the T'ang Dynasty in the year 635. A-lo-pên, bearer of the "Luminous Religion," was received with honor by the emperor; translations of sacred books were made; and a monastery under royal sanction was built. It is said that the emperor himself studied the religion and ordered its dissemination.

The "Luminous Religion" referred to on the monument was Nestorianism, a sect condemned as heretical by the Council of Ephesus in 431 because of its belief that in Jesus the divine and human existed as two distinct natures. The Nestorians separated themselves from Byzantine Christianity and spread eastward into Persia. Their missionaries followed the caravans along the trade routes of Central Asia, crossing into China on the ancient Silk Road.

The China into which the Nestorians came was at the zenith of its power. The T'ang Dynasty then ruled what was probably the most powerful and wealthiest empire in the world. Trade with India and the Near East was flourishing. Nestorian communities were established in the trading centers of the empire and for some decades enjoyed considerable success. However, in 845 the emperor, an ardent Taoist, issued an edict proscribing Buddhism and ordered all monks to return to private life. Apparently Nestorians were included in the persecution since three thousand foreign monks were referred to in the edict. The Nestorians fell on evil times and by the end of the T'ang Dynasty (907) had almost completely disappeared. Later under the Mongol Dynasty (1271–1368) the Nestorians made something of a comeback but then vanished altogether. Nestorianism may have introduced to the Buddhists the practice of praying for the dead, but apart from this there is no evidence that they had any lasting influence on Chinese life and thought.

Nestorians were in China for at least two and a half centuries. Why did they fail to win a foothold? Kenneth Scott Latourette gives these reasons:

> Nestorian Christianity appears never to have ceased to be primarily the faith of a foreign community. . . . Nestorianism seems to have depended chiefly upon foreign leadership and support.
>
> In the second place, Nestorianism arrived at a time when no especial need for a new faith was felt. . . . The older native faiths were popular and strongly entrenched. . . .
>
> In the third place, the Nestorian missionaries were separated from the center of their church by immense distances and could look for little assistance and inspiration from the main body of their fellow believers.[1]

The problems faced by the Nestorians—a foreign community, foreign leadership and support, immense distances—would be faced again and again by those missionaries who followed.

The Franciscans.   With the collapse of the T'ang Dynasty, the empire was torn by internal disorder. China lost control of the passes of Central Asia and access to the trade routes to the West. Revival of Christian efforts in China had to wait more than three hundred years for more auspicious circumstances.

Strangely enough, this opportunity came with the Mongol conquest in the thirteenth century. Genghis Khan and his Golden Horde swept out of Central Asia to overwhelm not only all of China, but Persia, northwestern India, parts of Russia, and even as far west as Poland. His grandson, Kublai Khan, consolidated the vast empire and brought it peace. Trade and commerce across the land bridge to Europe began again. Among the merchants making the long trek was Marco Polo, whose account of his travels and the fabulous civilization which he found in China aroused intense interest in that faraway land.

Pope Nicholas III was undoubtedly influenced by this report when he initiated a new effort to carry Christianity to China. A Franciscan by the name of John of Montecorvino arrived in Cambaluc (Beijing) in 1294 bearing a letter from the pope addressed to the Emperor Kublai. It had taken him three years to make the trip. In the meantime Kublai had died, but the missionary was welcomed by his successor and soon won the favor of the court which was then remarkably open to foreign influence and religion. In his letters back home, John speaks of erecting two churches in the capital and of baptizing six thousand converts. These included a number of young boys whom he bought (!) from pagan parents. Many of his converts were aliens in the service of the Mongols. For thirty years John labored in Cambaluc, never returning to Europe. As long as he lived, the church enjoyed the benevolent support of the court. In his letters he writes pathetically of loneliness, of growing old before his time, and pleads for the appointment of additional priests.

When John's missionary letters arrived in Rome, they created a sensation. Additional missionaries were appointed, but most of those sent died on the long, dangerous overland trek. Yet the work did prosper, as there are records of Franciscan centers in a number of Chinese cities.

During the latter part of the fourteenth century, the Franciscan mission began to decline. The reasons seem to parallel those for the failure of the Nestorians six hundred years earlier. Most of the converts were non-Chinese people living on the fringes of the empire. There was no evidence that any Chinese were trained for the priesthood. The church at home, suffering from the ravages of the Black Plague, was not able to support the effort across the vast distance. The Mongol empire disintegrated in 1368, again bringing disruption to the overland trade routes. The Franciscans were identified with the Mongol invaders, and when their dynasty fell, the Franciscan presence came to an end. With the ascension of the Mings, all Christian influence disappeared from the Chinese empire.

The Jesuits. Two hundred years were to pass before another attempt would be made. During these centuries China lost all contact and consciousness of Europe. Under a native dynasty, China became more and more disdainful of all things foreign and more locked into its proud traditions of the past. Confucianism reigned supreme.

In Europe it was the Age of Discovery. The Portuguese made their way around the Cape of Good Hope to India, the Spice Islands, and beyond. National states were on the rise. The Renaissance was in the air, bringing new technologies and science. Within the Roman Catholic Church the counterreformation was bringing renewal.

The Jesuits were spearheading a new missionary advance, and it was destined that they would make the next attempt to "open China." As in the case of the Nestorians and Franciscans, they followed the footsteps of the traders. The Portuguese had been able to establish a trading center at Macao in the mid-sixteenth century. For the next three hundred years this was the center for European commerce. That indomitable missionary, Francis Xavier, (1506–52), had opened a Jesuit mission in Japan in 1549, but always the pioneer, his restless soul was then possessed with a passion for doing the same for China. Portuguese authorities at Macao were bitterly opposed to his efforts, fearing that the introduction of a foreign religion into China would disrupt the delicate balance which they had achieved in their relations with the Chinese officials. Xavier failed in his efforts and died on a small, now-forgotten island off the coast of the mainland.

Success came when a permanent Jesuit residence was established at a small city not far from Canton in 1583. One of the Jesuits was a brilliant young man named Matteo Ricci, who was skilled in mathematics, astronomy, and clock-making. More than any other person, the Jesuit success story can be attributed to him. Initially they aroused great suspicion and endured many rebuffs. At first Ricci and his associates dressed in the saffron robes of Buddhist priests to indicate the religious nature of their mission. But when they became aware of the general disrespect paid the Buddhist clergy, they changed their dress to that of the scholarly class. This proved to be something of a breakthrough in winning the support of the official class and the respect of the common people.

In 1601 Ricci was able to establish residence at the capital city of Beijing. Another breakthrough was achieved when the Jesuits were asked to undertake the reform of the calendar when it was discovered that serious errors had distorted Chinese calculations of the times and seasons. Ricci, by his patience, scholarly ways, respect for Chinese customs and culture, and attempt to adapt Christianity to Chinese teachings and practice, won the confidence of the rulers. When he died in 1610, he left instructions that his funeral and grave should conform as nearly as possible to Chinese custom, and he was buried with the pomp and ceremony reserved for a Chinese scholar. In 1982 the four-hundredth anniversary of Ricci's birth received some notice in the People's Republic. His grave in Beijing, vandalized during the Cultural Revolution, has been completely restored.

Roman Catholicism flourished in China during the seventeenth century. It was able to survive the dynastic change that came in 1644 when the Ming Dynasty was overthrown by the barbaric Manchu warriors who swept over China from north of the Great Wall. The Jesuits now courted the favor of the new rulers and offered their assistance in the casting of bronze cannon, astronomy, and the art of diplomacy. For these favors they were rewarded by the warm personal esteem of the emperor, a grant of money, and a plot of land on which they later built the Nan T'ang Cathedral, still used for regular worship today.

Other Roman Catholic orders entered China with the Spanish and French. A native Chinese was consecrated bishop in 1685. Not until the twentieth century would a second Chinese bishop be appointed! In 1692 an edict of toleration protecting church buildings and permitting freedom of worship was proclaimed. By the end of the century there were about seventy-five foreign priests in China. Half of these were Jesuits. Christian centers had been established in all the provinces with the exception of Gansu (Kansu). Christians probably numbered about 300,000.[2]

Controversy and Confrontation (1700–1800)

The eighteenth century was not as kind to Roman Catholic missions as had been the seventeenth. A series of events brought to an end the earlier period of rapid growth, and by the end of the century, the number of believers was probably fewer than it had been in 1700.

One of the elements that undoubtedly contributed to the retarded growth was what has become known as the "Rites Controversy." The dispute, which lasted the better part of a century, concerned issues which are still relevant today. Can Christianity be accommodated to the philosophy and practices of an alien culture without losing its own distinctive nature? As we have seen, Ricci and the Jesuits who followed him made every attempt to adapt Christianity to Chinese customs. They used classical Chinese names for God which had pagan connotations but to which they gave a monotheistic interpretation. They were tolerant of Confucian ceremonies honoring the ancestors—accepting the rites as a cultural, not a religious matter. They altered the Roman Catholic liturgy and practice in places so that it would not offend Chinese proprieties.

Other missionary orders, principally the Dominicans and Franciscans, felt that the Jesuits had gone too far. A basic fundamental issue involving the very nature of the Christian faith was at stake. When Christianity is introduced into another culture, invariably the question arises as to how much of the Western tradition can be discarded as unnecessary accretion. What is the core of the faith which cannot be surrendered even though it is a scandal to those who first hear it? How much of the foreign culture can become an appropriate vehicle to carry Christian concepts and values?

The issue was undoubtedly complicated by jealousy between the various missionary orders. The Jesuits had been there first, knew and appreciated the Chinese classics and customs, and were the court favorites. The Dominicans and Franciscans felt that they were being deprived of legitimate opportunities for ministry and that the Jesuits, because of their long years in China, had lost touch with the realities of the Christian faith as interpreted by Rome.

As the dispute grew in intensity, appeals were made to Rome, which sided first with one party and then the other. In 1704 the pope dispatched a special representative to China to seek a solution. The legate, Charles Maillard de Tournon, probably had an impossible task, and his youthful years and lack of experience in the Far East did not help. He chose an interpreter from the anti-Jesuit party which immediately caused irritation and misunderstanding. His audience with the Chinese emperor, the great K'ang Hsi, ended in disaster as the foreigners dared to disagree with the emperor on a matter of interpretation of the Chinese classics! It was becoming clear that the legate would decide against the Jesuits.

Up until this time, the emperor probably had never considered the Roman Catholic faith a foreign threat. Were the missionaries not "his Jesuits" who had served him and the empire well as advisors and technicians? But when the nature of the controversy became clear and the possibility that a decision was to be made in faraway Rome that would bind Chinese subjects, the emperor took decisive action. He simply could not tolerate what he felt was external interference in the internal affairs of his domain. He issued a decree ordering the legate to leave, banishing certain missionaries, and commanding all those who wished to remain to abide by the principles and practices of Matteo Ricci.

When the legate heard of the edict, he issued one of his own. He condemned the Confucian and ancestral ceremonies and threatened excommunication to those who disobeyed.

The issue was now squarely joined. Priests and the Catholic faithful had to decide between the emperor and the pope's representative. Again there were appeals to Rome, and attempts were made to find some way out of the dilemma. The matter dragged on until 1742 when Pope Innocent XIII issued a decree which was a final rejection of the Jesuit position and ordered the Society to comply. The long controversy was ended.

The aftermath of the controversy was a divided and weakened Christian mission in China. Emperors had become alienated. Intermittent persecutions took place during the next hundred years as Christianity was viewed increasingly as a hostile and alien force.

Did the Rites Controversy affect the ultimate success of Roman Catholic missions in China? Opinions have differed. Some believe that the papal decrees ruined the mission and that if the Jesuits had been left to themselves, necessary accommodations with adequate safeguards could have been made and that the Christian mission in China would have continued its remarkable growth with the possibility that China would have become a Roman Catholic nation. Others believe that the persecutions which followed were inevitable due to the increasing rigidity and authoritarianism of Confucian orthodoxy during the later days of the Manchu Dynasty.

Latourette's appraisal is as relevant today as it was when he made it in 1929:

> The most serious indictment which can be brought against the papal decision is that it established a tradition for making the Church unadaptable to Chinese conditions and beliefs. It tended and still tends to keep the Roman Catholic Church a foreign institution, one to which China must conform but which refuses to conform to China. Among semi-civilized or barbarous peoples . . . this relative inflexibility was an advantage, for to them the Church came as the vehicle and agent of an unmistakably higher and more powerful civilization and the older cultures offered but a feeble resistance. . . . It is significant, however, that in the only countries where Christianity has triumphed over a high civilization, as in the older Mediterranean world and the Nearer East, it has done so by conforming in part to older cultures. Whether it can win to its fold a highly cultured people like the Chinese without again making a similar adaptation remains an unanswered question.[3]

It is still an open question. At an international conference on China held in Montreal, Canada, in October 1981, Roman Catholic Bishop Michael Fu Tieshan of Beijing cited the issue posed by the Rites Controversy—foreign interference—as a problem which still affects relations between Chinese Roman Catholics and the Roman papacy.

The Arrival of Protestant Missionaries (1807–38)

Robert Morrison, a Scottish Presbyterian under the appointment of the London Missionary Society, arrived in 1807 in Canton, the only city of China that was then open for trade. The British East India Company and the Chinese merchant guild, called by Westerners the Cohong, held the monopoly for the trading of goods which took place in the foreign settlement, known as the "Thirteen Factories," along the river bank. Foreigners were permitted residence in Canton only during the trading season and were subject to many restrictions including arbitrary arrest. Wives were not permitted, and foreigners were denied the privilege of riding in sedan chairs! Enormous profits were made by the merchants, both Chinese and foreign, who had to put up with each other under these rather trying circumstances.

Morrison had been refused passage by the East India Company, which was unalterably opposed to the work of missionaries within their preserves. He arrived in an American ship and began immediately the study of the Chinese language. Being of a scholarly disposition, he made rapid progress. His residence in Canton was precarious until it was legitimized by his appointment as translator by the same East India Company that had once refused him passage. Although opposed to the work of the missionaries, the traders often found them indispensable because of their linguistic skills. Morrison spent his time translating the Bible, preparing a Chinese-English dictionary, and writing a Chinese version of the Shorter Catechism and other pamphlets. In his journal entry for July 16, 1814, he records a historic occasion:

> At a spring of water issuing from the foot of a lofty hill by the seaside, away from human observation, I baptized in the name of the Father, Son, and Holy Spirit . . . Tsae A-ko. . . . . May he be the first fruits of a great harvest, one of millions who shall believe and be saved from the wrath to come.[4]

In 1819, twelve years after his arrival, Morrison completed the herculean task of translating the Old and New Testaments with some help from his colleague William Milne. In the first twenty-five years of the Protestant missionary effort, only ten Chinese were baptized. These were difficult, lonely years. Morrison's wife died of cholera. Milne's wife died of dysentery. Milne himself died a few years later. All were under forty.

New volunteers began to arrive. The first American missionary, Elijah Bridgeman, under appointment of the nondenominational American Board of Commissioners for Foreign Missions, arrived in 1830. Bridgeman began a boys' school and literary work with the aid of a press which friends at home had donated. His wife, Eliza Jane Gillett Bridgeman, opened a school for girls. In 1834 the first medical missionary, Peter Parker, and his wife, arrived also under appointment of the American Board. In 1835 he opened the Canton Ophthalmic Hospital with space for forty in-patients. He specialized in the treatment of the eye because these diseases were so common. The hospital was an instant success and more than nine hundred patients were treated during the first three months. His surgical skill became legendary, and his example encouraged the introduction of Western medicine into China in the succeeding years.[5]

In these early days Protestant missionary activity was cautiously confined to Macao and Canton. A great emphasis was placed on the translation, printing, and distribution of the Scriptures and Christian literature in preparation for the day when they could be carried to the great cities of the empire.

Opium Wars and Unequal Treaties (1839–60)

The next period in the relationship between China and the Western powers is not a happy one. Events of this era cast a long shadow into the future, affecting the reputation of the Christian mission in China for the next hundred years. Two wars were fought, actually with little loss of life but with enormous consequences for China's international relationships. Patriotic Chinese of every persuasion, Christians and non-Christians alike, deeply resented the humiliation which was imposed by the unequal treaties.

It all began with the rapid expansion of trade through the port of Canton which outgrew the merchant guild system. In 1834 the monopoly of the British East India Company was ended in the interest of free trade. What had been a cozy relationship between merchants became a matter of government protocol. National honor was now at stake.

Exports from China, principally tea and silk, were in great demand in the West. These were paid for in Indian cotton which was needed by China's infant textile industry. All went well until China's domestically grown cotton began to take care of its needs. What could be used for import into China to continue the lucrative trading exchange? British merchants came up with an ideal product readily available in India, easily transportable, in great demand in China, and enormously profitable: opium!

There had long been a market for opium in China. In the nineteenth century its use was on the increase because the Chinese discovered that it could be smoked. Periodically the government took steps to outlaw the use and import of opium but with little success. Bribes, blackmail, incompetence, the self-interest of officials, the enormous profits involved, and the vacillating policies of the central government made its control all but impossible.

As the trade increased and opium became a serious social problem, anti-opium campaigns began to spread. In 1839 a new incorruptible commissioner of trade at Canton began to enforce the prohibitions against all opium imports. Meeting resistance from the merchants, he detained three hundred and fifty foreign traders in the Canton Factories for six weeks until they agreed to deliver up their cargoes of opium. Twenty thousand chests of opium were publicly burned.

Dissatisfaction among the British with the Canton system had been smoldering for some time. There were complaints over the treatment of British subjects who had been convicted and punished according to capricious and cruel Chinese law. The Manchu officials continued to regard British diplomats as tribute-bearing foreigners from a vassal state. Now the forceful detention of British subjects and the confiscation of British cargo offered an excuse to settle the issue by force of arms.

The war, which consisted primarily of a series of naval engagements around Canton and along the coast, was hopelessly one-sided. The Manchu dynasty was totally unprepared for the conflict and was soon ready to sue for peace.

The first of the infamous unequal treaties was signed at Nanjing in 1842. The significant terms of the treaty were that (1) the merchant guild system at Canton was abolished in exchange for free trade regulated by fair and regular tariffs; (2) Hong Kong, then a barren island, was ceded to the British; (3) five "treaty ports"—Guangzhou (then called Canton), Xiamen (Amoy), Fuzhou (Foochow), Ningbo (Ningpo), and Shanghai—were open to British residence and trade; (4) an indemnity was paid by China to cover the confiscated opium and the cost of the war; (5) British subjects were granted extraterritoriality when residing in the "treaty ports," which meant that they would be subject to British law and trial. Similar treaties were signed with the United States and France, who, though not involved in the conflict, were granted the same concessions.[6]

Missionaries who were citizens of the foreign powers signing the treaties gained two important privileges: (1) the right of residence in the treaty ports, and (2) legal protection of their own country's laws. Travel into the interior was not protected by the treaties. However, increasingly missionaries did travel inland, establishing their stations and sometimes suffering the consequences.

But the Treaty of Nanjing did not really settle the issue. Both sides were unsatisfied. The British wanted more. The Chinese had acted under duress and were often slow or unwilling to comply with the concessions which they had granted. The exchange of diplomatic representatives was still refused.

A minor incident in 1856 provoked a new war. Canton authorities, professing to be searching for pirates, seized a Chinese-owned craft of Hong Kong registry flying the British flag. The crew, all of whom were Chinese, were detained. On this flimsy excuse, Britain went to war again. This time France joined in, using the pretext that a French priest had been murdered in Guangxi (Kwangsi) Province, even though he was outside the protection of a treaty port. Again the war was brief and one-sided. Canton was briefly occupied. The Taku forts guarding the sea approach to Beijing were stormed. The Chinese sued for peace.

The Treaty of Tientsin (Tianjin) was signed by China in 1858 with Britain and France. Similar treaties were signed with the United States and Russia although neither had taken part in the conflict. Significant terms of the treaties included the following: (1) Additional ports in North China, Formosa, and along the Yangtse were opened for trade. (2) Foreigners were given the privilege of travel throughout the empire. (3) The treaty powers were permitted to have diplomatic representation at the court in Beijing. (4) The Chinese were to pay an indemnity to provide for the cost of the war and property destroyed. (5) Religious toleration clauses, which differed somewhat in wording, were included in each of the treaties. The American treaty read like this:

> Any persons, whether citizen of the United States or Chinese convert, who . . . peaceably teach and practice the principles of Christianity, shall in no case be interfered with or molested.[7]

These clauses forced the recognition of Christianity upon an unwilling people and implicated missionaries in the treaty system.

Missionaries and the Colonial System

At this point the narrative must be interrupted with a discussion of the relationship between the missionary and the colonial system which was introduced into China by the treaties of Nanjing and Tientsin. From the standpoint of many Chinese patriots today, both Christians and non-Christians, Marxists and otherwise, the missionary movement was compromised by its association with the colonial powers and the treaties which they forced upon the Chinese people in the mid-1800s. In 1979 Zhao Fusan, from the Institute for the Study of World Religions in Beijing, charged that "Christian missions paved the way for colonial aggression into China."[8] Bishop K. H. Ting (Ding Guangxun), president of the China Christian Council, has made the same point:

> The recognition of the historical relatedness of the missionary movement to western economic, political and military penetration into China is all-important to any understanding of what Chinese Christians have strived to do and be, and to any consideration as regards future relations with Chinese Christians.[9]

In order to understand the Christian church in China today, we must try and understand these charges, painful though this may be.

(1) A starting point is the observation that from the beginning the colonial masters displayed considerable hostility to the missionary movement. Perhaps they understood the issues quite clearly: the arrival of the missionary would sooner or later undermine the whole system of exploitation which they found most profitable. Once converts were made, they would have to be accepted on equal terms, and exploitation could no longer be excused. Morrison and other early missionaries were denied passage on the ships of the East India Company. In 1793 one of the directors of the East India Company proposed the following resolution:

> The sending out of missionaries into our Eastern possessions is the maddest, most extravagant, most costly, most indefensible project which has ever been suggested by a moon-struck fanatic. It strikes against all reason and sound policy; it brings the peace and safety of our possessions into peril.[10]

(2) In fact, the missionaries did protest the worst aspect of the colonial system in China, which was the legalization of the opium trade. Missionaries were unanimous in this opinion. In Christian conferences held in China in 1877 and 1890 resolutions were adopted urging the

British government to suppress the traffic. Christians in England and the United States likewise denounced it. William Gladstone and the Earl of Shaftesbury led the attack on the traffic in the British Parliament, and in 1843 the House of Commons adopted the following resolution:

> That it is the opinion of this House that the continuance of the trade in opium, and the monopoly of its growth in the territories of British India, are destructive of all relations of amity between England and China, injurious to the manufacturing interests of the country by the very serious diminution of legitimate commerce, and utterly inconsistent with the honour and duties of a Christian kingdom; and that steps be taken, as soon as possible, with due regard to the rights of governments and individuals, to abolish the evil.[11]

However, the resolution did not have the force of law. Hong Kong, as Rudyard Kipling noted, was "east of Suez"

> Where the best was like the worst,
> Where there ain't no ten commandments
> And a man can raise a thirst.

The opium traffic continued. Not until 1917 was it finally brought to an end. In the words of the eminent historian, John King Fairbank, this was "surely one of the longest-continued international crimes of modern times."[12]

(3) Although they protested the opium traffic, the missionaries did enjoy the protection of the same treaties that legalized the trade. Only a very few raised their voices against the treaties themselves. Missionaries served as interpreters for the diplomats who negotiated them, and there is some evidence that in both the American and French treaties, the missionaries influenced the wording to grant themselves special privileges. In the treaty with France, the Chinese and French texts were quite different. It is suspected that the missionary interpreter inserted a clause, missing from the Chinese version, permitting "French missionaries to rent and purchase land in all the provinces and to erect buildings thereon at pleasure."[13]

(4) The worst aspect of the treaties was the "toleration clauses" which granted Christian converts the protection of foreign laws. In Latourette's judgment:

> This provision in part removed Chinese Christians from the jurisdiction of Chinese officials, for any alleged persecution could be referred by the missionaries to a consul or minister for presentation to the imperial authorities. It led to abuse, because not infrequently Chinese professed conversion to obtain the assistance of the missionary and the Consul in lawsuits.[14]

The record suggests that Protestant missionaries seldom resorted to this privilege. However, the French Roman Catholics consistently sought the legal protection of their consuls for their converts even in the case of law suits unrelated to religious matters. Because of abuses which did occur, the whole Christian community was implicated. It is little wonder that loyal Chinese condemned Christianity with the phrase "win a convert, lose a citizen."

(5) After 1925 most missionary bodies urged the repudiation of the "toleration clauses" and all special privileges for missionaries. Many American mission boards came out against extraterritoriality and other treaty privileges granted to foreigners. Under pressure from the Chinese nationalist movement, changes were made in the administration of treaty ports, collection of tariffs, and foreign courts, so that the more flagrant violations of China's sovereignty were removed. Changes in the system came to a halt in the early 1930s with the beginning of the Japanese penetration into China. It then became to China's advantage to retain the legal rights of the European and American powers in China as a barrier against Japanese encroachment. In 1943 the unequal treaties were finally abolished. But during the hundred years in which they were in effect, they had done great damage.

Reform and Revolution (1860–1912)

During the half-century following the signing of the treaties with the foreign powers, developments within the Chinese empire set in motion two parallel movements for change: reform and revolution. Both had national salvation as their goal. Each differed as to how this could be achieved.

China had been deeply humiliated by the events of the mid-1860s. The supremacy of the Chinese empire had been exposed as a myth. Western powers continued to make demands which the Manchu rulers were powerless to reject. Germany, a newcomer among the Western powers, using as a pretense the murder of two Roman Catholic priests in the province of Shandong (Shantung), seized the port city of Qingdao (Tsingtao). Russia demanded special rights in Manchuria.

Two other events took place which hastened the decline of the dynasty. The Taiping Rebellion devastated large areas of the nation for several decades before it was finally brought under control in the 1860s.[15] Then in 1895 Japan went to war with China over Korea, which was then a Chinese protectorate. The war was fought in Manchuria, in Korea, and at sea. China's armed forces were no match for Japan, which was then emerging as a world power. In the Treaty of Shimonoseki (1895), China was forced to cede Formosa (Taiwan) to Japan, to recognize the independence of Korea, and to grant special interests in Manchuria. Fifteen years later Japan annexed Korea.

A group of reformers within the Manchu regime believed that China's only hope was to adopt Western ways and technological skills but to retain traditional Chinese values and culture. Fairbank calls this effort a "leap halfway into modern times."[16] They set about establishing schools, translating scientific texts, modernizing the army and navy, sending scholars abroad for study, and beginning the construction of railroads.

They were blocked at every turn by the entrenched Confucian scholarly class. A showdown between these two forces came when the reformers were able to get the ear of the young emperor and made sweeping reforms during the "Hundred Days of 1898." A remarkable series of edicts were promulgated dealing with government administration, postal service, education, agriculture, armed forces, the penal system, police, and commerce. If the movement had been successful, China would have been well on the road toward becoming a constitutional monarchy. But the conservative elements were threatened and counterattacked. The Empress Dowager Tz'u-hsi effected a coup, deposed the young emperor, declared herself the regent, and rescinded the edicts. Some of the reformers were executed. The rest fled to Japan. The reform movement was at an end.

Here is one of the ironies of history. Japan, following the arrival of Commodore Matthew C. Perry's black ships in Yedo harbor in 1853, plunged into the twentieth century with a modernization program that surprised the world. China's attempt to do the same was blocked by reactionary conservative elements, and the course of Asia was changed.

Now enter the revolutionaries. In 1895 a young medical doctor, Sun Yat-sen, led an attempt to seize the Canton provincial offices, but the revolution was prematurely exposed and Sun fled abroad. For the next fifteen years Sun campaigned for the support of overseas Chinese and raised funds for his political party. In 1905 he published the "Three Principles of the People," which remains to this day the charter of the Kuomintang (KMT) party he founded. Roughly translated, the three principles are nationalism, democracy, and people's livelihood.[17]

With Japan as a base, Sun smuggled his publications into China to feed the smoldering discontent among the student groups. Ten attempts at revolution all failed. The eleventh one initiated at Wuhan on October 10, 1911, was successful.[18] There were simultaneous uprisings in other provinces. The mandate of heaven had passed from the inept Manchu Dynasty. Early in 1912 the emperor formally abdicated the throne. The new republic was born, with Sun Yat-sen as its first president.

During these turbulent fifty years, the missionary movement in China reached full acceleration. With the signing of the treaties, missionaries could now travel throughout the empire and were free to engage in evangelistic as well as educational, medical, and social service activities. This was part of the period which Latourette describes as "the great century" of missionary advance around the world. It was a time of renewed interest and enthusiasm for missions in Great Britain, the United States, and Europe. Missionaries came to China in increasing numbers. In 1864 less than a hundred missionaries were in China. Thirty-five years later the number had increased to 1,296!

Rapid Expansion. Missionaries traveled extensively throughout the provinces, preaching, establishing stations, distributing literature. By 1889 they were in all provinces of China, which then numbered eighteen.

American Presbyterians had begun mission work in Macao with the arrival of Walter M. Lowrie in 1842. Five years later he was killed by pirates off the China coast and his place was taken by his younger brother Reuben. Work in Ningbo (Ningpo) began with the arrival of a physician, D. B. McCartee in 1844. The next year a Protestant church was organized, possibly the first on Chinese soil. In 1850 the Presbyterians began a printing press in Shanghai. In 1861 John L. Nevius began work in Shandong (Shantung).

The Rev. and Mrs. Elias B. Inslee were the first missionaries appointed by the Southern Presbyterians after the division of the two churches at the time of the Civil War. Having buried his first wife and child in China during a previous term of service under the Northern Presbyterians, Inslee brought his bride, Eugenia E. Young. In 1867, three years after the guns were silenced at Appomattox, they arrived in Hangzhou (Hangchow), the southern terminal of the Grand Canal. In a letter home Inslee had this interesting comment about relationships with consuls and opium merchants:

> Mr. _____ has accepted the consulate again. It would doubtless have been more to his credit and that of the mission had he let it alone, for it involves a necessary connection with opium merchants and seamen that in my opinion ought not to exist.[19]

Eugenia Inslee started a girls' boarding school within their first year. Benjamin Helm, Matthew Hale Houston, and John Linton Stuart arrived the next year. Their work expanded up the canal as new stations were opened in Jiangsu and Shandong. In 1871 Houston was joined by his wife Evelyn Withrow, and in 1873 Stuart married Mary Horton, who served in China fifty years and became one of the most beloved missionaries of her day. By 1896 there were forty-seven Southern Presbyterian missionaries in six stations.

Church statistics for 1911 show an estimated Protestant constituency for all of China of approximately 370,114. Although a very small minority within the vast Chinese empire, it was still a substantial rate of growth.[20]

Diversity. By 1889 forty-one different Protestant missionary societies were at work in China. They came from different countries, traditions, theologies, and communions. As one would expect, there was great diversity in their policies and practice. Two of the great missionary figures of this day are examples of this diversity.

Timothy Richard, a Welsh Baptist, had a broad vision of the task of missions which included the reconstruction of the country for the benefit of the Chinese and of transforming all phases of Chinese life. He believed that the key to accomplishing this goal was through the leaders and educated scholars. He believed that Christianity could be adapted to Chinese philosophy and thinking. He was a prolific writer and editor, a pioneer in education and famine relief, and an advisor and consultant for leaders in the reform movement.

The missionary philosophy of Hudson Taylor, founder of China Inland Mission (CIM), was quite different. Taylor was convinced that the missionary task was to spread the gospel through evangelistic witness and preaching to the remotest corners of the empire as quickly as possible. He was a man of simple, daring faith who attempted the impossible. He gave little attention to the establishment of institutions although he did believe in the efficacy of medical work. His mission was interdenominational, conservative in theology, and operated on faith principles for support. CIM became the largest missionary organization in China, and its workers covered the realm from one end to the other.

There was little formal cooperation among Christians on a national scale except for comity agreements by which a particular missionary body would take responsibility for a particular geographical area. China was so large and transportation so difficult that there seemed to be room for all with little overlapping. This did mean that a hodgepodge of denominations, sects, and churches emerged in China with little rhyme or reason as far as China itself was concerned. In 1877 and again in 1900 large mission conferences were held in Shanghai though few Chinese attended since these were "primarily for the missionaries."[21]

Response to Human Need. From its inception Protestant mission work included a wide variety of responses to human need. The poverty of the peasants, the callous indifference of many officials, and the crushing burden of traditional practices were compelling reasons for this. Whenever possible the mission station included a school and a hospital or dispensary.

A phenomenal increase took place in educational work. Missionaries believed that it was the responsibility of the church to teach every believer to read the Bible. Mission schools were popular because education in accord with western standards was much in demand. In 1905 the ancient Confucian examination system for public office was abolished, removing the motivation for the study of the classics. In many cases the mission school was the only option available for girls. Primary and secondary school enrollment increased to 102,533 in 1911.[22]

The development of higher education was even more spectacular. By 1906 fourteen mission-related institutions of college rank existed. Among these was Hangchow College, opened jointly in 1897 by American Presbyterians North and South. Although church membership was a tiny fraction of the populace,

> Protestants, by their emphasis on higher education, were rapidly raising up a trained leadership for the Church and were in a position to have an influence upon the nation far greater than their numerical strength would have given reason to expect.[23]

In medicine Protestant missions had the field to themselves. In 1889 sixty-one hospitals and forty-four dispensaries treated 348,439 patients. Twenty-five years later the numbers had grown to 330 hospitals, 223 dispensaries, and 1,640,259 patients treated. Missionary physicians pioneered in the fields of medical education, research, leprosy, and humanitarian service during revolutions, plagues, and famines. The China Medical Missionary Association was the pioneer national organization of modern physicians which standardized medical terminology and published the first medical journal.[24]

Besides education and medicine, missionaries excelled in a long list of human welfare programs. Latourette lists eight of these contributions: community movements (public parks, the Red Cross, public morality); inaugurating changes (agricultural practices, organized athletics); peacemaking between warring forces; improvement of the status of women and girls (in regard to footbinding, concubinage, factory exploitation, education); combating opium; ameliorating the lot of the blind, the deaf, the dumb; famine relief; and care of orphans.[25]

Fairbank, the dean of China historians, writes:

> . . . the influence of mission schools and hospitals, of missionary ideals and activities in seeking out the common man, translating Western literature, initiating women's education, and assisting in ancient tasks of charity and famine relief, was considerable. This influence was highly disruptive to the old Chinese society, even though it was eminently helpful to the Chinese people.[26]

Women's Work.   A special word needs to be said about the work of women missionaries. The title of this chapter is "Wise Men from the West" because the earliest Catholic pioneers were all men and the records include for the most part only the names and exploits of the men. But since 1890 women missionaries have always been in the majority. Some were primarily wives and homemakers, assisting their husbands and raising their children under adverse circumstances. Some served as school teachers, principals, evangelists, doctors, nurses, and administrators. All worked untiringly at raising the status of women, educating young girls, and eliminating such practices as footbinding, child marriages, concubinage, and other practices which degraded the life of women in a Confucian male-dominated society.

One notable example of the many women missionaries in China would surely be Dr. Nettie Donaldson Grier, whom I knew as a boy as "Aunt Nettie." She arrived in China in 1893 and opened the Presbyterian mission station at Xuzhou (Suchow) with her husband, the Rev. Mark Grier, in 1897. Through her good will, kindness, and medical skill, she overcame little by little the prejudice and hostility of the people. She founded a women's hospital to which patients were brought in wheelbarrows from distances up to fifty miles. Her service went on in spite of warlords, bandits, Yellow River floods, and the death of both her husband and her only son. She is remembered in Xuzhou as a skilled surgeon, a hospital superintendent, a friend of the destitute, a trainer of nurses, a founder of churches, and an evangelist of souls. She worked in China for forty-five years.

Antiforeign Reaction.   Throughout this period the missionary advance was met by recurring antiforeign demonstrations and outbreaks. These became more numerous as the century came to a close. The record cites incidents where Chinese Christians were massacred, missionaries were killed, and foreign property destroyed. During this time many examples of faith, courage, and devotion emerged as Chinese Christians and missionaries faced martyrdom.

To determine the reasons for these outbreaks is not difficult. Nationalism caused some of it. Some patriotic Chinese blamed all the ills which had overtaken the dynasty on the foreigner who, in their eyes, had invaded their country, demanded special privileges, and exacted humiliating treaties. If only the foreigners could be expelled, the former glory of the empire could be restored. Superstition also caused some hostility. Rumors circulated about the "evil eye" of the foreigner, the use of children's eyes to make medicine, horrible things that were allegedly done in the orphanages, bad luck which the railroads brought by disturbing the harmonious balance of nature, and the desecration of time-honored traditions. Some reaction came with the general breakdown of law and order that inevitably accompanied the end of a dynasty. Undoubtedly some of the causes could be traced to the arrogance, insensitivity, and tactlessness of some missionaries and other foreigners.

The outbreaks were not primarily antimissionary or anti-Christian. They were antiforeign. But the missionaries and Christian converts suffered the most because they were in the most exposed and isolated regions. In spite of all their good works, the missionaries had not been able to rid themselves of the taint of foreignness. Christianity was still a foreign religion, and its foreignness, rather than any distinctive Christian dogma or practice, made it offensive. As the human body reacts to a foreign object in its blood stream and seeks to reject it, so the Chinese body politic was reacting to the foreign presence in its midst.

The antiforeign movement gained momentum when the Empress Dowager and the reactionary forces in the dynasty seized control in 1898. The intensity of the movement was strongest in the northern provinces which were the scene of China's humiliating defeat by the Japanese. Here the railroads, linked with foreign interests and power, were being built. Here the government ordered the mobilization of local militia, the I Ho Tuan ("Righteous Harmony Fists"—given the name of "Boxers" by Westerners) to defend China against further encroachments.

The "Boxers" in Shandong (Shantung) Province adopted the slogan, "Protect the country, destroy the foreigner." Reports began coming into the capital city of Beijing (Peking) of a thousand Roman Catholics being massacred, of English missionaries killed, of the destruction of a Presbyterian mission station, and of attacks on railroad engineers. When the Empress Dowager gave her encouragement, the movement spread to other provinces.

The situation became so serious that in June 1900 an international armed force attempted to advance from Tianjin (Tientsin) to the capital, where it was suspected that an attack on foreigners was imminent. The Taku forts, commanding the approach to the city, were taken by force. The Empress Dowager took this attack as a declaration of war. Against the moderate counsel of some advisors, she issued an edict on June 24 ordering the killing of all foreigners throughout the empire.

This began the siege of the legation quarter in Beijing into which many missionary refugees had fled from the northern provinces. The foreign community, including legation guards and some Chinese Christians, held out until the siege was lifted on August 14 by an international force which fought its way in from the port city of Tianjin. The court fled to Xian (Sian). Beijing was looted by the invading army "with a sordidness more despicable than the madness of the Boxers."[27]

Probably more than 30,000 Roman Catholic Chinese and 47 foreign priests and nuns were killed. The number of Protestants who lost their lives is estimated at about 1,900 Chinese, 134 missionaries, and 52 missionary children.[28] The loss would have been much higher if officials in the south and other parts of the country had not disregarded the dowager's edict. Southern Presbyterian missionaries in Xuzhou were advised by their friend the telegraph operator in time to escape.

On the political scene, the events of the "Boxer Year" brought new demands from the foreign powers for concessions and indemnities, strengthened the forces in the country for revolutionary changes and reform, and hastened the downfall of the dynasty.

Terrible as were the events of 1900, the persecutions did not have any permanent ill effect on the missionary advance. The heroism of Chinese Christians and foreigners left a lasting impression on the public. Plus, the eyes of Christians around the world had been focused on China, so that when the call for new volunteers was made, it did not go unanswered.

Nationalism (1912–49)

The dominant force of China's public life after 1912 was nationalism. This was one of the "three principles of the people" on which the new republic was built. Nationalism had its inception in the frustrations of a great nation with a proud history that had for too long been humili-

ated by powers from abroad and betrayed by leaders at home. Nationalism had been nurtured with high hopes when the yoke of the Manchu
Dynasty was being broken, but these hopes were shattered when Sun
Yat-sen's republic was torn apart by factionalism, rival armies, and
warlords. Nationalism had been revived by World War I and by American President Woodrow Wilson's fourteen points which stressed the
right of national self-determination. But this hope turned to cynicism
over the big power politics at Versailles when the Allies gave in to
Japan's demand to take over Germany's sphere of influence in
Shandong.

Nationalism could be both antiforeign and pro-foreign at the same
time—rejecting foreign influence and accepting foreign technology. In
this it was quite different from the antiforeignism of the Empress Dowager and the Boxers, for it looked to the future, not to the glories of the
past. It accepted the modern world but insisted that China should seize
its rightful place in it.

Nationalism was expressed in the creation of a new student class
that had studied Western—and Marxist—political theory. It was the
force behind the May Fourth Movement of 1919 and the Shanghai factory workers' demonstrations of 1925. Nationalism was sometimes anti-Christian, sometimes irrational, sometimes idealistic, always
unpredictable.

Nationalism, at least for a time, was able to combine the likes of
Chiang Kai-shek and Mao Zedong in the same camp. It was the force
that enabled Chiang to unify most of the country after the period of the
warlords. The same force unified the country for the long, exhausting
war against Japanese aggression (1938–42).

How did Christianity fare during this era of intense nationalism?
How did they relate to each other? These are critical issues, for the
answers help us to understand the Christian church and its leaders today
in China.

Missionaries and Change.   Much the missionaries did aided
and abetted the nationalistic movement. Many, perhaps most of the
revolutionaries were educated in mission schools. A number of the sev-
enty-two martyrs buried in the Mausoleum of Revolutionary Heroes in
Canton were Christians. Sun Yat-sen as well as Chiang Kai-shek were

Protestant church members. Most missionaries supported the cause of Sun and his overthrow of the Manchu Dynasty.

Yet it must also be said that the same missionaries who enthusiastically supported change in the early years supported the status quo in succeeding years. This is the judgment of John King Fairbank:

> To get a balance sheet on this problem, I would suggest first of all that the missionaries began as subversives, undermining and attacking an old order that was overdue for change. In the latter half of the nineteenth century the Protestant missionaries in particular contributed very heavily to the process of social change, which eventually became a social revolution. . . .
>
> But if the first impact of Christianity was a tremendous stimulus to change, gradually after 1900 another phase began, superimposed on the first one. The missionary contribution in the twentieth century continued to be one of leadership toward reform, but at the same time, the missionary institutions and their administrators became part of the established order.[29]

From the vantage point of the 1980s, one must wonder whether most missionaries understood either the depth or the intensity of the Chinese nationalist movement. In its long years of history, China never had to deal with other countries as equals. Those outside the sphere of Chinese culture and civilization were either barbarians or vassal states. Because of this, China experienced a deeper identity crisis and a deeper humiliation under foreign power and influence than did India or countries in Africa.

Institutional Work. This was the great period of expansion in the building of mission hospitals and schools. For much of this time the missions had virtually no competition in making Western medicine and education available to an eager public. Missions made tremendous contributions in the alleviation of suffering and in the training of leaders for church and nation. By 1931 six medical colleges were supported by Protestant missions. In that year an astounding ninety percent of all the nurses in China were Christians![30] A major effort was made to attack the problem of illiteracy through the Mass Education Movement, associated with the name of Y.C. James Yen. Because of such emphasis, a much higher percentage of Christians (sixty percent of the men and forty percent of the women) were able to read than in the nation as a whole.[31] Because of the great number of Christians in rural areas, a special emphasis was directed toward the improvement of agriculture and the quality of village life.

More and more emphasis was placed on higher education. In the four years between 1920 and 1924 enrollment of college students in Protestant schools doubled. Because of the great expense of higher education, support for the thirteen Protestant universities and colleges became ecumenical, cutting across denominational lines.

But there were problems. Government regulations affecting middle schools increased sharply after 1924, increasing the tension between nationals and foreigners. Religious instruction was curtailed. Government regulation required principals of these schools to be Chinese nationals. This provision later turned out to be a blessing in disguise. Nationalistic movements—some of which were antiforeign and anti-Christian—swept through the schools.

Another issue was the disproportionate share of personnel and financial support being pumped into an educational system that was beyond the capability of the local Christian community to support. Some church leaders were concerned that the mission schools were losing their distinctive Christian character. Almost inevitably these institutions were patterned after Western models—even in the choice of names such as "Yale-in-China."

Mission universities and hospitals struggled with the problem of maintaining expensive institutions with high Western standards yet relevant to the needs of an agrarian Chinese society. This dilemma is seen in the development of the Peking Union Medical College which began as a mission institution. Supported by Rockefeller philanthropy with the Johns Hopkins University Medical School as a model, it became the shining example of Western medicine in Asia. It established a Chinese medical elite, but in many ways it remained a foreign institution, an "American transplant,"[32] isolated from the society in which it had been planted.

Development of an Indigenous National Church

The same problem of indigenization related to the establishment of a national church, but with the church the issue was much more critical, a matter of survival. The church could not remain an American or a British transplant and live.

Latourette writes of the "rapid transfer of responsibility to Chinese leadership" among Protestants during this period.[33] In comparison to the Roman Catholics, who consecrated only one Chinese bishop in two hundred years, this was certainly the case. However, from the vantage point of the 1980s, one wonders whether the transfer of authority was fast enough or extensive enough. It was certainly much slower than in Korea which was influenced by the Nevius methods. John L. Nevius, a pioneer Presbyterian missionary in Shandong, had worked out some principles advocating strong emphasis on self-government, self-propagation, and self-support, but he had been unable to get his colleagues in China to adopt them. These same principles proved to be of tremendous significance in the rapid development of an indigenous, self-reliant church in Korea.

Some observers believe that progress toward establishing an indigenous church was hampered by the emphasis being given to the institutions. The same planners who were committed to the ideal of a self-governing, self-propagating, self-supporting church had also set up other institutional structures which continued to depend on foreign grants, experience, and administration. Thus the emphasis on institutions with Western standards negated the emphasis on a self-sufficient, self-reliant church.

Nevertheless, progress was made along some lines.

(1) Church membership continued to rise though probably not as fast as it had before 1914. Baptized Protestant communicants reached 567,000 in 1936 which was a doubling of membership in the previous twenty-two years. The total Christian constituency was much higher than that and certainly exercised a leadership role in the nation far more significant than these numbers would suggest.

(2) The number of ordained Chinese pastors increased dramatically from 764 in 1915 to 2,196 in 1936—a three hundred percent increase in twenty-one years. This is even more significant when compared with the decline in the number of China missionaries. The number of Protestant missionaries reached the high-water mark of 8,325 in 1926. After that date numbers declined because of the general exodus of missionaries from the country during the civil war of 1926–27 and the drop in missionary giving at home during the Depression. Progressively more and more of the leadership of the church thus came into Chinese hands.[34]

(3) Movement toward a national Christian identity also took place. In its early years the Protestant community was divided into different denominations unrelated to each other. In 1922 the first National Christian Conference was held with a majority of the 1,200 delegates being Chinese. In that same year the National Christian Council was organized, and by 1929 its leadership was in the hands of Chinese elected from the various Chinese churches. For the first time Christians from all over China were represented in one national body. From the beginning the Christian churches in China were active in the development of the ecumenical movement. The Chinese delegation at the International Missionary Council's Madras Conference in 1938 took the lead in representing the younger churches of Asia and Africa. When the World Council of Churches was organized in Amsterdam in 1948, Dr. T. C. Chao, professor at Yenching University, was elected one of the six presidents of the council.

(4) Tracing the organization of the great number of Protestant denominations that developed during this period is not possible, but one example is the Church of Christ in China. This church had its beginnings in the union of Presbyterian churches that took place in 1906 with the organization of the Synod of Central China combining the work of some American Presbyterian missions. In 1918 it adopted the name The Church of Christ in China (CCC, Chung Hua Chi Tu Chiao Hui) and sought a wider union with other than Presbyterian bodies. The constituting First General Assembly met in 1927 with eighty-eight commissioners (of whom sixty-six were Chinese) from eleven synods, forty-six districts representing a membership of more than 120,000. The church combined Congregational, Methodist, and Baptist elements and became the largest denomination in China.[35]

(5) The vitality and diversity of the Christian movement continued to express itself in the emergence of new indigenous groups as well. These were started, for the most part, by charismatic Chinese leaders and developed independently apart from the denominations founded by the missionaries. The largest of these was the True Jesus Church, established by Paul Wei and Barnabas Tung in the 1910s. The movement emphasized the literal interpretation of the Bible, faith healing, ecstatic utterances, and communal living. In 1926 the Little Flock was begun by Watchman Nee (Ni To-sheng) in opposition to formal church orga-

nizations, emphasizing Bible study and evangelism. In 1921 the first Jesus Family congregation was started by Ching Tien-ying on the principles of communal living, hard work, prayer, and daily worship.[36]

In National Defense

In the 1930s, resistance to Japanese aggression united the country and mobilized the forces of nationalism as nothing before had been able to do. This time the aggressor was not a Western but an Asian power. For the first time missionaries were viewed as allies in the defense of China's nationhood.

Japan had begun its relentless march toward world empire with the first Sino-Japanese War of 1895 when Formosa (Taiwan) was seized and Korea came under Japan's sphere of influence. In 1905 Japan fought a war against Russia and won, thus eliminating the other contender for power in the Far East. Japan entered World War I on the side of the Allies, seized the German port of Qingdao (Tsingtao), and demanded special concessions in Shandong. In 1931 Japan engineered the "Mukden" (Shenyang) incident as an excuse for invading Manchuria, and the next year the puppet state of Manchukuo was proclaimed, with the last "boy emperor" of the Manchu Dynasty enthroned. In 1937 at the Marco Polo bridge, not far from Beijing, all-out war against China began.

As the Japanese armies moved south and west along the railroads, mission compounds became safe havens for thousands of Chinese refugees. What happened in Xuzhou (Suchow) is told by my father:

> When the Japanese rolled into our city, it was "a night to be remembered." We were under artillery fire and incendiary shells set the city afire. That night we cut a hole in the bottom floor to get closer to the ground, if necessary, "and wished for the day." Twenty-five hundred refugees, mostly women and children, fled to us for protection and food. Dr. Grier, Dr. and Mrs. McFadyen and we, protected them while our Chinese leaders fed them. . . . Licentious Japanese soldiers prowled around our buildings like beasts of prey, but not a single woman or girl in our compounds was touched. Charlotte escorted groups of women through the burning city to places of safety. She organized a sanitary squad to scatter lime and swat the fly, for cholera time was approaching and our refugees were packed like sardines with no sanitary facilities available. However, the Lord was with us for there were more births than deaths among our refugees during that long hot summer.[37]

From pulpits and in the press, missionaries told the story of Japan's aggression. They gave wide publicity to the "rape of Nanking." Back home in the United States they lobbied against the sale of arms, scrap iron, and high octane gasoline to fuel the Japanese war machine. Because of the missionary voice and conscience, public opinion was mobilized for the support of the embattled Chinese republic.

Some missionaries remained in the eastern occupied provinces as long as the United States was a neutral power. After Pearl Harbor they were placed under house arrest, interned in camps, and later repatriated home. Some made the long trek to the West with the retreating Chinese people. Many of the Christian colleges moved westward, establishing their campuses in Sichuan (Szechwan) and Yunnan, where they continued their educational programs.

When victory came in 1945, Christian leaders and missionaries returned to the occupied provinces to begin again. It was a land that had been ravaged by war and enemy occupation, but there were high hopes for a new beginning.

Unknown to those at the time, however, the missionary era in China was fast drawing to a close. Marxist socialism had appeared on the horizon in the 1920s as a cloud no larger than a human hand. By the 1940s it had the force of a hurricane. It is necessary now to turn to this force in order to understand the new China and the new church.

3

Red Star in the East

"Who was it that brought the conqueror from the east
    and makes him triumphant wherever he goes?
Who gives him victory over kings and nations?
    His sword strikes them down as if they were dust.
    His arrows scatter them like straw before the wind.
He follows in pursuit and marches safely on,
    so fast that he hardly touches the ground!
Who was it that made this happen?
    Who has determined the course of history?
I, the LORD, was there at the beginning,
    and I, the LORD God, will be there at the end."
                                        (Isaiah 41:2–4 TEV)

At the same time Christian missionaries were striving to win the soul of China, another force was working for the same end. The Chinese Communist party (CCP) was on the road to power. The CCP sought to bring about some of the same reforms as the missionaries such as literacy, elimination of footbinding, and an end to superstitious practices. But there were fundamental differences, and no love lost between the two camps. Christians were committed to a policy of moderation and gradualism. The CCP opted for the radical solution of violence and class struggle.

In 1921 the CCP numbered fifty-seven members. Twenty-eight years later it ruled the most populous country on earth. How did it happen?

Peasant Uprisings

Chinese Communist party leaders like to trace their roots to pre-Marxist popular uprisings of the peasant class. In this way they wish to show the distinctive Chinese quality of their brand of communism.

One of these peasant movements was the Taiping ("Great Peace")

Rebellion that ravaged the empire during the last century. The founder of the movement, Hung Hsiu-chuan (1814–64), was a religious fanatic who had been influenced by the reading of the Bible and certain visions he had which convinced him that he was the younger brother of Jesus Christ. His mission on earth was the establishment of a heavenly kingdom in which there would be complete equality. Men and women would be treated the same. All persons would contribute their possessions to a common treasury and receive support from it. Land would be redistributed, and families would be grouped into mutually dependent units. A strict ethical code would govern personal conduct. All idols would be destroyed.

The rebellion spread like wildfire across the Yangtze valley, feeding on the dissatisfaction of peasants who had lost their land. Many native Chinese had little loyalty for the foreign Manchu Dynasty. The walls of Nanjing were stormed in 1853 and this city then became the capital of the "Heavenly Kingdom." Armies of the rebels reached the outskirts of Tianjin later that same year, but then the movement began to recede. The ruling Manchus were able to beat back the rebels with the services of foreign mercenaries. These included the colorful American adventurer Frederick Townsend Ward, who was killed in battle, and the British General Charles George Gordon. Huang's leadership was challenged by lesser generals, and "The Heavenly Kingdom of Great Peace" came to an end because of internal strife, fratricide, and assassinations. To present-day Communists, the Taipings were the precursors of revolution against a decadent feudalistic society.[1]

The May Fourth Movement of 1919

Another uprising of a different nature took place at the end of World War I. Japan, one of the victorious Allies, claimed German concessions in the province of Shandong and the port city of Qingdao as her share of the spoils. China's representatives at the Versailles Peace Conference were pressured to concede to these demands. It seemed that Woodrow Wilson's principle of self-determination did not apply to the people of China! Here was another example of the hated "unequal treaties" imposed by foreign powers. When word of the agreement reached Beijing, more than 3,000 students assembled on May 4 at Tiananmen (Gate of Heavenly Peace) and issued a manifesto protesting the action. Strikes broke out all over China. The concessions were repudiated, and China never signed the Versailles Treaty.

The actions precipitated by the May Fourth incident intensified the mood of nationalism then sweeping the country. The new popular leaders whom this movement catapulted into positions of prominence agreed on two goals: China should free itself from the stranglehold of Confucian conservatism by modernization, and a strong, united China could then throw off the shackles of the foreign colonial system. But soon they were to differ sharply as to how these goals could be achieved. Disagreement divided the two top May Fourth leaders, the educator Hu Shih and the editor of the reform newspaper Ch'en Tu-hsiu. Hu advocated educational reforms and liberal democracy and later became an ambassador to the United States. Ch'en believed that only a radical revolution could solve China's problems and turned toward communism.

The Communist Party under Russian Tutelage (1921–24)

The appeal Marxist socialism had for China is not difficult to understand. The Soviet success in Russia offered an example of hope for a quick solution to China's misery. The betrayal at Versailles was additional proof that the Western liberal democracies could not be trusted. The Soviets, with great fanfare, repudiated the "unequal treaties" signed by the former Tsarist regime and gave up their former privileges.[2] Russian agents representing the international Communist apparatus Comintern were dispatched to China to give direction in the formation of the CCP.

The birth of the party took place during July 1921 in Shanghai. Twelve Chinese were present. Ch'en Tu-hsiu, the hero of May Fourth, was chosen as the first chairman. A young library assistant named Mao Zedong from Peking University was one of the twelve. Although he seemed to have been more of an observer than a participant, he was the only one present who would have any lasting influence on the party.[3]

In the early years Russian influence dominated the party's policies and practice. Emphasis was on organizing factory and industrial workers in the large cities. General strikes and mass uprisings in the urban areas were the pattern that had worked in Russia. It was the only example they had to follow. The peasants and the countryside were ignored.

First Coalition with the KMT (1924–27)

In these early years the CCP enjoyed only modest growth. Its rival, the older and much larger bourgeois party of the Kuomintang (KMT) did not consider it strong enough to be a threat. Even its Soviet supporters had little hope that it could win China for the socialist cause. They were, in fact, putting most of their bets on the other horse!

In January 1923 Lenin's envoy, Adolf Joffe, signed an agreement with Sun Yat-sen promising Soviet support and technical assistance for the KMT. Sun's trusted lieutenant Chiang Kai-shek was sent to Moscow for indoctrination and training. Lenin appointed Mikhail Borodin as his envoy to Canton to serve as senior adviser to the KMT. In 1924 at the insistence of their Soviet advisers, the CCP signed an agreement with the KMT under which the two parties would collaborate in overthrowing the warlords and in establishing a new united China based on Sun's "Three Principles of the People." The CCP would retain its own separate party structure, but individual members would become members of the KMT and were given some positions of leadership.

The CCP at first profited from the alliance. They now enjoyed an aura of respectability. Party membership grew by leaps and bounds after the May Thirtieth Movement of 1925—a series of strikes caused by the killing of ten anti-Japanese demonstrators by the police in Shanghai's International Settlement.

But the alliance was not to last. Each of the three parties had entered it to further its own ends. Back in Russia the Soviets had found it useful to infiltrate and use bourgeois nationalist parties. The same technique could be used in China. The KMT needed the technical assistance that Russia had offered and which the Western democracies had refused to give. But more and more the KMT became fearful of foreign domination. Sun's "Three Principles" of nationalism, democracy, and people's livelihood were sufficiently vague for the CCP to accept, but once these goals became clarified, there was bound to be trouble. It was only a question of time before one would double-cross the other.

The KMT struck first. Sun Yat-sen died in March 1925, and the leadership of the party was soon shared by leftists and the military commander Chiang Kai-shek. In January 1926 Chiang seized power, ousted the leftist leaders and some Soviet advisers. Inexplicably Moscow still favored collaboration with the KMT and Borodin returned to

Canton when a compromise was worked out. He continued his support of the KMT and urged the CCP to do the same.

In July 1926 Chiang began his Northern Campaign to smash the warlords and reunify China. Through a series of brilliant maneuvers, he succeeded in defeating some of the warlords in battle and winning others over through diplomacy. The capital was moved from Canton to Wuhan, and then Chiang moved down the Yangtze to seize Shanghai and China's industrial heartland. Communist organizers in Shanghai had prepared the way for him and had paralyzed the city through a general strike. The city fell with little loss of life.

Then Chiang struck again. On the morning of April 12, 1927, he ordered the destruction of armed CCP units and labor leaders throughout the city. He claimed that evidence seized by Beijing officials in a raid on the Soviet Embassy had incriminated the CCP and their Soviet advisers in a plot to seize control of the government. The Communist organization was smashed, and many of its leaders were liquidated. Borodin was dismissed and returned to Russia in disgrace. CCP chairman Ch'en Tu-hsiu was blamed for the fiasco and expelled from the party. But the fault was more fundamental. Russia's China policy had ended in disaster.

Enter Mao Zedong

The Communist party of China was now in shambles. It had received little popular support. Its leadership had been decimated. Its base of power in the urban centers had been crushed. It had followed blindly the direction of its Soviet advisers which had led to failure.

At this point the man enters the scene who was to lead the party for the next forty-nine years. What kind of man was Mao Zedong? Mao was born in the year 1893 in the village of Shao Shan, forty miles from Changsha, the capital city of Hunan. His parents were moderately wealthy peasants. He attended primary school and worked on the family farm.

Two incidents in his childhood left lasting impressions for the rest of his life. At age thirteen he had a violent clash with his tyrannical father. He ran away from home but returned because of his mother's pleading. The breach with his father, however, was never healed. The second incident occurred a few years later when a group of merchants came to his town and reported an uprising in the city of Changsha. There was a famine in the land and some starving people went to the governor with petitions for food. The callous indifference of the Manchu official infuriated the populace, and they rebelled, but in the end the uprising was brutally suppressed and its leaders beheaded.

At age eighteen Mao left home to attend the Changsha Middle School and began to read everything he could get his hands on. At this time China was caught up in the death throes of the Manchu Dynasty and the revolutionary movements which followed. Mao served in a revolutionary army for six months and then returned to his books.

At age twenty-five Mao traveled to Beijing where he was able to get a job as library assistant at the university thanks to the help of a former teacher. It was not much of a job and paid only eight dollars a month, but it did put him in touch with some of the leading revolutionary thinkers of the day. During the summer of 1920 Mao read the *Communist Manifesto* and from that time on considered himself a Marxist.

Returning to Changsha, Mao became director of the First Teacher's Training School, edited a student newspaper, and began agitation for the ouster of the corrupt provincial governor. It was an unequal struggle, and Mao was soon forced to leave town. Soon after this experience Mao attended the first meeting of the CCP in Shanghai.

Mao was sent back to his native province with responsibility for organizing students and a labor movement in the Anyuan coal mines. When the CCP Central Committee met the second time, in the summer of 1922, Mao journeyed to Shanghai to attend but "forgot the name of the place where it was to be held, could not find any comrades, and missed it.'"[4] He supported the alliance with the KMT and went to Canton to work with the united front. In 1926 Mao returned to his native Hunan to inspect peasant organizations and political conditions in the countryside. He wrote up the results of his investigations in his first published work, *Report on an Investigation of the Peasant Movement in Hunan*. It quickly became one of the classic documents of the Communist movement. In his report Mao insisted that the revolutionary elite, most of whom were city dwellers, must take the peasant movement seriously, for it was in the countryside, not the cities, that the revolutionary movement would find its true source of strength:

All the wrong measures taken by the revolutionary authorities concerning the peasant movement must be speedily changed. Only thus can the future of the revolution be benefited. For the present upsurge of the peasant movement is a colossal event. In a very short time, in China's central, southern and northern provinces, several hundred million peasants will rise like a mighty storm, like a hurricane, a force so swift and violent that no power, however great, will be able to hold it back. . . . They will sweep all the imperialists, warlords, corrupt officials, local tyrants and evil gentry into their graves. Every revolutionary party and every revolutionary comrade will be put to the test. . . . There are three alternatives. To march at their head and lead them? To trail behind them, gesticulating and criticizing? Or to stand in their way and oppose them? Every Chinese is free to choose, but events will force you to make the choice quickly.[5]

These were heretical words, for it had long been believed that peasants were incapable of making revolution. But within a short time Mao would be proven right.

Rebuilding on a Peasant Base (1927–34)

When the final break with the KMT came, the CCP ordered attempts in various parts of the country to seize control and organize popular uprisings. One of these, the "Autumn Harvest Uprisings," was led by Mao in Hunan. It was a complete failure, and Mao barely escaped with his life. He gathered a few thousand survivors of the campaign and took refuge in the craggy mountains of his native province.

There he began to put into practice some of the principles concerning peasant organization about which he had written. The first "soviet," or base area, was established. Local councils of peasants were established. Indoctrination began. Land was seized from the wealthy landlords and distributed to the peasants. In the early days the peasants retained ownership of their land. The communes were to come later. In 1928 Mao's position was greatly strengthened by the arrival of another guerilla army under the command of Zhu De, a professional soldier. In 1929 the base area was moved to the border of Jiangxi (Kiangsi) Province where they were joined by General Peng Dehuai, who had defected from the KMT army. Their combined forces now numbered about 10,000 men. In November 1931 in Ruijin, Jiangxi (Kiangsi), the Soviet Republic of China was proclaimed as a "democratic dictatorship of the proletariat and peasantry."

During this time Mao had to fight on two fronts. The Moscow-trained Central Committee, called the "twenty-eight Bolsheviks," were intent on keeping Mao out of control of the party. Mao was demoted and removed from the Central Committee because of the failure of the Autumn Harvest Uprising. At one time he may have been under house arrest. There was opposition to the way he was organizing the peasants. However, it was hard to argue against success. Mao's movement in the countryside was succeeding; whereas the Communist movement in the cities and elsewhere in China was going very badly indeed.

On the other front, Mao had to contend with the KMT. As his base areas were enlarged, he came under increased attack. During 1932 and 1933 Chiang Kai-shek organized four "extermination campaigns." Each failed. But in late 1933–34 a fifth campaign was launched with a systematic blockade and massive troop penetrations into the base areas. The Red Army was unable to hold their own in positional warfare. The entire base area was threatened. Then on the night of October 15, 1934, the main body of approximately 100,000 broke through the KMT lines and escaped toward southwestern Jiangxi. The legendary Long March had begun.

The Long March (1934–35)

The trek was a giant end run around those areas which were then controlled by the Nationalist armies of Chiang Kai-shek. The Red Army first drove southwest through the province of Guangxi, and then turned northward into Guizhou (Kweichow). Because of blockading Nationalist forces, they swerved again to the south into Yunnan. From there the army marched north across the high mountain plateaus of Central Asia, passing through Sichuan (Szechwan), across sparsely settled Gansu (Kansu), and then turning to the east into Shaanxi (Shensi). The journey ended at Yanan one year after the departure from the base area. They passed through eleven provinces, traversed eighteen mountain ranges, and crossed twenty-four rivers, including the Tatu gorge and the mighty Yangtze.

The march began under the control of the Moscow-trained central party members, the "twenty-eight Bolsheviks," and their Russian advisers. It was not a good beginning, and blunders were made during the route of march. Not until January 1935, at the historic party congress at Zunyi (Tsunyi), was Mao elected party chairman. From then on he was the undisputed leader.

It is hard to overestimate the importance of the Long March for the Chinese Communist party. In one sense it was a 370-day, 6,000-mile retreat ending in an isolated, wretchedly poor region of China's northwest. Of the 100,000 men and women who began, less than 10,000 arrived at the destination. Yet, on the other hand, it was a deliverance, for it removed the bungling, inept interference of the Russian Soviets. It became for the Communist party a national epic comparable to the children of Israel's exodus from Egypt. Almost without exception, all the leaders of the party for the next forty years would be chosen from those who had taken part. Participation in the Long March was a badge of honor, a necessary prerequisite to advancement in the party hierarchy.

On the trek Mao and his lieutenants learned two lessons of inestimable value, without which they would never have won China. First, of necessity, they learned to identify with the peasants—how to live with them, how to think like them, how to organize them. Mao compared the revolutionary soldiers to fish in the sea. The peasantry was the sea in which the revolutionary army must swim! Second, Mao learned and perfected the principles of guerilla warfare. In the celebrated quotation from Mao's writings:

> The enemy advances, we retreat
> The enemy halts, we harass
> The enemy tires, we attack
> The enemy retreats, we pursue.[6]

During the long, protracted war against Japan, Mao's armies were able to penetrate enemy-held areas and organize resistance movements against the Japanese. It was a style of warfare that Chiang Kai-shek's armies never learned.

The Yanan Period (1935–45)

In contrast to the annihilation campaigns of Jiangxi and the exhaustion of the Long March, the Yanan (Yenan) decade provided a "breather" for the CCP. American visitors to Yanan during this period were impressed with the relaxed, jovial, good-natured camaraderie of the Communist leaders. Mao presented the image, not of a guerilla leader, but of a sage.[7] A university was established for training party cadres. A more moderate position on class warfare and land expropriation was adopted. It was a time of schoolteaching and experimentation.

During this period missionaries gained differing views of the Chinese Communists. Many found little difference between Communist bands and the bandits who roamed the countryside. Both were outlaws who attacked and were attacked by government forces. Missionaries in the path of the Long March tell of brutality, villages decimated, and Christians killed. John and Betty Stam of the China Inland Mission were murdered in December 1934 by militia thought to be part of a Communist army. On the other hand, a few missionaries had become so totally disillusioned with the KMT that they sided with the Communist cause. Among these were James G. and Mary Austin Endicott of the United Church of Canada, who befriended the rebels and became their apologists.

Warfare between the KMT and the CCP was still smoldering, but there were no annihilation campaigns. Yanan was far removed from the power centers of the republic. After the Japanese seizure of Manchuria in 1931 and their growing encroachment on Chinese sovereignty after that time, Chiang's attention turned toward this new and more ominous threat.

In December 1935 a bizarre incident took place in Xian (Sian), which remains something of an enigma. Chiang Kai-shek, while inspecting troops in the northern provinces was seized by one of his own generals Chang Hsueh-liang and held captive for thirteen days. Chang's father had been one of the Manchurian warlords and had been assassinated by the Japanese. Chang, with his army, had left Manchuria and was growing impatient with Chiang for not standing up to the Japanese. Chiang's position had been that it was necessary to bide for time, build up the national resources, and avoid a showdown. During this tense situation, Zhou Enlai arrived from Yanan and pled for Chiang's release on the grounds that a united front against Japan demanded a live Chiang and KMT support.

On Christmas Day Chiang was suddenly released and flew back to his capital in Nanjing. There was general relief and celebration all over China. Chiang Kai-shek became a national hero. Whatever agreements were reached in Xian were never made public. Chiang's captor claimed that he had demanded, and received, assurances of a united front against Japan. Whatever the case, following the incident the KMT and the CCP did enter into a second coalition in order to prepare for the inevitable conflict with Japan.

The Japanese began their all-out war against China in the summer of 1937. The conflict was to last eight long years. The Japanese war machine seized all the important cities along the coast and advanced along the railroads. Chiang traded space for time and followed a "scorched earth" policy of destroying industrial areas and crops to keep them from falling into the hands of the Japanese. He moved the capital from Nanjing to Wuhan, and when that city fell, he moved further up the river to the wartime capital of Chongqing (Chungking).

By the time the United States entered the conflict after the Pearl Harbor attack in December 1941, Japanese armies were bogged down in China's vast interior. It was not worth the cost of men and equipment to push further westward. There were more important battles to be fought in the Pacific. So in the China theater there was stalemate.

As the long years wore on, the strength of the nationalist government (KMT) began to wear down. In all probability it was only the massive United States military support that kept it going, but the stalemate was a situation which the CCP could exploit. They were able to infiltrate the countryside that was nominally under Japanese rule, establish their base areas, organize the peasants and wage guerilla warfare, following the pattern they had learned in fighting the KMT. By 1945 when the war against Japan was won, the Yanan government claimed nineteen liberated base areas, seventy to ninety million people under their rule, an army of 910,000, and a militia of two million.

Civil War (1945–49)

Peace came suddenly in Asia with the dropping of the bomb on Hiroshima. Neither the Chinese Nationalist nor United States forces expected the end to come quite so suddenly. But CCP General Zhu De acted immediately. On August 10, 1945, the day the Japanese sued for peace, he unleashed the Red Army units in the liberated areas, ordering them to take over the Japanese garrisons and to seize their arms.

Both sides then made a rush to move their troops to take over government administration and military equipment from the defeated Japanese. The Nationalists were aided by United States planes and ships. The Red Army had the support of the Soviet armies in Manchuria who had entered the war just days before the end. Very quickly the coalition between KMT and CCP broke down as each attempted to gain the superior position.

The United States tried valiantly but in vain to bring about a genuine coalition government. General George C. Marshall was dispatched to China as President Harry Truman's personal envoy to make this effort. Peace teams composed of Nationalists, Communists, and United States officers were dispatched to the troubled areas to work on truce negotiations. But it all ended in failure.

Civil war broke out and grew in intensity during 1947. Already the KMT had lost the confidence of the people because of the utter corruption of the government. Public order and discipline began to crumble. Chiang Kai-shek, against the counsel of his United States advisers, stubbornly insisted on committing some of his best troops to the defense of the cities and industrial centers of Manchuria. Here the Communists were in positions of strength with Soviet support. Supply lines for the Nationalists were long and precarious. Chiang's armies were isolated in the cities, surrounded, and finally cut to pieces.

A gigantic battle was fought for the strategic railroad center of Xuzhou (Suchow), two hundred miles north of Nanjing. Five hundred thousand men were involved on both sides of the conflict. In December 1948 Xuzhou fell with heavy loss of life on both sides. My seventy-two-year-old father, Dr. Frank A. Brown, was in Suchow during the siege and tells of his experiences beginning the night when the Communist armies entered the city:

> **December 1.** Last night was a night "to be much remembered," . . . I will jot down the events as they occurred.
>
> *6:00* P.M. Mrs. Stella Walter arrived at the airport in our car, with some of the baggage. An American pilot is just leaving for Nanking and assures her he will be back in two hours and take us all to Shanghai. By ten o'clock we hope to see the lights of Shanghai.

7:00 P. M. Walter and I arrive with plenty more trunks, bedding and what not. A Catholic priest joins our party. . . .

8:00 P. M. Nine-Ten o'clock, searching the skies for a plane does not help.

11:00 P. M. A sound of rushing planes, for everything that has wings on this big air field is leaving for the south loaded down with the high command and every soldier that can climb on board.

MIDNIGHT. Walter and I explore the control tower. Lights all on, but instruments and utensils all left in disorder. Men all gone.

2:00 A. M. I investigate the offices downstairs and find them looted, with soldiers prowling around in the dark. I get out, for though I have usually got along well with soldiers of all armies, it is not healthy to meet them looting in the dark!

The night is cold so we sit out in the car to keep warm. Southward a few miles the flashes of the big guns light up the sky incessantly. The enemy is very near.

DAYBREAK. Two little "spotter planes" from Nanking circle overhead for reconnaissance. We notice 50 gal. gasoline drums have been placed all around the field close to the empty army trucks that still line the field. It may be that the nationalists are about to bomb with incendiaries and set all the works afire. We move out of range and wait, for our plane that never comes. So back we go homeward. Evidently the Lord still has a work for us to do here.

The roads are crowded with huge retreating armies—trucks, tanks, infantry, one amphibian tank, all mixed together heading for the Southwest. . . . A doomed army is in full retreat. The private soldier is brave enough, as Chinese Gordon discovered 100 years ago. But many of the higher officers are cowardly, selfish and inefficient, with the result that the army has no will to fight, as we have known for some months past.

Am anxious tonight for this old city. "THEY" arrived before midnight, and went from door to door reassuring the inhabitants. Came to our hospital gate and said they knew there were three Americans here, but not to fear.

December 2. "THEY" put up notices today, promising liberty of worship, protection of property, safety for foreigners, etc. Sounds good. . . .

December 7. Saturday I found 20 wounded government soldiers [Nationalists] on the floor of our gate house. Hospital dares not take them in as regular patients. I called for volunteers and each day we washed their faces. They are almost starving. Hospital gives them a little food, though we have none to spare, and daily dresses their wounds. . . . One of the prisoners is dying of tetanus. I tried to make him a little comfortable—he has no bed. He begged for a little lamp which I gave him. I suppose he does not want to die alone in the dark. . . . Pastor Tai takes drugs and bandages sent to me and distributes them to four groups of wounded P.O.W.s in our city: He is well received by the guards. We are doing our best, but it is so little.

December 8. Walter and I visit patients in our wards—just sit by their beds, talk with them, and hand them Gospels and tracts. Seven years ago Dr. Junkin and I were doing this kind of work when we were interned on Pearl Harbor day. . . . It is a comfort to walk down the long wards, so clean and quiet, with the staff working to cure some of the misery amid this cruel war. They are upholding the great tradition of the past 52 years since this hospital was founded. They show the effect of the long years of training by the McFadyens and by Dr. Grier. As you walk at night among these 20 hospital buildings on this compound, and recall their history, you feel that you are on holy ground. Faith built them all—faith of the sending church, faith of the missionaries, faith of the Christian Chinese who are now carrying on.[8]

The end was near. In January 1949 Beijing and Tianjin fell. In April the Red Armies crossed the Yangtze and took Nanjing. Chiang Kai-shek and the remnants of his government and army evacuated to Taiwan. Then on October 1 Mao Zedong made his historic proclamation from Tiananmen Square in his new capital city of Beijing: "The Chinese people have stood up. . . ." The People's Republic of China had begun.[9]

Former Presbyterian Mission hospital in Xuzhou (Suchow) still in use after seventy years; large building in rear is recent addition

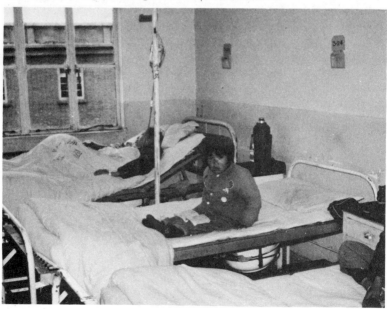

Patients in ward of former mission hospital in Xuzhou

A Revolution Is No Dinner Party

a time to be born, and a time to die;
a time to plant, and a time to pluck up what is planted;
a time to kill, and a time to heal;
a time to break down, and a time to build up;
a time to weep, and a time to laugh;
a time to mourn, and a time to dance; . . .
a time to love, and a time to hate;
a time for war, and a time for peace.

(Ecclesiastes 3:2–4,8)

The coming to power of the Chinese Communist party in 1949 was the most massive revolution in world history. However one measures it—from the standpoint of the number of people involved or the radical changes which were imposed—here was revolution on a massive unprecedented scale. Yet the events of the revolution are not well known in the West, and even less understood. A controlled press, the lack of outside observers, the emotional bias of all the participants made objective reporting all but impossible. Those who tried to tell what they witnessed speak of enthusiasm and despair, joy and terror, self-sacrifice and vengeance, heroism and hatred, self-discipline and uninhibited, uncontrolled violence.

As was true for the French Revolution, "it was the best of times; it was the worst of times." Or in the words of Chairman Mao:

> . . . a revolution is not a dinner party, or writing an essay, or painting a picture, or doing embroidery; it cannot be so refined, so leisurely and gentle, so temperate, kind, courteous, restrained and magnanimous. A revolution is an insurrection, an act of violence by which one class overthrows another.[1]

What do the events of the first years of the Communist Revolution mean today? From this distance of thirty years, the events may be viewed with less distortion and a clearer perspective.

When the Chinese Communist party (CCP) came to power in 1949, they inherited immense problems. The country had been wracked by war and civil strife for more than a decade. The economy was stagnant. Inflation during 1949 reached seven hundred percent. Railroads had all but ceased to operate according to schedule. The merchant fleet for the most part had left for Taiwan. Unemployment was widespread, and refugees crowded the cities.

The CCP itself numbered 4.5 million members, less than one percent of the people. Only two percent of the party were city workers. The party had little experience in urban affairs, and yet now the administration of some of the largest cities of the world was thrust upon it.

In one sense the revolution had been too successful, for the suddenness of the KMT collapse left them unprepared. Some years later Mao described the problem they faced: Socialism "came too suddenly," he said. "In 1949 our armies crossed the Yangtze, but our ideology did not cross the Yangtze."[2]

How in the world were they going to make it work? They did have considerable assets. The great mass of the people were sick and tired of war and the chaos of the past decade. They were willing to accept almost anything as better than what they had been through. The Communist party did have the experience of administering the base areas during the Yanan years. And they had a highly disciplined, ideologically motivated army.

The new rulers of China had two allies that would be much maligned in subsequent years but now stood them in good stead. First, the Confucian ethic compared the relationship of the ruled to the ruler as that of son to father and demanded complete obedience. The mandate of heaven had passed from the KMT, as it had from previous regimes, and now the new rulers should be followed and obeyed. The other friend was Soviet Russia, which provided the organizational model, the experts, hardware, and capital in those early years.

The System

To understand how the CCP made it work, it is necessary to look at the system of government which followed the Russian model. First, a word of caution: words and concepts do not necessarily mean the same even though they are translated into accurate English. This is another reason why it is so difficult to understand the Chinese Revolution. Not only is it Chinese; it is also Russian and Marxist.

Like a three-legged stool, the Communist hierarchy of power rests on three legs.

The Party. The first leg is that of the party. By "Communist party" one means something quite different from the "Republican" or "Democratic" party in the U.S. The CCP is the supreme authority, the final arbiter of conflict, the formulator of doctrine, the interpreter of orthodoxy. In Communist ideology, all power resides with the masses. But the party is the instrument by which the masses rule themselves. For this reason, it is supreme.

The hierarchy of the CCP looks like this:

Chairman
|
Standing Committee
|
Politburo
|
Central Committee
|
National Party Congress

Great power rests in the Politburo (twenty to thirty members) and in its Standing Committee (seven members). Since minutes and discussions are not made public, it is difficult to know how a consensus is reached. Often the announcements of decisions are delayed and not revealed until long afterwards. The Central Committee (one to two hundred members) is important to legitimatize and endorse decisions that have been made earlier by the leaders. When there is no agreement, meetings of the Central Committee are often delayed, or simply not held. During the turbulent years between 1962 and 1966 it did not meet once. The National Party Congress (one to two thousand members) meets irregularly, on an average of once every five or six years, and is useful in publicizing and interpreting party decisions. It is not a legislative body as the name would suggest but serves as the link between the central party apparatus and the party structure in the provinces. Like the Central Committee, when there is no consensus among the leaders, it does not meet. There were no meetings between 1956 and 1969.

The Government. The second leg of the stool is the administrative branch of the government with its separate hierarchical structure. Government ministries and departments run the day-to-day affairs of the country. Always the CCP sets the policy; the government agencies carry it out. Not only does the party issue directives at the top but has its members in key positions throughout the government structure who monitor decisions as to whether or not they are in accordance with approved doctrine. The government hierarchical structure looks like this:

Premier
|
State Council
(Ministries and Departments)
|
National People's Congress (NPC)
|
Chinese People's Political
Consultative Conference (CPPCC)

The premier is nominated by the Communist party and approved by the National People's Congress. The State Council corresponds roughly to a cabinet made up of vice-premiers, who control major functional systems, and the various ministers of finance, trade, foreign affairs, defense, health, education, etc. All vice-premiers and cabinet ministers are appointed by the Politburo. The National People's Congress is elected by corresponding provincial people's congresses who are elected by the people. The National People's Congress (three to four thousand deputies) approves changes in the constitution, adopts budgets, and enacts the legal codes. According to the constitution, it functions under the supervision of the Communist party. Non-party members may serve within the various ministries and in the People's Congress.

The Chinese People's Political Consultative Congress includes representatives from a great variety of people's associations throughout the country. Some non-Communist parties are included. Associations of women, youth, athletes, artists, trade unionists, and overseas Chinese are represented. Within the CPPCC is a religious group comprised of Buddhist, Islamic, Taoist, Catholic, and Protestant representatives. The Consultative Conference is advisory, but Christian members who have participated in it believe that their views and recommendations are taken seriously, and that they are able to make a significant contribution to the public life of the nation through this channel.[3]

The People's Liberation Army (PLA). The third leg of the stool is the army, but it is no ordinary army. The PLA cannot be understood as the counterpart of armies in other countries. It is the army of a party. It has an ideological mission as well as a defense mission. The chairman of the CCP is the commander-in-chief of the army. The army is recruited from the peasantry and is considered a select corps of model citizens who can be used in civil as well as military duties. The PLA operates some state farms, factories, and transportation facilities. It is the builder of roads and railroads. The army produces eighty percent of its own food. On an average a soldier spends fifty percent of his time on military duties, thirty percent on political study and activity, and twenty percent on productive labor.

In times of turbulence the army has assumed an active role in politics. During the Cultural Revolution, the army was the only leg that continued to hold up the stool when the other two legs (party and government) collapsed. In 1969 it dominated both the Central Committee and the Politburo.[4]

Motivation for Change

One of the most remarkable characteristics of China in this decade is the rapid change that took place among a people whom the West had thought of as changeless for a thousand years. How were so many people motivated for the sweeping revolutionary changes that were taking place? One must look beyond the structures of government to the dynamic process in which the people were involved.

Four Revolutionary Classes. First the people were made very conscious of class distinctions. One class was turned against another. Only in this way could momentum for radical change be built up. A coalition was formed between the "four revolutionary classes": workers (proletariat), poor and moderately wealthy peasants, petty bourgeoisie (shopkeepers), and national capitalists. The national capitalists demand some explanation. These were native Chinese business interests and companies that were not allied with foreign colonial interests and who had thrown their lot in with the CCP in the early stages of the revolution. These four revolutionary classes were recognized as having somewhat compatible interests, could share in the formation of the New China, and join forces in destroying the old.

Class struggle was the order of the day. The landlords, rich farmers, capitalists, rightists, and other "bad elements" were considered "enemies of the people" and had no rights. In the early days of the revolution a number of Christians were included among one or more of these latter groups and suffered harassment and persecution. To be classified as a member of one of the correct classes was all-important because class distinctions could be carried over to one's family and children. One might say that in the early days of the New China, class distinctions became more sharply drawn than ever before.

Mass Organizations. The central authority of the CCP was supreme. But in China's Communist ideology, this authority had to be closely linked to the sovereignty of the masses. This concept was called the "mass line" and might be considered the Communist version of Abraham Lincoln's "government of the people, by the people, and for the people." Expressed in Maoist terms, it was government "from the masses to the masses in an endless spiral."[5] First the party had to secure accurate reports from the peasants as to their opinions and problems. Next policy directives would be issued by the party to express the peasant viewpoint. Finally the masses had to be mobilized to adopt these policies as if they were their very own. To make the principle work, a constant relationship had to be maintained between the party leadership and the peasants. This helps to explain Mao's repeated attempts, often unsuccessful, to send party cadres back to the rural areas to reestablish connections with the peasantry.

To bridge the distance between the official structures of government and the people, mass organizations were created which reached the individual in his or her profession, peer group, and community. These national organizations included the All-China Federation of Democratic Women (76 million members in 1953), All-China Federation of Trade Unions (13 million members), Democratic Youth (34 million), the children's Young Pioneer corps (30 million), Sino-Soviet Friendship Association (68 million), and many, many more specialized associations dealing with the arts, sciences, and welfare activities. Communist party members dominated the key positions, but a broad representation of non-Communists was also included.

These organizations developed training programs, maintained social and recreational centers, and provided services such as libraries, medical care, pensions, and insurance. They sent representatives to provincial and national congresses and gave the citizens a sense of participation in the affairs of the country. Fairbank estimates that one half of the adult population of China was included in one or more of these groups and thus involved in programs, meetings, study, and agitation.[6]

Mass Movements.   Another phenomenon somewhat unique to Maoist communism is the mass movement, used as a powerful instrument for both control and social change. The Central Committee of the CCP would decide on the campaign target which could be the elimination of some social evil, the promotion of some new goal, or the interpretation of the latest shift in the mass line. A movement could be quickly launched and set in motion through the extensive apparatus of party, state, army, and the mass organizations. Enormous pressure could be quickly mobilized and concentrated on the target through the use of slogans, posters, marches, discussions, and peer pressure. Sometimes one individual would be chosen as an example and held up either for attack (such as the intellectual Hu Shih), or for emulation (such as the self-sacrificing soldier Lei Feng). Mass movements in the early 1950s included "eliminate the four pests" (flies, mosquitoes, bed-bugs, rats), "aid Korea to resist the United States," and many others.

The mass movements were a powerful weapon for political control and for mobilizing public opinion but often produced an overreaction and excessive violence. It was easier to turn on than to turn off and sometimes got out of control as party enthusiasts at local levels outdid each other in eliminating the evils which had been targeted for destruction. Fairbank cites as an example the campaign for the "Elimination of Counterrevolutionaries" in 1951, a reign of terror in the cities, characterized by mass arrests and mass executions.[7]

Thought Reform.   Accompanying the mass movements, which involved thousands of participants at a time, was a process of changing individual thinking and behavior through the use of small groups. Psychiatrist Robert Lifton suggests three stages in the process.[8] In the first stage group solidarity and togetherness are emphasized. In the second stage conflict and struggle are induced as each member engages in criticism of each other and then in self-criticism. Participants experience intense emotional conflict and are overwhelmed with feelings of guilt, shame, and humiliation. This prepares the members for the third stage which is one of submission and rebirth—something akin to a religious conversion experience. Confessions are written and rewritten until one is accepted by the group. The process was most successful among young people, less successful among older intellectuals. But even when the result was a *pro forma* confession, the participant was made dependent on the group, even though this was done unwillingly. Thus possible dissidents were neutralized.

Transition to Socialism

Whatever one may think of the means employed by the new masters of China, there is no doubt about one thing. They worked. Changeless China began to change. The human cost was enormous, but China began to throw off the shackles of the feudal past and move forward into socialism. To a remarkable degree, all parts of the vast country responded to the stimuli that were being applied to awaken and arouse the sleeping giant. The people of China were changing—from the northeast province nearest Russian Siberia to the borders in the south facing Vietnam, from the teeming cities along the Yellow Sea to the arid plateau of Central Asia. Villages and hamlets, factories and farms, schools and homes—nothing was quite the same as before.

Order was restored. Train service renewed. The railroad network was enlarged. Inflation was brought under control. But of most significance was the social transformation of the country. In 1950 three key laws were enacted which became the basic building blocks of the new society: marriage reform, agrarian reform, and urban reform.

Marriage Reform. The new marriage law of the People's Republic of China made a complete break with the male-dominated Confucian tradition. The new law abolished the feudal marriage system based on the superiority of man over woman and adopted the principle of equal rights for both partners. Bigamy, concubinage, and child betrothal were abolished. The exchange of dowries was prohibited. Marriages arranged by parents or other third parties were declared unlawful. Both husband and wife were to have equal rights to family property. Article eight of the code summed it all up:

> Husband and wife are in duty bound to love, respect, assist and look after each other, to live in harmony, to engage in production, to care for the children and to strive jointly for the welfare of the family and for the building up of a new society.[9]

Certainly the new law did not immediately remove all inequality between the sexes, or bring complete harmony for the family, or insure free choice of occupation. New tensions and problems were created such as the separation of husbands and wives due to work assignments. But recent visitors to the New China who knew the old have remarked that one of the most radical and beneficial changes has been in the changed role of women.

Agrarian Reform. Mao had said, "Whoever wins the peasants will win China. . . . Whoever solves the land question will win the peasants."[10] Thus, the importance of agrarian reform for the CCP: could it solve China's land problem that had defied solution for a thousand years?

The Agrarian Reform Law of June 1950 announced that the principle aim of land reform was "to confiscate the land of the landlord class and distribute it to the landless poor peasants."[11] The landlord class would be eliminated and there would be no more tenant farming. One-fourth of the country's agricultural production was affected by the decree. Three hundred million peasants would receive land from the distribution. The implementation of the law took three stages.

In stage one land reform squads would come to a village, explain the desirability of land reform, classify the villagers into different classes (poor peasant, middle peasant, rich peasant, landlord), and instigate a period of class struggle by which poor and middle peasants would be set against the wealthy landowners. Through accusation meetings and testimonials, unpopular landowners and "local bullies" would be held up for mob ridicule and denunciation. Not only landlords but other persons of influence and authority who might become centers of resistance were included. There would be a trial and the accused would be either executed,expelled, or led through a process of confession and reform. The property of the landlord would then be divided up between the poor and middle class peasants. Fairbank estimates that between two and five million people were executed by ''people's courts'' over the three-year period from 1949 to 1952.[12]

The second stage began with the organization of peasant associations or cooperatives. This was accomplished through the voluntary cooperation of the peasants. The reasoning was that small plots were inefficient, and that everybody would profit from the sharing of farm equipment, establishment of village industries, and more efficient marketing. Farmers would retain ownership of the land plots. According to a resolution adopted by the Central Committee in 1957, small scale village-sized cooperatives were to last for ten years.[13]

The cooperative stage, however, was short-lived. As a half-way station between private ownership and collectivization, they did not prove efficient. Basic agricultural problems were not solved. The year 1956 was a disappointment in farm production.

The third stage came quickly in 1958 when all cooperatives were replaced by communes. The passage from private to public ownership of property was now complete. Through this process, ''the inveterately property-conscious peasant, through propaganda, practice, and steady pressure [was led] to become . . . 'a socialist without knowing it.' ''[14]

Urban Reform.   Social transformation in the cities was more complicated. The CCP had control of heavy industry, the mines, and the railroads which had been nationalized or taken over at the time of the KMT collapse. But ''national capitalists,'' recognized as one of the four revolutionary classes and an ally of the Communist movement in the early days of the revolution, owned and operated a high percentage of light industry and commercial enterprises. Their expertise and management was needed. Outright confiscation would create chaos and disorder. Compromise, at least temporarily, was needed.

So the 1950 Law on Labor Unions, the third building block for social transformation, was far less radical than the other two. The law dealt only with the establishment of labor unions and their role in overseeing factory working conditions and negotiating with management over wages and benefits. The capitalists were left in control of their factories. For a while they flourished. Production sharply increased as did their profits.

At this point the leadership of the party seems to have been divided as to the next course of action. Some believed that the compromise worked out with the smaller capitalists should be continued in order that production, greatly needed for the reconstruction program, could be increased. This was the "rightist line." The "leftist line" held that the rising power and influence of the private sector of the economy should be curbed in line with orthodox party ideology. It was a debate that has recurred again and again up to the present time.

Mao sided with the leftists and in 1952 launched the twin movement—"Three Antis" and "Five Antis"—to break up the remaining merchant and manufacturing class. The "Three Antis" campaign, directed against corruption, waste, and authoritarianism, was aimed at government functionaries and bureaucrats who had used their influence in collaboration with the capitalists for their own gain. The goal of the "Five Antis" campaign was the elimination of bribery, tax evasion, fraud, stealing economic information from the government, and cheating in labor and materials. It was aimed at bringing the merchants and manufacturers under control. In the first six months of 1952, 450,000 companies were investigated for evil practices then under attack. Seventy-six percent were convicted. There were exorbitant fines, confiscation of property, and increased regulation and party control. The "national capitalists" were thus effectively neutralized. In January 1956 the remaining independent manufacturers and merchants "dutifully celebrated, with firecrackers and dancing, their own demise as a social class."[15]

The International Scene

The transition to socialism at home was carried out in the context of international turbulence and conflict. Soon after the establishment of the People's Republic in 1949, Mao traveled to Moscow, the first of only two trips he ever made outside of China. After weeks of hard bargaining with Stalin, a thirty-year mutual aid and friendship treaty was signed. But the benefits for China were less than expected. Three hundred million dollars in aid was received, but most of it was in the form of loans rather than outright grants. And a price had to be paid in the form of concessions and special interests for Russia in Manchuria. It was clear that Stalin intended to treat China as a satellite, similar to the Soviet bloc nations in Eastern Europe.

Relations with Russia improved dramatically with the beginning of the Korean War. Did the rulers of China know in advance of the Korean conflict? Evidence is divided. It is interesting to speculate that had the conflict not occurred, a *rapprochement* between China and the United States might have taken place decades earlier.[16] Whatever the case, the Soviet-armed North Korean invasion of South Korea in June 1950 certainly succeeded in destroying all chances of a Sino-American reconciliation. Was this the intent of those in Russia or North Korea who masterminded the campaign? United States forces were committed to the defense of South Korea and the Formosa Straits, should that be necessary. General Douglas MacArthur's drive to the Yalu River and the border of China's northeastern provinces precipitated the intervention of massive Chinese armies of "volunteers" under the command of Marshal Peng Dehuai of Long March fame. American troops were forced into a disastrous winter retreat. Then in turn China's attempt to take all of Korea by force of manpower also failed. The war dragged on in stalemate. Truce talks began in July 1951 and continued for nearly two years. In the end a negotiated armistice was signed in July 1953.

For China the war was a costly undertaking. The nation suffered 900,000 casualties, one of whom was Mao's own son who was killed in a bombing raid. The country was drained of economic resources at a time when they were sorely needed for reconstruction. But for the CCP the war also had its benefits. China emerged from the conflict a military power. The People's Republic had indeed "stood up" and had fought the United States to a standstill. The war effort had also mobilized the people at home in a great patriotic effort against a foreign enemy. This had united the country and speeded up the process of nationalizing its industries.

The First Five-Year Plan (1953–57)

By 1953 the CCP had consolidated its grip on both the countryside and the cities, and an armistice was signed ending the war in Korea. China was now ready for a major advance in development and modernization. This was to be accomplished through the first Five-Year Plan. The plan followed the Russian model which placed great emphasis on heavy industry and large production units. Perhaps against their best judgment, the Chinese administrators were persuaded by their Russian advisers that the agricultural sector would have to be neglected. The aim was to increase dramatically the production of steel, cement, machine tools, the development of mining, and the construction of railroads and dams.

During this period came the high-water mark of Russian influence. After the death of Stalin in 1953, China was received by Russia on more equal terms. Soviet special concessions in Manchuria were discontinued, and Soviet aid was increased. By 1956, 10,000 Soviet technicians were at work in China. Chinese engineers were sent to Russia for training. Study of the Russian language became compulsory for advancement within the party or industry.

The results of the first Five-Year Plan were spectacular in some areas. Sharp increases were made in the production of heavy industry, and the cities prospered. But for other sectors of the economy, the results were disappointing. The rural areas were falling further behind. During 1956, 500,000 peasants migrated into Shanghai, causing problems there. The contradictions and ambiguities of the Five-Year Plan began to be debated within the party leadership. Was the Russian model the best model for China? What about the imbalance which had developed "between the large production units and the small and middle-sized industrial units, between heavy and light industry, between regions of advanced development and average regions, between cities and rural areas"? The debate heralded a new shift in doctrine between "the two lines" and leads into the next period of China's history.[17]

But first we must turn to the religious scene and see how the church fared during these first years of the New China.

Tiananmen Square in Beijing

Author, Rev. G. Thompson Brown with Tiananmen (Gate of Heavenly Peace) in background

5
Christianity and the New China

How shall we sing the Lord's song
in a strange land?
(Psalm 137:4 KJV)

How did the Christian movement fare in the New China? It was a time of the testing of wills, of conflict of emotions, and of agonizing realignments. Many Christian institutions and agencies were taken over by the state. Relationships that had held the churches and Christians together were torn apart. It was a time of conflict between Christians and of alienation of missionaries, mission boards, and ecumenical councils. Above all else it was a time of clashing loyalties. The overwhelming number of Christians were patriotic Chinese committed to the welfare and the unity of their people. For the most part their sympathies had been with the KMT in the civil war, for the CCP was avowedly atheistic and was viewed as anti-Christian. Yet toward the end of the struggle, many Christians welcomed a change because of the corruption and incompetence of the Nationalist government. Many could not help but rejoice over some of the reforms which the CCP enacted. Christians had always been a very small minority, and there was now tremendous pressure to renounce their religious faith, along with their discredited political views. Some did. But for others loyalty to Christ was too deep. K. H. Ting speaks for them:

> However, Chinese Christians felt that there is something in Jesus Christ that makes us unwilling to depart from Him. "Thou has the word of eternal life, to whom shall we go?" That seems to be the thought that existed in the minds of many Chinese Christians. In spite of all the political reaction that had appeared in the name of the Christian faith, we felt there is something in Christian faith that speaks to us about things more ultimate than what the newspapers were talking about, and that speaking we need to hear.[1]

The Communist View of Religion

To understand the situation faced by the Chinese Christians, one must try to understand the Communist view of religion. That is not as simple as it might seem.

Religious freedom was guaranteed in Article 88 of the 1954 Constitution: "Citizens of the People's Republic of China enjoy freedom of religious belief." This guarantee was in line with classical Marxist dogma. Religion originated in primitive society because people were unable to explain or cope with the dreaded forces of nature. As classes of society developed, the upper classes found in religion a useful tool by which to control the lower classes. It became a tool of exploitation as expressed in Marx's famous dictum: "Religion is the opiate of the people." By focusing attention on the world of the spirit, the exploiters could take the minds of the exploited off their present condition of misery.

With the overthrow of the upper classes by the proletariat and the establishment of a classless society, the *raison d'être* for religion should disappear. Religion should wither away like a melon whose vine has been cut. This demise could take many years. But during the transitional period leading to the Communist state, force should not be used to eliminate religion for this would only make things worse. Religion is but a symptom, and once the root causes have been eliminated, then the symptom will disappear. So goes the theory.

Mao reiterated the classic position on religion in this statement made in 1927:

> The idols were set up by the peasants, and in time they will pull down the idols with their own hands; there is no need for anybody else to throw away prematurely the idols for them. The agitational line of the Communist Party in such matters should be: "Draw the bow full without letting go the arrow, and be on the alert."[2]

The cryptic phrase about drawing the bow seems to imply that the Communist party should always be on guard but should interfere in the worship of the idols only if this becomes a tool of exploitation of one class by another.

The Maoist position on religion can be better understood in the context of Mao's thesis, "On the Correct Handling of Contradictions

Among the People," which is considered his major contribution to Communist philosophy. In Maoist thought a "contradiction" refers to the struggle of opposing forces within a given situation, similar to the Hegelian dialectic of thesis and antithesis. But Mao made a distinction between two kinds of "contradictions." One is "antagonistic" and relates to differences between the "people" and the "enemy." The "enemy" meant the capitalists, feudalists, landlords, colonialists, and all who exploit the people. The second kind of "contradiction" is "nonantagonistic" and refers to differences which arise within the people. The first kind of "contradiction" must be met with force and destroyed. But the second kind can be dealt with through dialogue, discussion, debate, and education. In fact "nonantagonistic" contradictions may even be helpful in refining a new position. Differences over religion are considered "nonantagonistic" contradictions.

> We cannot abolish religion by administrative orders; nor can we force people not to believe in it. We cannot compel people to give up idealism, any more than we can force them to believe in Marxism. In settling matters of an ideological nature or controversial issues among the people, we can only use democratic methods, methods of discussion, of criticism, or persuasion and education, not coercive, high-handed methods.[3]

This noninterference with religion was the official doctrine. Actual practice, however, was quite different. This varied from place to place, depending on the local party functionary and on the particular rightist or leftist line that was being followed at that time.

To summarize the CCP's position on religion:

(1) *Religious freedom is narrowly defined.* It is something that is permitted within the four walls of a mosque, temple, or church, or something that takes place within the privacy of one's home. This freedom does not include the right of religious ceremony or display in public places.

(2) *Party and government have an obligation to promote atheism.* The state is not neutral. Atheism should be promoted through education, scientific research, and propaganda, but not by force.

(3) *A distinction is made between superstition and religion.* Superstitious practices are harmful to the people and cannot be tolerated. The state has an obligation to protect innocent and gullible people from ex-

ploitation by fortune tellers, shamans, and the sellers of magical po-
tions. Religion is viewed as something quite different. Though
misguided, it does have some legitimacy due to its historical and social
origins.

(4) *Christianity is a special case.* Christianity was viewed with a
greater degree of antagonism and suspicion because of its historical
links with the Western powers who oppressed China and with the capitalistic system that exploited the people. Christians could be singled out
and deprived of their rights as citizens, not because of their religious
faith, but because of their "rightist sympathies" or because of their
relationship with foreign missionaries. This was particularly true in the
early years of the People's Republic when China and the United States
were at war in Korea.

The Chinese Christian Movement in 1949

As the People's Republic of China came to power in 1949, it
faced a Christian movement that had a considerable following. Although the baptized membership was but a tiny fraction of the population as a whole, its influence was all out of proportion to its size.
Through a history of more than three hundred years it had a com-
mendable record of educational and social welfare programs and institutions. Although concentrated in the maritime provinces of the
east, there was an extensive network of chapels and centers throughout all the provinces. Chinese churches had relationships with more
than one hundred foreign mission boards, societies, orders, and international councils. In previous years, this had been an asset. It was
now a liability.

Statistics for the year 1949 are hard to come by, for China was then
in civil war and church affairs were in a complete state of disarray.
However, the following compilation gives some estimate of the size of
the Christian movement at that time.[4]

	Roman Catholic	Protestant	Total
Church Membership			
Baptized Members	3,274,740	936,000	4,210,740
Catechumens	194,712	600,000	794,712
Christian Constituency	3,469,452	1,536,000	5,005,452

	Roman Catholic	Protestant	Total
Clergy			
Chinese	2,698	2,024	4,722
Foreign	2,090	939	3,029
Total	4,788	2,963	7,751
Middle/High Schools	189	240	429
Universities	3	13	16
Hospitals	216	322	538
Total Missionary Personnel	4,441	4,091	8,532

The problem faced by Chinese Christian leaders was clear, and it was urgent. The issue was the survival of the Christian church in an environment which was hostile and for which the church was ill-prepared. How were they to "sing the LORD's song in a strange land"?

Two alternatives were open: first, to go underground; second, to work out some accommodation with the new rulers of China. Except for some indigenous sects and independent churches, most of the Protestant denominations and leaders chose, in some degree, the second option. In the beginning there were some encouraging signs that some *modus vivendi* could be worked out. The platform of the New Democracy included other non-Communist parties and groups. After all, the constitution did guarantee religious freedom, and initial contact with Communist leaders after they had taken up the reins of government were friendly. But to make an accommodation work, Christians would have to convince the new government of their loyalty and support. Relationships with missionaries and overseas mission boards and agencies would be a major obstacle, but even this did not seem to be insurmountable.

In December 1949, just a few months after the proclamation of the People's Republic, the National Christian Council of China sent a pastoral letter to all its constituent churches calling on Christians "with the greatest enthusiasm" to "give praise and glory to God for that awakening of the social conscience which we see spreading day by day under the New Democracy." The letter cited the accomplishments of the Protestant churches during their one hundred years of history in China, including education, the emancipation of women, schools for deaf and dumb, day nurseries, welfare of workers, and

rural reconstruction. The letter called on the churches to engage in
self-examination, to repent of past previous faults, "to hasten on to
real implementation of independence and self-support," and "to
make a determined struggle against the inequities of the economic
order and against social evils." The pastoral letter ended with a ringing appeal for support for the new era:

> Our doctors, nurses, teachers and social workers need to develop a
> yet greater spirit of service and sense of social mission. Our city and
> rural pastors and evangelists need better training in social service.
> Our Churches must put themselves positively behind the movement
> for increased production, and raise the people's standard of living;
> they must take a deeper interest in farmers and laborers, and those in
> society who are in special need of help; they must demonstrate within
> the life of their own fellowship the spirit of Christian equality, love
> and mutual aid; both within and without the Church they must sup-
> port all kinds of cooperative organizations and movements. They
> must seek to bring more abundant life, both spiritual and material to
> their own members and to all the people they serve.[5]

About this same time, a group of Christian leaders representing
most of the major denominations issued a "Message from Chinese
Christians to Mission Boards Abroad." The letter was remarkably
friendly, realistic about the present conditions, and somewhat optimistic about international cooperation in the future. It stressed the radical
nature of the revolution which had taken place and the necessity of
rigorously scrutinizing China's traditional heritage. As Christians they
felt "the urgent necessity of re-examining our work and our relationship with the older churches abroad in the light of this historical change
in China." However, they said there was no need to reexamine their
faith, "for our fundamental faith in Christ is not to be shaken, and
under the New Democracy, freedom of religious faith is definitely stip-
ulated." The Communist view that Christianity had been implicated
with imperialism and capitalism was admitted. But the authors of the
letter went on to say:

> We do realize and so wish to assert that missionary work in China
> never had any direct relationship with governmental policies; mission
> funds have always been contributed by the rank and file of common
> ordinary Christians and church members; missionaries have been sent
> here for no other purpose than to preach the Christian gospel of love,

and to serve the needs of the Chinese people. The central Christian motivation will not and can never be questioned, but these other social implications can very easily give rise to misunderstanding and accusation.

Specifically, three points were made as to future policy: (1) Policy determination and financial administration should pass to Chinese leadership wherever this had not yet been done. (2) There was "nothing in principle which makes the future position of the missionary untenable, or renders his service unnecessary." An open mind toward the new political environment would be necessary. The future contribution of the missionary would not be along administrative lines: "To BE, to SHARE, and to LIVE will be a significant contribution in itself." (3) Financial support would still be welcomed, provided there were no strings attached, but it should be considered temporary in nature.[6]

The Rise of the Three-Self Movement

At this stage of history there emerged a man who was to dominate the Protestant church scene for the next decade. Y. T. Wu (Wu Yao-tsung) is not an easy man to understand. Some spoke of him as a "marginal Christian," others as a "patriotic Christian citizen." Some felt that he had given up key elements of historic biblical Christianity. Others called him a "prophet before his time." Frank W. Price, a Southern Presbyterian missionary, wrote of him:

> Y.T. Wu is like an Old Testament prophet: his soul is seared by the social sins and injustices that he sees around him, and his words, though quietly spoken and written, lash and cut. He has made a thorough study of socialist and Communist theories and seeks a truly Christian answer to their challenge; some, therefore, think of him as a radical. But he is also mystical and a man of prayer.[7]

Mr. Wu, converted to Christianity as a young man, gave up a promising career in the customs service to become a YMCA secretary. He attended Union Theological Seminary in New York and was influenced by the worldwide Christian socialist movement of the 1930s. In China he founded a Christian weekly known as *Tian Feng* ("Heavenly Wind"), which focused on social and political issues. He became more and more sympathetic to the Chinese Communist ideals and became acquainted with Zhou Enlai. In 1948, at the height of the civil war between the Nationalists and the Communists, Wu wrote a controversial article for *Tian Feng* entitled "The Present-Day Tragedy of Christianity," to which many trace the origins of the Three-Self Movement. He said that the situation of the Chinese Christian Church was tragic:

> Because China is today face to face with the greatest change in its history, and in this period of great change the Christian Church, besides the negative reactions of feeling sorry for itself, and trying to escape reality, has nothing to say or do.[8]

He deplored the close connection that existed between the Christian Church in China, Western capitalism, and the United States in particular. He wrote that though Christianity claimed to be above political ideology, actually it had become the tool of reactionary forces opposed to social change. He saw the world breaking into two camps, one desiring and one resisting social change, and he feared that the church was on the wrong side. The article recognized the "many honorable persons and many noteworthy accomplishments" of the church but declared that basically "Christianity has no understanding of today's revolutionary movement." The article ended with a ringing affirmation of the ultimate victory of the risen Christ:

> It is this that proves that the risen Jesus is forever our light and our strength. In spite of our stupidity, weakness and selfishness, he still forever stands before us, beckoning us forward to a rebirth of mind and soul.[9]

The article created quite a sensation and Y. T. Wu was forced to resign as editor of *Tian Feng*. However, with the victory of the Communist forces the next year, his leadership in the church and the New Democracy was assured.

In May 1950 he led a group of Christian leaders to meet with Premier Zhou Enlai in Beijing to discuss future government relations. Zhou's remarks were to the effect that no new or furloughed missionaries would be permitted to enter China, that those missionaries then in China might stay if there was no question of their political activity, and that neither missionaries nor Chinese Christian leaders should visit areas affected by the land reform movement then in progress. Zhou urged the church to rid itself of all imperialistic foreign influences, implying that if this was done, government protection would follow. It was probably at this meeting that Zhou remarked to the Christian delegation:

> So we are going to go on letting you teach, trying to convert the people. . . . After all we both believe that truth will prevail; we think your beliefs untrue and false, therefore if we are right, the people will reject them, and your church will decay. If you are right, then the people will believe you, but as we are sure that you are wrong, we are prepared for that risk.[10]

During the meeting, Y.T. Wu discussed with the premier the preparation of a paper which would become known as the "Christian Manifesto." The first draft was written by Wu and approved by the premier. Wu returned to Shanghai and presented it to Christian leaders there. There was considerable opposition to the document. Many refused to sign it the way it was and asked for revisions. Wu resisted the changes on the grounds that the premier had already approved the draft. But the group insisted, and Wu returned to Beijing and secured Zhou's approval for the suggested changes. A second meeting was held in Shanghai, but there were still objections and demands for moderation in the language. Finally the group was told there could be no further changes since this was the "official form" approved by the premier. The Anglican bishops withdrew and issued their own statement.

The "Christian Manifesto" was published in July 1950 over the signatures of forty prominent Christian leaders. By this time war had broken out in Korea, anti-American sentiment was rampant, and patriotic fervor was high. A massive campaign was launched to get Christians all over China to sign the statement. It is reported that by 1952 at least 400,000 Christians had signed it.

The "Christian Manifesto" began with the acknowledgement that Protestant Christianity had "made a not unworthy contribution to Chinese society." Nevertheless, since most of the "missionaries who brought Christianity to China all came themselves from these imperialistic countries, Christianity consciously or unconsciously, directly or indirectly, became related with imperialism." The Manifesto called on Chinese Christians to heighten their "vigilance against imperialism, to make known the clear political stand of Christians in New China, to hasten the building of a Chinese church whose affairs are managed by the Chinese themselves." Christians should support the "Common Political Platform'' and under the leadership of the government ''oppose imperialism, feudalism, and bureaucratic capitalism.'' The church should purge itself of imperialistic influences. America was singled out for denunciation for ''its plot to use religion in fostering the growth of reactionary forces.'' More specifically, those churches and organizations relying on foreign personnel and financial aid should discontinue these relations within the shortest possible period of time and work toward self-reliance.[11]

In October 1950 the biennual meeting of the Chinese National Christian Council was held for the purpose of adopting the Manifesto and implementing means to bring about ''Three-Self Reform.'' Missionary members of the council were excluded. The Manifesto was adopted, perhaps under considerable duress. Although the Chinese National Christian Council lingered on, it was eclipsed by a new organization created to implement the new direction set by the Manifesto.

In April 1951 the newly organized Religious Affairs Bureau of the government invited 151 Protestant leaders to a conference in Beijing to deal with the problem of Christian institutions formerly receiving mission aid. The conference voted

> . . . to thoroughly, permanently and completely sever all relations with American missions and all other missions, thus realizing self-government, self-support and self-propagation in the Chinese church.[12]

In order to carry this out, the Protestant Three-Self Patriotic Movement was established. Y.T. Wu was elected chairman. The ''Three-Self'' formula (self-government, self-support, self-propagation) had been taken from a page in the old missionary tradition, but it was applied in a new radical way. When T.C. Chao (Chao Tsu-chen), dean of the Yenching University School of Religion, resigned his position as one of the six presidents of the World Council of Churches in 1952 in protest against the action of the WCC Central Committee in approving United Nations intervention in the Korean War, the break with all international and ecumenical relationships was complete.

Orientation to Communism

With the establishment of the Three-Self Movement, pressure to purge the church of imperialistic influences increased. The next step was the initiation of training classes for preachers and other Christian leaders. These were begun in Shanghai in the fall of 1953 under the sponsorship of the Three-Self Committee and the Religious Affairs Bureau of the government. Soon they spread to various other parts of the country. Study classes lasted from several weeks to three to four months in length. The subjects included patriotism, the contrast between the old and the New China, the nature of imperialism, and the meaning of the Three-Self Movement. The climax of the course was a personal autobiographical essay required of each participant. Students were expected to tell how they had been affected by imperialistic influences and how their thinking had changed. A confession of wrong doing and an affirmation of complete support of the New China was required. The process was much the same as that for secular study and discussion groups which had been held all over the country since 1949 and were required for all sectors of society.

Along with the training sessions came one of the most difficult and painful aspects of this period—the accusation meeting. Those singled out for the special treatment included missionaries, persons who had refused to sign the ''Manifesto'' or seemed lukewarm in their support, and those who had held positions of importance before 1949. Often a close associate of the person to be accused was chosen for the denunciation. There was a set pattern for the accusation. It began with a sweeping denunciation of the accused in strong, bitter language. A list of specific charges followed. Charges included cultural aggression, support of American imperialism, being a ''running dog'' of the foreigners, connection with missionaries, or of just being a ''bad element.'' The accusation concluded with a demand that the government punish the offender in an appropriate way. The New China News Agency of Shanghai for May 15, 1951, carried an article on ''How to Hold a Successful Accusation Meeting'' and offered this advice:

> The order of arrangement of the accusers is very important; they should be arranged as follows: first high tension, then moderate, then another of high tension, etc.; only so can the accusation meeting be a success. When the accusations have succeeded in deeply stirring people, clapping and applause may be used as a form of expression.[13]

It seemed that no one was exempt from the possibility of an accusation. Dr. T. C. Chao was one of the most influential supporters of the "Manifesto," but later he was accused by faculty, students, and workers at Yenching for supporting "American imperialism in utilizing Yenching to promote its cultural invasion of China." He was dismissed from the university and suspended as a priest of the Anglican communion.

The most celebrated accusation case was that of the Rev. Wang Mingdao. It is also one of the most difficult to justify. Wang was pastor of an independent Protestant church in Beijing and an extremely popular itinerant evangelist. He was not related to any overseas mission board and his church was entirely "self-governing, self-supporting, and self-propagating." However, he had steadfastly refused to sign the "Manifesto" or have anything to do with the "Three-Self Movement" because of the liberal theological views of its leaders. He also believed that the church should not become involved in what he felt were political campaigns. In July 1954 a public denunciation meeting was held against him in Beijing. Wang was placed on the platform and never said a word during the denunciations. However, popular sentiment supported Wang and the denunciation fizzled. He went back to his pulpit and continued his own attacks on the Three-Self Movement. A year later he was denounced again and arrested. After a year in prison, he was released in broken health, having signed a confession. Later he repudiated the confession and again was arrested. He remained in prison twenty-two years and was finally released in late December 1979 at the age of seventy-nine. Today he is reported in fairly good health although partly blind and deaf. His case is documented by Amnesty International.[14] Other leaders of indigenous Christian sects such as Watchman Nee of the Little Flock and Isaac Wei of the True Jesus Church suffered the same fate as Wang Mingdao.

Roman Catholic Resistance

Roman Catholics in China had suffered more than their Protestant counterparts in the Communist-occupied areas of China before 1949 and were less optimistic of the future. Two factors made accommodation more difficult for them than for the Protestants and resistance more inevitable. First was the continued Vatican recognition of the Nationalist regime on Taiwan. Second was the necessity for the papacy to make all appointments of bishops. Both these factors accentuated the foreign nature of the church in the eyes of the Chinese. One native Chinese bishop had been consecrated in the seventeenth century. No Chinese bishop had been consecrated during the next two hundred years. In 1949 four-fifths of the bishops and two-fifths of all priests were foreigners.

Relations between the Vatican and the PRC broke down almost immediately because of the "Riberi Affair." Archbishop Antonio Riberi, a diplomat of the Holy See, was sent to China as apostolic nuncio in 1946 by Pius XII. In 1949 when the People's Republic was established, Riberi remained at his post although his accreditation was to the departed Nationalist regime. The Vatican continued its recognition of the Nationalists, who had set up their seat of government in Taiwan. This produced a nearly impossible diplomatic impasse. According to protocol, the presence of an official diplomatic officer of such a rank would have required recognition of the new government. Otherwise his presence would have been *persona non grata,* and he should have left. It appears that the People's Republic of China waited patiently for two years for some signs of recognition. At a conference with Catholic leaders in Beijing in January 1951, Premier Zhou Enlai is reported to have said, "It is necessary for Catholics to remain united with Rome in the spiritual field."[15]

Archbishop Riberi continued to warn of the dangers of communism and urged all missionaries to stay at their posts in the face of persecution and possible martyrdom. He encouraged the organization of the Legion of Mary, which proved to be a very effective lay Catholic movement in many areas as a means of strengthening parish life and continuing services when priests were under surveillance or not available. But the militant nature of the organization, translated in Chinese as the "Army of the Holy Mother," brought down the wrath of Communist party officials.

Criticism of the papal nuncio came to a head in May 1951 when he repudiated the patriotic church movement then in progress. He was placed under house arrest and later escorted by third-class railroad coach to the Hong Kong border and unceremoniously expelled from the country.

Initially the PRC made attempts to organize Roman Catholics along the same lines that had proved so effective with the Protestants. In 1951 an organization called the "Three Autonomies" (similar to the Protestant Three-Self Movement) was pushed. The Catholic bishops countered with a statement entitled "The Church in China: Declaration of Principles." The document claimed the church was moving toward a gradual assumption of control by native bishops, rejected any pressure from outside to organize its inner life and structure, denied any imperialistic connections, warned of the dangers of schism from Rome, prohibited all priests from political activity, and strictly charged Catholics to love their country.

In spite of mounting pressure for participation in the "Three Autonomies" movement, it was largely unsuccessful. A new name was tried—the "Anti-imperialist Movement for the Love of Country and Church." This proved somewhat more successful, but still only a small number supported it. Later it was known simply as the Patriotic Association. When a parish was known to have a "patriotic priest," attendance at mass would drop dramatically. The government was unsuccessful in getting any Catholic of any stature to take the leadership of the movement. As late as 1954 it was reported that 115 out of 143 dioceses were still resistant to the patriotic movement.

Examples of devotion and courage by Catholic priests and lay people abound during these years. How many suffered long years in prison, and even death, will never be known. Two names stand out as examples of the high caliber of Christian witness in the face of the mounting pressure.

Father John Tung (Tung Shih-chih) of Chongqing was asked to speak at a mass meeting on June 3, 1951, to denounce Riberi on behalf of the patriotic church. He gladly agreed to speak and began by saying that he feared the attack on Riberi would be followed by an attack on the pope and then one on Christ. As an alternative to that course, he offered himself:

> Gentlemen, I have only one soul and I cannot divide it; I have a body which can be divided. It is best, it seems, to offer my whole soul to God and to the Holy Church; and my body to my country. If she is pleased with it, I do not refuse it to her. Good materialists, who deny the existence of the soul, cannot but be satisfied with the offering of my body.[16]

He continued by saying that if he spoke against his conscience his confession would only deceive the authorities, sowing further discord between government and church. He admired the courage of the Communists who were capable of facing death without fear; he prayed for their conversion, and he hoped that his "poor speech," which had the approval of neither the church or state officials, would help bring about reconciliation between the two. A month later he was imprisoned. Reports in 1965 indicated he was working in a labor camp in a remote area and in good spirits.

Father Beda Chang, director of the Bureau of Chinese Studies in Shanghai, was arrested in August 1951 along with two other priests. The were charged with opposing student control of their Catholic schools, supporting the Kuomintang, and engaging in counterrevolutionary activities. Father Chang died in prison three months later and there was evidence that he had either been beaten to death or gone into a coma after long and repeated questioning. The courageous example of Father Chang served to stiffen the Catholic resistance, and the churches of Shanghai were crowded for requiem masses held for the martyred priest.[17]

By 1955 the percentage of Catholics who refused to cooperate with the patriotic movement had dropped to about thirty percent. Only ten percent were actively following the party line, and the remainder were somewhere in the middle. But as the year wore on, the balance began to tip in the direction of the Patriotic Association. The arrests of foreign and native priests and the continued harassment of the lay people were having their effects.

Shanghai was still a center of resistance. On September 7, 1955, the blow fell here. During the night, Bishop Gong Binmei (Kung Pinmei), twenty-one priests, two nuns, and from two to three hundred lay Catholics were arrested. Later in the month an additional fifteen to twenty priests and between six and seven hundred additional laypeople were arrested. Bishop Gong was accused of being a spy and saboteur. There were similar roundups in other major cities. Along with the arrests were denunciation meetings and study-and-discussion groups sponsored by the Catholic Patriotic Association. Organized resistance was broken.

By this time many of the bishoprics were vacant due to death, old age, expulsion, or imprisonment. Some had been vacant for a long time, even before 1949. Undoubtedly this had become a critical problem for the hierarchy and for the welfare of the Catholic community. In February 1958 the Patriotic Association issued a call for the election and consecration of new bishops to meet the critical shortage. Two priests in Wuhan were the first ones elected by popular vote of priests in that area. Names of these first two candidates for consecration were sent by cable to the Vatican. The Chinese hierarchy insisted that the election was according to canon law. The Holy See replied, however, that the elections were invalid and warned the consecrating bishop and the two priests of excommunication. The priests were consecrated anyway. By mid-1958 between twenty-five and thirty new bishops were consecrated. Many of these were undoubtedly loyal servants of the church who feared that if they rejected the election, party lackeys would be put into office, thus further compromising parish life within their diocese.

These consecrations are now held by the Vatican as "valid" but "illicit." That is, although they were irregularly performed, they do have validity for the proper functioning of parish life in China. The Vatican has refrained from calling the church in China "schismatic." That would be the case only if it had separated itself from Rome "knowingly, willingly, and obstinately." But, in the words of Carlo van Melckebecke, a former bishop in China, that is hardly the case:

> We know they are desperately trying to maintain the faith, to keep the church alive, to give their Catholic people the sacraments they need. . . . Even if some of their actions are materially wrong, we are not in a position to judge their persons and even less to condemn them.[18]

The End of the Missionary Era

How did the missionary community fare during these days? During the later days of the civil war there had been guarded optimism about the possibilities of working under the "new regime." In 1948 Dr. E. E. Walline reported to the meeting of the China Council of the Presbyterian Church, U.S.A., that missionaries "are entering into a period of great opportunity in China." The Methodist Board of Missions, at its annual meeting in January 1949 "pledged to carry on its missionary work in China despite dangers and obstacles created by the Chinese civil war.'' During 1948 new missionaries were still being appointed to China by mission boards, and the old hands were returning after furlough.[19]

There was certainly work to do. Missionary letters written in 1948 tell of these activities.

Refugees.

What fills our hearts with deep distress . . . is the pitiful plight of millions of poor refugees in North Kiangsu and Southern Shantung. Not only have they been harassed and despoiled by communist, and sometimes by government, soldiers, also, but actual famine prevails over large sections of our field, due to two successive crop failures. Hundreds of thousands have passed through Suchowfu going south in open freight cars, and tens of thousands are remaining here, some starving. We are trying to do something for them through the American Advisory Committee and the International Relief Committee. But time is against us, and unfortunately nature will not declare a moratorium on starvation, so during these next two months (April and May) multitudes will starve to death.

Church Activities.

Presbytery has just been meeting, also our summer training class for leaders with a registered attendance of about eighty. Reports of giving throughout the field is most encouraging. Churches throughout our own field are reporting many accessions on profession of faith. Schools and hospitals at the peak. We have matchless opportunities for service—greater than ever before—but of course are much under-manned.

The "Five-Cakes Movement."

The Christians in our Suchowful city churches of their own accord have started a "Five-Cakes-Movement" (Wu Bing Yun Dong), with the slogan that five bean cakes (large discs of dried soy beans, from which the oil has been pressed) will save a life until harvest. They hope to secure enough through their contributions to purchase 2,000 bean cakes and thus save the lives of 400 starving Christians in the country.

Forebodings about the Future.

I feel like one who is standing in the twilight, and trying to keep back the dark. But I'm no pessimist, as I said. The night is coming—it seems almost to be upon us—but "the morning cometh too." . . .

Eternal Optimism.

It is true that the fall of the capital of Shantung, Tsinan, 200 miles to the north, has shattered the morale somewhat, and that some of our doctors are leaving. It is true that our railroads, north, south, east and west are being cut and repaired every few days. And it is true that last summer, American Consul "alerted" us and advised women and children to leave, but the situation has improved since then. We do not feel that we have a call from the Lord to leave his work yet, for it seems more important than ever.[20]

As the Nationalist armies disintegrated, and the victory of the People's Liberation Army became imminent, agonizing decisions had to be made about whether to leave or whether to stay. In some cases it was obvious that the presence of missionaries would be an embarrassment and a danger for the Christian community, and it was best to leave. In other cases the church leaders pled with their missionary colleagues to stay with them. Mission boards, in most cases, left the decision up to the individual missionary.

Attempts were made to work with the new rulers of China by those who stayed. After all Christian missionaries had lived and worked and given their loyalty to many differing regimes and governments during the long, tumultuous years. There had been other revolutions, and in each case some *modus vivendi* had been worked out. And the "Message from Chinese Christians to Mission Boards Abroad," which has already been quoted, indicated that missionaries would still be welcome.

In response to the new situation, the Board of World Missions of the Presbyterian Church, U.S., soon after the People's Republic had been established, adopted the following policy statement which makes clear this desire to continue work under the new government of China:

It is the earnest desire of the Presbyterian Church, in full cooperation with the Church of Christ in China, to continue its Christian service under the Communist regime. The Christian people of the United States are eager to maintain the close bonds of friendship with the people of China and to express that friendship concretely in a continued program of cooperation with the Chinese church and to assist those institutions, including Christian hospitals and Christian universities, that are an essential part of the Church's ministry to the Chinese people. As evidence of this continuing policy, missionaries

> are remaining at their posts of service in China and new missionaries
> have already gone or are preparing to go. We trust that this mission-
> ary service will still be welcome to China.[21]

The attempt was made. It is important that this be noted. But it
soon became apparent that, with the new political environment, missionaries would not be welcome. They were subjected to travel restrictions. Foreign property was exorbitantly taxed. The presence of
missionaries became more and more an embarrassment and threat for
Chinese Christians and the institutions which they served.

With the entrance of Chinese troops into the Korean conflict, all
possibility of an accommodation ended. The United States froze Chinese assets in America in December 1950. China retaliated. The Administrative Council of the PRC demanded that all Christian churches
in China and related hospitals and schools break relations with American mission boards. One by one Protestant universities and colleges
were taken over by the government. Roman Catholics estimated that at
the end of 1951 nine-tenths of their educational facilities had either
been destroyed or confiscated by the government.

It seems that certain influential missionaries, perhaps those with
most popular appeal, were singled out for denunciation. It was important to discredit the Christian movement through its foreign "imperialistic" connections. Methodist missionary the Rev. Olin Stockwell,
who had been quite friendly with the incoming Communists, was arrested at his residence in Chengdu, Sichuan, in November 1950. He
was imprisoned for two years on charges of espionage. Dr. William
Wallace, Southern Baptist hospital superintendent at Wuzhou, died in
prison in February 1951. Gene Carleton Lacy, bishop of the Methodist
Church in Fuzhou (Foochow), suffered a heart attack after considerable
harassment and house arrest for a year. He was buried at night, without
a funeral.[22] Roman Catholics suffered more. Bishop Francis X. Ford of
Maryknoll was placed under house arrest and then transported to
Guangzhou (Canton) for deportation. Richard Bush quotes from
sources which tell of his harassment and maltreatment in route. His
health deteriorated and he died and was buried in Guangzhou in February 1952.[23]

When the denunciation meetings began in early 1951, Dr. Frank
W. Price, Presbyterian missionary in Shanghai, was one of the special

targets. His accuser was his former colleague, the Rev. H.H. Ts'ui (Ts'ui Hsien-hsiang), general secretary of the Church of Christ in China. He was charged with being an adviser to Chiang Kai-shek and taking orders from the U.S. State Department. Accusers claimed that Dr. Price once arranged for fifty Chinese students to go to America and stay in American homes "to poison the minds of the Chinese young people."[24] For months, Dr. Price had a small suitcase packed in case police should arrive to take him to prison. He heard mob slogans against him broadcast over the radio. But strangely enough the police never came. He and Mrs. Price were denied exit permits for two years but were allowed to continue living in their home in Shanghai. Permission to leave was finally granted in October 1952 after they turned over their Shanghai residence, frozen mission bank account, and mission seals to the government-approved church organization. Thus ended Southern Presbyterian mission work in China which had begun in August 1867.

Another celebrated case was that of Bishop James E. Walsh of Maryknoll. He was director of the Catholic Central Bureau of Shanghai and was the only Catholic missionary left within the People's Republic after 1954. He had a fair degree of freedom until he was arrested in October 1958. He was held without trial for violating unspecified Chinese laws until March 1960 when he was indicted in a mass trial with thirteen other Roman Catholics. The charge was collusion in sheltering spies, collecting restricted state information, setting up counterrevolutionary activities, and maintaining clandestine radio communication with U.S. imperialists. His sentence was for twenty years. He was suddenly released in July 1970 as a part of the general relaxation of tensions between the U.S.A. and the PRC. After his release, while in Hong Kong, Bishop Walsh reported to the press that he had been well treated while in prison, that the government had brought about changes in the life of the country which were beneficial, and that he hoped for some amelioration in the church situation in the future.[25] Bishop Walsh died at his home in Maryknoll, New York, in August 1981.

One of the last and most colorful of the China missionaries was Ellen Nielsen, a missionary of the Danish Missionary Society in Takushan, Manchuria. She became a Chinese citizen and supported herself through the sale of milk and butter from her three cows. Her letters report evangelistic services of considerable success. She

served a small Christian community until her death in 1960 at the age
of 89.[26]

In reviewing this difficult and painful period, it is well to remember
the nature of the times. During some of these years, Chinese volunteers
were fighting American soldiers and other U.N. troops in Korea. Chinese casualties were estimated at 900,000. The Chinese people knew
only what the papers and the radio broadcasts told them and nothing of
the other side of the Korean conflict. The United States had pledged
support for a regime in Taiwan that claimed sovereignty over all of
China and vowed to return to the mainland in force. The People's Republic was understandably nervous about spies and counterrevolutionary agents. Once a mass movement was unleashed, it became difficult
to control and easily went to extremes which the leaders had not anticipated. We have only to remember the actions Americans and our own
government took against loyal Japanese living along theWest Coast
during the early days of World War II to understand what war hysteria
can do.

Dr. Price summarized this "end of an era":

> Under the spell of ardent nationalism and surrounded by powerful
> Communist pressure, the Chinese people are repudiating the Western
> forms and imperialist associations of Christianity, but they have not
> repudiated all Christian faith and teaching.[27]

That faith was still very much alive as is evidenced in this hymn
written by an anonymous Christian in Beijing, possibly Wang
Mingdao, beautifully translated by Francis Price Jones:

> Father, long before creation
> Thou hadst chosen us in love;
> And that love, so deep, so moving,
>   Draws us close to Christ above.
>   Still it keeps us,
>   Still it keeps us,
>   Firmly fixed in Christ alone.
>
> Though the world may change its fashion,
>   Yet our God is e'er the same;
> His compassion and His covenant
>   Through all ages will remain.
>   God's own children,
>   God's own children,
>   Must forever praise His name.

God's compassion is my story,
  Is my boasting all the day;
Mercy free and never failing
  Moves my will, directs my way.
    God so loved us,
    God so loved us,
  That His only Son He gave.

Loving Father, now before Thee
  We will ever praise Thy love;
And our song will sound unceasing
  Till we reach our home above,
    Giving glory,
    Giving glory,
  To our God and to the Lamb.[28]

Learnings

What can be learned from the withdrawal of Christian missions from China after nearly 150 years of witness and service? This question was addressed by the Division of Foreign Missions of the National Council of Churches at a three-day conference held at Stony Point, N.Y., in June 1951 which was attended by missionaries who had recently returned from China. The experience of their last months in that country was still very fresh in their minds. The conference used a questionnaire which had been mailed to a large number of Protestant missionaries. One-hundred-fifty-two responses, representing missionaries from twenty-two boards, were received.

Among the questions asked were these: (1) "What lessons have you learned from missionary experience in China which would be suggestive of what *should not be* repeated in other missionary fields?" (2) "What lessons have you learned which, in your opinion, *should be* incorporated in mission work in other fields?"

The first seven answers to each question, showing the concerns with the highest number of votes in rank order, is most enlightening. The negative lessons—in response to question (1)—were

(1)   Much *talk* about self-support but not enough *action* in that direction.

(2)   Educational and medical work outstripped the development of the church in size of institution and quality of leadership.

(3)   There was too much foreign-owned and controlled property in many places, including large houses in high-walled isolated residence compounds.

(4)   Too little effort was made by the church to help the farmers in the villages or exploited factory workers in cities.

(5)   Too many missionaries had an inadequate understanding of the Chinese language, customs, culture, philosophy.

(6)   Too many missionaries kept too much control too long over institutions, funds, policies, methods, and activities.

(7)   The church as it developed remained too western in character—not sufficiently indigenous as to thought patterns, worship, architecture and activities.

The positive lessons—in response to question (2)—were

(1)   Everything which has been done to improve the lot of women, girls, and children is all to the good today. We have been pioneers from the beginning in the education and welfare of women and children.

(2)   The degree to which we carried developments of National Leadership, including Lay Training, is very advantageous today.

(3)   Having Chinese principals for the schools and colleges since 1927 (a government requirement) has been of inestimable value. The same is true where Chinese doctors have been superintendents of hospitals.

(4)   Medical service and public health work have been effective means of service to the people, important expressions of Christian compassion, and examples and stimuli to the public authorities for the development of health services.

(5)   The longtime democratic participation by Chinese church leaders in arranging the local distribution of field budgets and of the location and assignments of missionary personnel has proven of great value in recent years.

(6)   The building up of strong Christian character, which gives high moral standards of living, has been achieved in countless individual men and women.

(7)   The development of appreciation for the values of corporate worship, fellowship in work and prayer is a great contribution to the life of Christian Chinese.

The conference itself had a message addressed to the mission boards. A strong affirmation of the mission was made:

> The taking of the Christian Gospel to China and the establishment of the Church of Jesus Christ among the Chinese people, we believe to be the plan and work of God, ultimately triumphing over all the human weakness of the missionary movement.

Faults and mistakes were also acknowledged:

> We humbly confess great faults in the planting and development of the Church, such as the divisions of our denominations, the large-scale neglect of rural masses, the inadequate training and use of lay workers, the provision of property and support on a Western scale unsuited to the Chinese scene.

There was rejoicing over the achievements of unity:

> We rejoice in the considerable measures of cooperation and of union which have latterly been achieved in important sectors of the Chinese Church. Recognizing that the initiative and the choice rest with the Church in China itself, we are sure that whatever relations may hereafter obtain between us and the Chinese Church, should be characterized increasingly by an interdenominational and international approach through the agencies appropriate thereto.

There was a readiness to follow the leadership of the church in China:

> Unwilling and unable to attempt predictions of the development of Chinese and of world affairs, we quietly affirm our wholehearted readiness to cooperate in full mutuality with the Church in China when that Church desires such a relationship. Whatever we could do that might be helpful to the Christian Church in China should be centered not in a foreign missionary enterprise, but, carrying forward a change already well begun, should center in the Chinese Church. We expect to learn from the life of the Chinese Church in these present years, and to be strengthened in heart by its response to the Spirit of God.[29]

Donald MacInnis, director of the Maryknoll in China History Project, points out one striking omission in the report:

> Nowhere do these missionaries, recently living in the midst of the greatest revolutionary upheaval in modern history, refer to that cataclysmic event, or to the social forces that brought it about, nor do they point to the need to understand and relate to such events in the future.[30]

The conference report does speak of the "immense revolution of China" with the possibility of this occurring in other lands. This, they said, sharpened the urgency of their recommendations. Perhaps this was all they could say at that time. They were writing in 1951, all too close to their experience to see it clearly.

Eighteen months later Dr. Frank W. Price, in his own evaluation of the "end of the era," is more forceful:

> Communism is a judgment, a warning and a challenge. It may in unexpected ways bring about what we have long hoped for—a Christian church rooted in the soil of China, and not dependent on the missionary finances and personnel of Western countries. The Communist attack on superstitions and bad social customs remove some age-long obstacles to the extension of the Christian religion. . . .
>
> All Asia is in ferment. What has happened in China may happen in other Asiatic countries. Christian missions and the new Christian Churches of Asia are on trial.
>
> **I would say to missionaries in every land—work as if this were your last year; prepare the church where you are for the storm that may come.**[31]

Former Gin Ling College for Women in Nanjing with statue of Mao Zedong

Pictures of Mao Zedong and Hua Guofend hanging in sanctuary of the Mo En Protestant Church in Beijing

6

The Great
Leap Forward

What gain has the worker from his toil?
(Ecclesiastes 3:9)

The year 1956 marked a turning point for the People's Republic of China. It was a time of confusion and crisis for international communism. In February Nikita Khrushchev made his secret report denouncing Stalin to the Twentieth Congress of the Communist party of the Soviet Union. The shift caught China by surprise and led to questions about the Russian leadership. There followed the uprisings in Poland and Hungary, which sent shock waves throughout the Communist world. The monolithic nature of international communism could no longer be taken for granted.

Within China cracks were beginning to appear within the leadership of the CCP. Gao Gang, party veteran and boss of the Northeast Provinces (Manchuria), was dismissed and killed himself. He was accused of establishing an independent power base with Soviet help and promoting provincial interests in opposition to the central government. It was the first of many purges to come. Disenchantment with the results of the first Five-Year Plan was growing. Rural areas had suffered from neglect. Was the Russian model for development the right one for China? A great deal had been accomplished during those first six years. But the massive social reforms had produced considerable dislocation and dissent. The party apparatus had grown too fast for its own good. In the beginning there were 1,200,000 revolutionaries. These had been succeeded by 10,340,000 elite party functionaries.

"Let a Hundred Flowers Bloom"

One particular concern was the attitude of the intellectuals. Some who had vigorously supported the revolution had become lukewarm or openly hostile. Hu Feng, an old time fellow-traveler for the Communist cause before liberation, took up the cause of the individual rights of authors, protesting the bureaucratic supervision that was being required. He was denounced as a counterrevolutionary and arrested. This created quite a sensation, and perhaps because of the incident, Premier Zhou Enlai, in a report to the Central Committee in January 1956, spoke of the necessity for gaining the support of the intellectuals again. Their scholarship and technology were needed. Only forty percent of the intellectuals fully supported the party, forty percent had traveled only halfway, and the remainder were either indifferent or counterrevolutionary.[1]

In order to regain their support the party launched in May 1956 a campaign known as the "Hundred Flowers"—taken from the slogan, "Let a hundred flowers bloom, let a hundred schools of thought contend." Mao stated that Marxists should not be afraid of criticism, that it was needed for correction and reform, and he urged the citizens of China to be frank and open in their grievances. The invitation for criticism was addressed primarily to the intellectuals, and it was suggested that the faults and shortcomings of the party cadres and functionaries be made known.

Questions have been raised as to the motive for launching the campaign. One view holds that it was a sincere attempt to invite criticism which would be helpful in bringing about badly needed reform within the party bureaucracy. Mao believed that he had overwhelming support for the party, and that no real criticism of the system would surface. The other view holds that the campaign was a cynical attempt to "smoke out" the opposition which was developing so they could be detected and cut down.

Whatever the case, the deluge of criticism which came down on the party and state was something for which few were prepared. The whole country cut loose with a barrage of complaints through forums, discussion groups, letters to the editor, speeches, and publications. Students denounced arrogant party officials. Business leaders exposed disastrous orders from party administrators. Teachers hated the long hours required at Marxist study meetings. Scientists complained of unqualified officials being advanced to high positions because of party connections. Some even called for an end to one-party rule, advocating a multiparty system and the right to establish legal opposition parties. Again and again came the recurring refrain—people wanted more freedom to speak, freedom to move, freedom to publish, freedom to disagree.

The party was totally unprepared for this outburst which they had invited. Thus this time of freedom to criticize was short lived. Weeds were growing in the garden of the hundred flowers and had to be cut down! In June 1957 *The People's Daily* launched a counterattack. Many critics were leaving the path of national unity, the editorial said. They were openly advocating a return to the bourgeois-democratic system. This would lead to class struggle and violence. It could not be tolerated. "Correct criticism" was still welcome, but the article left no doubt as to what was meant. The period of the "Hundred Flowers" was suddenly brought to an end.

The aftermath was the antirightist campaign of 1957. All summer long there were public hearings, accusations, and self-criticism. Hundreds of thousands of intellectuals and party cadres were sent to the villages for reeducation.[2]

A Great Leap to Increase Production

In November 1957 Mao returned from his visit to Moscow where he attended the fortieth anniversary of the Russian October Revolution. It was his second and last trip outside China, and the visit left him disillusioned with Russia. Although an appearance of unity was preserved in their joint communique, his talks with Khrushchev had not gone well. He felt that with Stalin's death, his position of seniority within the Communist camp should have been recognized. Nor was Russia as generous in economic aid as had been expected.

One of the basic problems was that the Russian model of economic development which had been slavishly followed in the first Five-Year Plan had not worked well for China. Heavy industry, requiring massive injections of capital, had been emphasized at the expense of light industry. Cities had been emphasized at the expense of the countryside. The agricultural sector was stagnant while the urban population was growing at an unhealthy thirty percent. Food production was becoming a problem. The gap between peasant and city worker was increasing. Elitism was creeping back into the structure. Central decision making had not been practical in a country as vast as China with limited com-

munication and transportation facilities. And China's one major re-
source—man- and womanpower—had been underutilized.

A radical new Chinese model of development was needed. Such a
model would "walk on two legs"—both industry and agriculture
would be emphasized. Economic decisions would be decentralized.
Small, self-contained industries would be planted in the countryside.
The model would utilize "human power" in place of "capital power."
There would be a mass mobilization of rural labor unmatched in China's long history. Such a model would require a massive herculean
effort to move forward. It would be motivated by Maoist ideology.
"Dare to think! Dare to act!" said Mao. "The main factor is man, not
weapons." Such an effort would "overtake Great Britain in fifteen
years." It would be called "The Great Leap Forward."

Some were skeptical. Technocrats and administrators wondered
whether it would work. The ranks of the economists had been depleted
by the antirightist campaign, and so the planning was done by those
unfamiliar with production goals. The Russian advisers shook their
heads in skepticism. Khrushchev, using the strongest language in the
Communist dictionary, called the experiment "Trotskyism." But
"politics was in command" and the campaign was launched in early
1958.

The first reports were encouraging. There was a bumper harvest in
1958. Production goals were increased and time tables shortened. A
sense of euphoria prevailed. In August the Beidaihe (Peitaiho) Resolution was issued which called for the most radical development yet—the
establishment of mammoth people's communes:

> . . . the establishment of people's communes . . . is the fundamental
> policy to guide the peasants to accelerate socialist construction, com-
> plete the building of socialism ahead of time, . . .
> . . . Chinese society *will enter into the era of communism* where
> the principle from each according to his ability and to each according
> to his needs will be practiced.[3]

A sympathetic observer, Edgar Snow, wrote that "in the whole
history of the People's Republic there had never been such an abrupt
and sweeping change ordered by so loosely worded a directive."[4] It
should be remembered that no Communist state, not even Russia,
ever claimed to have arrived at the utopian Communist era to which

the directive pointed. Although the language of the communique indicated these changes might take a number of years, this was forgotten in the rush to bring in the era of communism which was just over the horizon. Smaller cooperatives were merged into mammoth organizations. All of China's rural people would be placed in more than 26,000 communes. One such commune in Guangdong numbered 276,358 people and included 738 dining halls to feed the multitudes. Individualism was frowned upon. Privately owned plots of land became a thing of the past. Late marriages were encouraged. Romantic attachments were taboo. Children were cared for in live-in nurseries, so the productivity of the parents would not suffer. Six-hundred thousand small blast furnaces were put into operation. The people were urged on to greater and greater efforts. Examples of workers remaining on duty for twenty-four hours at a time were praised and publicized.

Catastrophic Results

Undoubtedly the face of the nation was changed with dikes and dams, roads and factories, forestation and lakes, embankments and irrigation. But the net effect of the Leap must be judged a catastrophic failure. Disappointing statistics began to pour in during 1959. Early production reports had been inflated to meet the ideologically set goals and had to be revised downward. The 1959 harvest was well below average because of bad weather. Much of the industrial output was of such poor quality it could not be used. Such was the case with the iron and steel produced in the backyard furnaces. Serious engineering errors were made in project designs, resulting in the waste of materials and energy.

The year 1960 was no better. A drought in the north and floods in the south undid the hard work of the peasants. Food shortages developed, requiring the importation of grain. Repairs and maintenance were neglected in the reckless use of machines, resulting in worn out equipment. This led to an overall production in 1961 and 1962 which was less than it was before the Leap began. Productivity of farmers and laborers suffered because everyone was paid the same according to the egalitarian wage system. Incentive was lacking. In the end the Great Leap simply collapsed from general overwork and exhaustion.[5]

Showdown at the Central Committee

At the meeting of the Central Committee held at Lushan in August 1959, the magnitude of the disaster was becoming apparent. Mao was on the defensive. Peng Dehuai, the minister of defense, led a blistering attack on the Great Leap Forward and indirectly on Mao himself. He was supported by Zhu De, the hero of the Long March. Liu Shaoqi was more moderate but clearly supported a move to the right, away from the radical leftist position of Mao. Zhou Enlai, ever the peacemaker, worked for some kind of compromise.

Mao almost lost control. In the end he got his own way on some issues, but on others there was compromise. Peng Dehuai was dismissed. Lin Biao was appointed minister of defense in his stead, an appointment that all would soon regret. Mao's self-criticism over his failures in the Great Leap is most revealing:

> I am a complete outsider when it comes to economic construction, and I understand nothing about industrial planning. . . . But, comrades, in 1958 and 1959 the main responsibility was mine and you should take me to task. . . . Who was responsible for the idea of the mass smelting of steel? . . . I say it was me. . . . In June I talked about 10,700,000 tons. Then we went ahead and did it. It was published in the Peitaiho communique. . . . With this, we rushed into a great catastrophe, and ninety million people went into battle. . . .
>
> . . . I do not claim to have invented the people's communes, only to have proposed them. The Peitaiho Resolution was drafted according to my suggestion.
>
> I have committed two crimes, one of which is calling for 10,700,000 tons of steel. . . . As for the people's communes, the whole world opposed them; the Soviet Union opposed them . . . you can share some of the responsibility for this.[6]

Mao turned over many of the day-to-day affairs of the country to Liu to whom he had earlier relinquished the presidency of the republic. Liu and his pragmatic protégé Deng Xiaoping ran the country while Mao retired from public view—for a while.

The rightists were now in control, and the country swung back from the disastrous radicalism of the Great Leap Forward. The size of the communes was drastically reduced. Ownership and administration of property was transferred from the communes to the much smaller, village-sized production brigades. Pay incentives for better work or for those with greater responsibility were reintroduced. The experiments of mass dormitories, dining halls, and live-in nurseries were abandoned. Family life returned to normal. Private plots of farm land were once again permitted. Farm production increased accordingly. Once again China had changed courses—this time to the right—and for a while there was an uneasy truce between the two camps within the party leadership.

The Break with Russia

Relations with Soviet Russia continued to deteriorate after Mao's visit to Moscow in 1957. Khrushchev visited Beijing in 1959, but the summit meeting did little to heal the breach. In 1960 the Soviets abruptly withdrew all their technicians from China and discontinued all developmental assistance. Fourteen hundred Russian advisers left the country, abandoning many projects. Of the 300 industrial installations which Russia had agreed to help, only 154 had been completed at the time of the withdrawal.

Mao writes, "We spent the whole of 1961 arguing with Khrushchev." In April and May of 1962 there were skirmishes between soldiers along the border of the Ili river in the far northeast. Again in 1963 there were clashes between Soviet customs officers and Chinese railway employees. By then the break was complete and has continued to this day.

What were the reasons? One was ideological. China charged that Soviet Russia was "revisionist." By this China meant that Russia had betrayed the principles of its own October Revolution, was reverting to capitalism, and had been in collusion with American imperialism. It should be remembered that Khrushchev had met with President Dwight D. Eisenhower at Camp David during the summer of 1959 and backed down at the time of the Cuban missile crisis in 1962. Russia was critical of the Great Leap Forward from the beginning and felt that China was engaged in reckless experiments that were doomed to failure. China had been guilty of one-up-manship in claiming to have arrived at the Communist state before Russia.

Perhaps a deeper reason for the break was divergent national interest. China and Russia share a long common border stretching across the whole distance of Asia. In places it is still ill-defined. On the Russian side it is sparsely populated, and the Soviets feel vulnerable to possible pressure from the south. Russia refused to back up China in her dispute with India in 1958 and took the side of China's rival. Both China and Russia are competitors for leadership among Communist parties and revolutionary movements in various parts of the world. China, as a Third World country, has claimed a dominant role which the Soviets have not acknowledged.

Then there is the matter of temperament. Somehow neither side was able to hit it off with the other. The Russian technicians in China were aloof, kept to themselves, appeared to the Chinese as arrogant and crude. They had the same frustrations as a generation of "China changers" had before them—and less patience. Most of the Chinese intellectual class had been trained in the liberal Western tradition. Changing to Russian language and thought forms did not come easy. The common Marxist revolutionary heritage was not the common bond as one might have expected, for the origins of the Chinese revolution were quite different from that of the Russian. China was Confucian and oriental; Russia was Byzantine and European. The two did not easily mix.

Church Life Goes On

Protestant Christianity showed remarkable resiliency as it moved into the 1950s. In spite of the turmoil, accusation meetings, and political activity at the top echelons of the church, Christian life at the grass roots continued to show vitality and even some growth. There were reports of ordinations, baptisms, student conferences, Bible study, and evangelistic meetings. Some churches, closed during the time of the great land reforms, reopened. Bibles, books of sermons, commentaries, and devotional literature continued to be published and sold in book stores.

The number of churches undoubtedly dropped. There were numerous consolidations. Weaker churches closed. Some church buildings were confiscated by party officials. Some Christians were harassed by the government. But Christian life and witness, worship and devotion went on. Francis P. Jones estimates that church membership probably dropped as much as forty percent in the early years of the Communist rule, but then that gains made during the mid-1950s resulted in numbers probably seventy-five percent of the 1949 figures.[7]

Information about church life becomes increasingly scarce during the 1950s, and what information we have comes from either *Tian Feng*, the occasional visits of Chinese Christians outside of China, or the few Western Christians permitted to visit the PRC during these years. Richard Bush writes that reports of these visitors during 1955–57, "all affirmed that church life was vigorous, that worship was vital, that evangelism or 'extension' was going on, that Sunday schools, YMCA, and YWCA were active."[8]

This time of comparative freedom was during the period of the "Hundred Flowers" when "blooming and contending" was encouraged. Christians, along with the intellectuals, quickly responded to the call for criticism. They spoke out openly about the discrimination against their children in the schools, harassment in places of employment, the seizure of church buildings, abusive language by officials, and the denial of religious freedom guaranteed by the constitution. Christian leaders took their complaints to the provincial and municipal consultative conferences on which they served as representatives.

Defense Against Atheism

Two addresses by Christians during this period are worthy of note as examples of the vigorous theological thinking of some Protestant leaders. The Rev. Marcus Cheng, a prominent evangelical and vigorous supporter of the Three-Self Movement, addressed the People's Political Consultative Conference in Beijing in March 1957 during the "Hundred Flowers" period on the subject of respect for religious belief. Cheng followed Y. T. Wu, who had spoken to the assembly citing a number of problems that had arisen in the implementation of the policy of religious freedom. But Cheng went further. He had some very forthright things to say about the abusive treatment of Christians by party cadres:

> Therefore believers have freedom to preach their faith, and unbelievers have freedom to criticize religion, and the attempt in this controversy to discover the truth should be carried out calmly, without abuse or name-calling. You speak out your atheism and I will preach my theism, and in this controversy you must not take to abusing my mother, defiling my ancestral graves or reviling my ancestors. In the eyes of us Christians, God is the Supreme Being, and the churches are His temples, the place where Christians worship Him. In the ar-

gument over theism and atheism you must not revile God, or blaspheme His name; you must not take our churches by force.[9]

He went on to say that the antireligious propaganda which was translated from the Russian was inappropriate for China, for social conditions were quite different. He cited the example of many of the revolutionary martyrs who were Christians and the example of Jesus, the carpenter, the Son of God, who spent most of his years in common labor among laboring people. While continuing to stress the saving grace of Christ upon the cross and salvation in Christ's blood, he affirmed that Christian doctrine had been enriched through the study of Marxist political economics.

The second address was made by Bishop K. H. Ting, president of the Nanjing Theological Seminary, to his students in June 1957 on the subject "Christian Theism."[10] The address is a brilliant defense of theism against the Marxist position. In this the most articulate statement of Christian theology during this period, Ting expressed differences between Christians and Marxists in some critical areas.

Christianity and the Idealism-Materialism Question. Christians believe that the Marxist classification of thought as either materialistic or idealistic is a great oversimplification. Christianity cannot be classified as either idealistic or materialistic. Its true nature is revealed in the incarnation of Jesus Christ and thus transcends this and all other human lines of philosophical thought.

Is Christianity an Opiate? Religion may at times have been used as an opiate, just as many other things in the world (literature, art) have also been used as opiates. But the use of Christianity as an opiate does not belong to the essence of Christianity. Jesus Christ refused the opiate offered him when he was bearing the sins of humanity on the cross. Christians have likewise refused the opiate of religion by opposing the oppression of the poor by the rich.

The Existence of God. Human reason can come to the conclusion that there is a certain order in nature. By reason we can go no further. But faith is higher than scientific demonstration. Religion is betting one's life on the existence of God. Ultimately we come to know God through revelation in Jesus Christ, who has said, "I am the way, the truth, and the life." The truth of this is borne out by countless Christians.

Environment and Sin.   Atheistic thinking attributes all the ills of society to a bad social system. Christians in the past thought too little about the social order and have been helped by this emphasis. But the question of sin is still fundamental. In the New China the level of morality has been raised, and for this Christians should be grateful. But the question of personal sin has still not been solved. Sin is not just a matter of social progress. Sin can only be healed through forgiveness, salvation, and grace.

The Reason for Unbelief.   Why then is there so much unbelief? There are two reasons. The first is moral and spiritual. To believe in God makes certain demands upon a person. In order to avoid facing this issue, people from the beginning of history have drugged themselves by a denial of God's existence so they could continue to sin, avoid responsibility, and stifle their conscience. When this happens, unbelief becomes the opiate! The second reason for unbelief is the failure of the church to show forth the light of God. This is especially true when the church has been on the side of those who oppress the people.

Faith and Fellowship.   Theism and atheism are matters of personal faith and do not pertain to governments. Christians should not be influenced by governments who claim to be Christian but are self-righteous and use this claim for political purposes. On the other hand, the Communists are atheists, and Christians do not approve of their atheism but can welcome their political leadership and their frank attitude regarding questions of belief. It is a great responsibility for the Chinese Christians to establish a church in a socialist country, for that has never been accomplished before. But Christians of China can take heart, for although the church is weak and without prestige, the Lord of the church can use this weakness to show forth God's might.

Steady Decline

This period of "blooming and contending," when freedom of expression was encouraged, was short-lived. As we have seen, it was followed by the antirightist campaign when many of those who dared to speak out were sent to work camps or publicly denounced and humiliated. For Protestant Christians this campaign began when 130 Christian leaders were called to Beijing late in 1957 by the standing committee of the Three-Self Movement. At the meeting an attack was made on six prominent church leaders for having spoken out in criticism. Among these was Marcus Cheng. His speech before the People's Political Consultative Conference was used against him. Although denounced, he apparently continued in his position as pastor. Some of the others denounced were dismissed from their church positions and joined the ranks of the factory workers. Taking the cue from the Beijing accusation meeting, extremists in various parts of the country sought out Christians who had been lukewarm or uncommitted to the socialist cause, had them denounced, and sent off to the work camps. There is no way of knowing how great this number was. Christians met with the same treatment meted out to the many others accused of rightist tendencies during this period. Because of their international relationships, many Christians were more vulnerable to public attack.

The antirightist campaign was but the prelude for the Great Leap Forward which began in 1958. Christians, along with other citizens, were caught up in the great upheaval of this era. The massive public works projects and the regimentation of life in the communes made church worship and activity much more difficult. Pastors were expected to engage in other productive labor. There was no set time when church worship could be conducted regularly. Yet the reports in the papers complaining of "irregular" church services, such as faith healing, exorcism, praying for rain, and solicitation of funds, indicated considerable church activity was still going on.[11] After 1958 most Sunday schools and youth activities disappeared. Worship was the only thing left. Sources of information after 1958 become fewer and fewer, but the few reports we do have indicate that church life was steadily on the decline.

In the midst of the Great Leap Forward, one new development did take place: the unification of churches and worship services. *Documents of the Three-Self Movement* contains a number of descriptions of how this was done in various parts of the country. A meeting in the city would be called by the Religious Affairs Bureau and the Three-Self Committee. After some discussion, all would agree that unification would be a good thing because the number of churches was more than needed, the differences between denominations were not important, the savings in buildings and energy would benefit the social progress of the country.

For example, in Taiyuan, the capital of Shanxi Province, it was decided to unify all Protestant churches under a ministerial staff of three or four persons. All other pastors were told to "throw themselves into the Socialist construction of our mother country." All church property was turned over to the Three-Self Committee. All former governing committees and boards were abolished. Regarding religious teachings:

> All books used in the interpretation of the Bible shall be examined and judged, and those containing poisonous thoughts shall be rejected. Only teachings favoring union and socialism shall be used. . . . There shall be no more preaching about the Last Day, or about the vanity of this world. This is negative and pessimistic teaching. Instead we shall emphasize the need for the union of faith and practice, the dignity of labor, the control of nature, and the dividing line between ourselves and our enemies.[12]

In Beijing the number of congregations was reduced from sixty-five to four. In Shanghai two hundred Protestant congregations were reduced to twenty-three. Some of the support for the merger of worship services undoubtedly came from the Christians themselves for practical considerations. Dr. Francis P. Jones cites evidence for believing that government interference was minimal. However, the reference to the control of Christian teaching and theology in the Taiyuan merger does sound ominous—especially in view of what was to come in the mid-1960s. Dr. Jones also reports that after the first wave of enthusiasm for the mergers, a reaction did sometimes occur, and the congregations were free to return to their former denominational preferences.[13]

In 1960 Nanjing Theological Seminary still had a student body of eighty-five. There were only twenty-five students in 1964, but observers who visited the seminary that year were favorably impressed with the quality of the curriculum and the minimal attention given to Marxist teaching. The last seminary class graduated in 1966. The Bible Society continued to print Bibles up to 1958 and possibly longer. It was merged with the Christian Literature Society and other Christian publishing houses in 1958 but continued to keep a rather large supply of Scriptures in its book store and warehouse until 1966. *Tian Feng* continued publication as a weekly until 1956 when it became a biweekly. Halfway through 1960 it suspended publication, apparently for financial reasons, and then resumed publication as a monthly.

Thus slowly, but inexorably, church life and activities waned. At such a time reports coming out of Hong Kong seemed all the more remarkable. Some young people coming out of the People's Republic during the 1960s immediately sought a church, having only recently been converted to the Christian faith in China! Somehow the church in China during this difficult time had found a way to nurture its own inner life and to communicate its faith in a convincing and appealing way to those outside.

7

The Great Proletarian Cultural Revolution

Help us, O God of our salvation,
  for the glory of thy name; . . .
Why should the nations say,
  "Where is their God?"
         (Psalm 79:9–10)

The Great Proletarian Cultural Revolution was an event without precedent in the history of world communism. It took "China watchers" and the whole world by surprise. No one could have predicted it. When the news of this new revolution suddenly burst on the world scene in the summer of 1966, observers were totally astonished at the rapidity with which the movement developed, the emotional fanaticism of the participants, and the party factionalism that was publicly displayed.

The movement was full of contradictions: a combination of circuslike theatrics and the somber spectacle of public executions, a near-deification of Mao along with a denunciation of all religion, a fundamentalism of "the little red book" with the public burning of the Bible, high ideals along with brutality. The time-honored Chinese respect for the elderly was reversed, and boys and girls in their teens assaulted senior party officials. The long-standing Chinese love for learning was upset as schools and universities were attacked and professors and presidents sent off to the countryside for "reeducation" through manual labor. It was all so un-Chinese! How and why did it happen?

The Cultural Revolution might be considered as a Chinese opera in five acts.

Act One: Setting the Stage (November 1965)

The Dramatis Personae. Five old men, average age 66, dominated the plot. All had been comrades since the early days of the

Chinese Communist party. All had shared the rigors of the Long March and the years of uncertainty at Yanan.

Mao Zedong, 73, the dominant personality of the Communist Revolution, still had enormous influence and popular prestige. Since the failure of the Great Leap Forward, however, he had withdrawn from the administration of national affairs and had become somewhat isolated from the party bureaucracy. He was not entirely happy with the direction in which administrators and party functionaries were leading the country. The massive party bureaucracy was becoming more entrenched, giving every indication of leading to a new elite privileged class. Would the old revolutionary ideals be lost?

Lin Biao, 58 and youngest of the five, had for seven years been defense minister since the ouster of Peng Dehuai for criticizing the master. Lin had been army commander in the Northeast Provinces (Manchuria) and had gained the decisive victory over the KMT armies there at the time of the liberation. He opposed a professional caste system for the army, believing in a peasant army of comrades like the old Yanan days. Lin was more of a Maoist than Mao himself. He was also a very ambitious man.

Liu Shaoqi, 68, president of the People's Republic since Mao had stepped down in 1958, was the party organizer, the organization man. He held the reins of the party apparatus and was more interested in stability and production than revolutionary idealism. Since the days of the Great Leap Forward, the ideological gap between him and Mao had been growing.

Deng Xiaoping, 62, had led the Red armies across the Yangtze River in the final assault on Nanjing and Shanghai. In the affairs of government he was the protégé of Liu and served as the party general secretary. He was known as a pragmatist, who once remarked, ''It hardly matters whether a good cat is black or white—as long as it catches mice, it is a good cat!''

Zhou Enlai, 68, had held the posts of premier and foreign minister since the beginning of the People's Republic. Suave and urbane, he was the consummate diplomat. He had the ability to survive in a top position of leadership, mediating between different positions, bringing a measure of stability to the administration when other prima donnas were veering off to one extreme or the other.

These five men held the power of the country in their hands. Mao and Lin were advocates of the leftist line—continuing the revolution. Liu and Deng were on the right—favoring stability and production. Zhou was somewhere in between, playing the role of the conciliator, but his sympathies undoubtedly were more on the side of stability than ideology. In Henry Kissinger's apt phrase, he "worked unobtrusively to assure the continuity of life rather than the permanence of upheaval."[1]

The Stage.   The stage for the opening scenes of the drama shifted from Beijing to the south. In the fall of 1965 Mao absented himself from the capital for about six months. It was the longest time he had been away. One might imagine he found himself stifled in the city which was firmly controlled by party administrators and functionaries. Any play for reform or a change of direction would have to be initiated elsewhere. Where best could such a move be made but in Shanghai—the largest city of China, the commercial and industrial center of the Yangtze valley? Here radicals were in positions of leadership. Here was the home base for all members of what was later to be called the infamous "Gang of Four."[2] Shanghai became the cockpit for the Cultural Revolution.

The Curtain Rises.   Strange as it may seem, the Cultural Revolution began with the publication in a Shanghai newspaper of a critique of a play which had been produced five years earlier in Beijing! The play was *The Dismissal of Hai Rui*. The playwright was Wu Han, deputy mayor of Beijing. In the plot, Hai Rui, a loyal official of the Ming Dynasty, was dismissed from office for his honest criticism of the emperor. The comparison with Mao's dismissal of Peng Dehuai was pointed and obvious. The drama critic was a young Shanghai journalist named Yao Wenyuan, who had allegedly been coached by Mao to attack the satire in which he had been portrayed as the villain.

Act Two: The Plot Thickens (Early 1966)

The controversy began to boil as newspapers around the country rallied to the support of Mao. Beijing papers were silent. The author of the play issued the standard self-criticism and the authorities in Beijing tried to soft-peddle the issue and keep it from getting out of hand.

But Mao's supporters were not willing to let the controversy pass, wishing to use it as a springboard for a general offensive against bourgeois elements who, it was said, had infiltrated the system. Still using Shanghai as a base, Mao organized an ad hoc committee including Lin Biao, who could deliver army support if needed, and Mao's wife, Jiang Qing, a former movie actress from Shanghai. This group soon had control of the media and launched a campaign against the "four olds": old habits, old ideas, old customs, and old culture. The official army newspaper very quickly added its support. The whole country was beginning to be aroused.

In May 1966 the first *dazibao* (big character posters) began to appear on the campus of Beijing University. The posters attacked the administrators of the university and the municipal government. They demanded that more peasants and workers be admitted to the university and that "red" (ideological) training replace "expert" (technological) training. Red Guards began to form. The president of the university was ousted. Entrance examinations were abolished on the grounds that these favored sons and daughters from bourgeois families. A new curriculum elevated Mao's writings to a central position.

Considerable public support developed for the student-led movement. The appeal for reforms had struck a responsive chord. High idealism was in the air. Service and self-sacrifice were rallying cries. Education in the universities had become elitist, and party cadres were unresponsive to the people's needs. Bureaucracy is often a popular whipping boy!

Act Three: The Red Guards (1966–67)

During all or most of this time, Mao had been out of the capital, withdrawn from public view. There was speculation that he was in ill-health or had lost power. Then in July, dramatically, he made his famous swim across the Yangtze at Wuhan. This signaled his good health and his return to active involvement in the momentous affairs that were beginning to sweep the country.

Soon after, he returned to Beijing and posted his own *dazibao* on the door of the Central Committee: "Bombard the Headquarters!" Was it an ultimatum addressed to the recalcitrant committee which had not met for four years? Or had the balance of power shifted to the leftist line advocated by Mao? Incredibly it would seem, Mao was advocating an attack on his own Communist party!

The Central Committee met August 1 for twelve days, during which time they in effect endorsed retroactively the direction of the Cultural Revolution already in progress. The committee identified as targets those elements which had infiltrated the party, held leadership posts, and advocated a return to the "capitalist road." Obviously, this meant Liu and Deng. Clearly the movement was being shifted from the cultural to the political sphere. It would sweep through the party and purge cadres and officials from top to bottom of all bourgeois tendencies.

The stage was now set for the Red Guards. Middle schools and universities were closed so that students could take part in the mass movement and spearhead the attack. Free transportation was offered on all trains. The press sounded the alarm. Students were brought to Beijing in large numbers. More than one million at a time were harangued by Mao in Tiananmen Square. It is said that 11,000,000 Red Guards assembled in the great square between August and November 1966. Mao and Lin wore Red Guard arm bands and urged them on under the slogan, "Revolution is not wrong; it is right to rebel." In Beijing one million students demonstrated for thirty hours outside the Soviet Embassy. The British Embassy was attacked and nearly destroyed.

From Beijing groups of Red Guards were sent out across the country on "Long Marches." They were charged to criticize everything, to distrust all cadres. They denounced bourgeois luxuries, taxicabs, Western style clothes, and long hair. Offenders were shaved bald. Armed with copies of a little red book called *The Thoughts of Mao Zedong*, they defied all order and were responsible to no one.

Party officials fought back. There was armed conflict between industrial workers and guards in Shanghai, Wuhan, Guangzhou, and Qingtao. Ninety thousand were reported killed in factional strife in the province of Sichuan.[3] Factions of the Red Guards attacked each other. When things got totally out of hand, the People's Liberation Army stepped in to restore order.

Off and on all through 1967, the Red Guards continued on their rampage. No one was immune as party officials in high positions of authority were assaulted. An eye witness account tells of an attack on the governor of a province:

> One day, my friend told me that Hu Yaobang, who was elected Governor of Shaanxi Province in 1965, had been arrested by the Red Guards and was being publicly punished by them daily. The next morning I went with a group of friends to see if the report was true. . . .
>
> Upon entering the square, we heard Red Guards—most of them middle school students about 15 or 16 years old—chanting a song of the Cultural Revolution. Loosely translated, the words were, "We must strike down the evil group! Let us, the students of the Revolution, rebel and form the vanguard." Suddenly all eyes turned to the Red Guards on one of the balconies. The 53-year-old Mr. Hu was dragged out by two of them. Around his neck was a thin, strong wire supporting a heavy wooden ball so large it obscured most of his body. Printed on the ball was the imperative, "Strike Down Hu Yaobang!" The words were marked with a red X, signifying that he was a reactionary. As soon as he was in view of the public, cries of "Strike down Hu Yaobang!" arose from the ranks of the Red Guards. When at last they quieted down, one of the two men who flanked him grabbed a microphone and ferociously screamed, "Hu Yaobang! Confess your crimes against Chairman Mao!"
>
> The brave Mr. Hu replied strongly, "I have never opposed Chairman Mao!" and the infuriated Guard replied, "You lie!" whereupon three Guards forced the small, aging man to kneel, as they screamed again, "Strike down Hu Yaobang! We will strike down all opponents of Chairman Mao!" Incredibly, Mr. Hu showed no sign of fear. Then the Guards punched him viciously all over his body, yelling, "You must confess! You lie! You must confess!" But he remained completely silent. One of the Guards reproached him threateningly for his obstinacy, pulling him up and hauling him into the building. The back of Mr. Hu's white shirt was thoroughly soaked with perspiration. I was very impressed with his composure and strength.[4]

The "brave Mr. Hu" is now chairman of the Chinese Communist party, and Mao's successor!

The movement reached its climax in Shanghai when the most radical elements of the Red Guards seized control of the city. By mid-September 1966, 1,500,000 Red Guards had poured into the city and were quartered in 1,500 reception centers. The whole life of the city was paralyzed. Municipal functions ceased. The Guards organized what was called the Shanghai Commune and appealed to Beijing for recognition. But now even the leaders who had urged the Red Guards on in the beginning were having second thoughts. There was no way a motley group of self-proclaimed rebels could manage China's largest city with its intricate systems of commerce, transportation, and industry. A halt was called, and by early 1967, after considerable turmoil, confusion, and fighting between factions, the administration of the city was returned to the municipal council.

Act Four: Picking Up the Pieces (1967–68)

In August Mao returned to Beijing from an inspection trip in Central China and decided that enough was enough. The propaganda levers which had been propelling the Red Guards forward were now thrown into reverse. Directives calling for the Guards to return to school were issued. Free passes on the trains were ended. They were told to stop the harassment of high officials. But Pandora's box had been opened, and it was not all that simple getting it shut. Students had found it much more interesting to make revolution than to attend classes! It was a long time before order was restored. The last outbreak of student violence came nearly a year later in the spring of 1969 on the campus of Qinghua University in Beijing, not far from where it had all begun.

The party structure and government administration at local and provincial levels had virtually ceased to function. These two "legs" of the state tripod of power had collapsed. Only the People's Liberation Army was still intact, and again and again it was called upon to restore order. As a temporary, transitional measure, the reign of the Red Guards was replaced by what was called "Triple Alliance Committees"—groups made up of representatives from the army, loyal party cadres, and the Guards.

As central authority was restored, the leftists were now in full control. The Red Guards had either eliminated the opposition or else it was lying low. In October 1968 Liu Shaoqi, who surprisingly had remained nominally the chief of state in spite of the vast amount of invective that had been heaped upon him, was dismissed from office and expelled from the party. Some time later he died in disgrace. His protégé, Deng Xiaoping, was paraded through the streets in a truck with a dunce cap pulled over his ears. He was dismissed but never expelled from the party.

In mid-1968 students were sent to the countryside in large numbers to work in the communes. It was not a move that many of them relished, but they were now tasting some of their own medicine. The universities were still closed, and the cities were overpopulated, unable to provide enough jobs for students who had no place to go. In the fall party cadres were likewise sent to the rural villages for reeducation through manual labor. In the province of Guangdong alone, 100,000 cadres were involved in the move.

Throughout the period Zhou Enlai was untouched although some abortive attempts were made by the radicals to do him in. Undoubtedly his stature increased as the factionalism and strife surged around him. Certainly, more than any other person he was responsible for bringing the country back from the brink of chaos to a semblance of order.

Act Five: The Aftermath (1968–76)

The long-delayed Ninth Congress of the Communist party was held in March and April 1968, marking the beginning of a new era. Fifteen hundred delegates met for twenty-three days. Rebuilding the decimated party apparatus was the top priority. New Central Committee and Politburo leaders were appointed, including many Red Army members and the Shanghai leftist faction. The Cultural Revolution was pronounced ended.

But in many ways the Cultural Revolution lasted longer than its official demise. As late as 1977 it again had to be officially declared dead! Today the Cultural Revolution is known as the "ten lost years," meaning the period from 1966–76, for during this time the leadership of the country was still, for the most part, in the hands of those later identified as the "Gang of Four." Jiang Qing and her clique dominated cultural affairs, exercising complete censorship over all the arts. Only six revolutionary operas could be seen. Artistic expression was brought to a standstill. Museums were closed. Even the prestigious Academy of Sciences was suspended.

It was also during this period, from 1968–70, that the cult of Mao Zedong reached its height. Mao pictures, badges, statues, symbols, and loyalty oaths filled the country. Quotations from the little red book of Mao's sayings were quoted with respect, adulation, and reverence. All kinds of success stories were attributed to the guidance of Mao and his infallible wisdom. This is illustrated by a quotation from an article in a Shanghai paper:

> The thoughts of Mao Zedong is the sun in our heart, is the root of our life, is the source of all our strength. Through this, man becomes unselfish, able to do everything; he is not conquered by any difficulty and can conquer everything.[5]

What was behind all this veneration is difficult to say. Perhaps Mao in his old age relished this kind of thing. A more plausible explanation is that Lin Biao encouraged it and made use of it to strengthen his own position.

Lin Biao dominated the Ninth Congress. He was officially recognized as the number two man in the hierarchy and Mao's heir apparent. As defense minister he controlled the army which wielded enormous power since the other organs of government had been decimated during the Cultural Revolution.

But Lin's days were numbered. A new struggle, known as the Lin Biao affair, was brewing. The problem with Lin seems to have been his overriding ambition. Almost as soon as the congress was over, Mao began to have doubts about Lin's loyalty. According to the official version of this bizarre affair, Lin, realizing that he was under suspicion, devised a *coup d'état* which included the assassination of Mao. The plot failed and Lin, together with his wife and son, attempted an escape by plane to the Soviet Union. The plane crashed in the People's Republic of Mongolia on the night of September 12, 1971, and all on board were killed. The story was not made public until months later. The Soviets, who undoubtedly would have investigated the crash, have never affirmed nor denied the story.

Lin was vilified as a traitor and denounced, first as a "leftist" and then, strangely, as a "rightist." Each side wanted the other to take the blame. During these years it was not really clear which faction was in control. In the "Anti-Lin, Anti-Confucius" campaign of 1973 it seemed that the "leftists" were calling the signals, but the next year Deng Xiaoping reemerged as Zhou Enlai's right-hand man, and this must have been a victory for the "rightists."

Mao's health was failing, but he could still intervene decisively at any point. He did so in the matter of reestablishing relationships with the United States. The negotiations were handled by Zhou Enlai, but such a radical change of direction could never have been consummated without the total support of Mao himself. With the end of the Vietnam War, Mao had come to feel that the "imperialism" of the United States was a lesser threat than the "hegemony" of the Soviet Union. In February 1972 when President Richard Nixon made his historic visit to China, both countries signed the Shanghai Communique, stating that they would move ahead to increase trade, cultural, and diplomatic relations. The United States affirmed it would eventually withdraw its military support from Taiwan, acknowledging that "all Chinese on either side of the Taiwan Strait maintain there is but one China and that Taiwan is a part of China."

A new era was just over the horizon.

The Church During the Cultural Revolution

The fury of the Red Guards descended upon the Christian churches, as it did on all religious faiths, in August 1966. A correspondent for the Hong Kong daily, *South China Morning Post*, in Shanghai at the time, tells what happened:

> The final page of the history of the Christian religion in Shanghai was written on August 24.
> On that day all the churches, active and inactive, whether conducted by their meager congregations or preserved by the Shanghai Municipal Bureau of Religious Cults, were stripped of the crosses, statues, icons, decorations and all church paraphernalia by the revolutionary students, wearing Red Guard armbands and determined to eradicate all traces of imperialist, colonial and feudal regimes.[6]

Bibles, religious tracts, and other books were carried out into the streets and publicly burned in huge bonfires. According to a Reuters correspondent in Beijing, the Mi Shih Tang Protestant Church was completely rearranged with a large white statue of Mao at the center.

Posters were plastered on the walls of churches and religious buildings such as this one found on the YMCA building in Beijing:

> There is no God; there is no Spirit; there is no Jesus; . . . How can adults believe in these things? . . . Like Islam and Catholicism, Protestantism is a reactionary feudal ideology, the opium of the people. . . . We are atheists; we believe only in Mao Tse-tung. We call on all people to burn Bibles, destroy images, and disperse religious associations.[7]

Cemeteries were desecrated and crosses removed from tombstones in a foreign cemetery in Beijing.

What happened in Beijing and Shanghai was going on all over the country. The homes of Christians were invaded and searched for incriminating evidence. "Confessions" of guilt were extracted from those accused of having contacts with people abroad. Teachers and doctors were demoted and assigned menial jobs. Pastors were sent to work camps in the countryside for reeducation. Suicides, broken bodies, and mental breakdowns resulted from the intense pressure and brutal treatment. The Rev. John Fleming, former Scottish missionary in China, wrote of what he heard when he returned in 1980 and talked with friends:

> I heard grim tales of the sufferings of these days: men and women attacked and persecuted because they were "old intellectuals"; highly qualified professional people who had been beaten up, had ribs crushed, eardrums shattered, elbows broken; eminent professors who had been put to scrubbing floors, washing windows and cleaning lavatories—while unqualified people took their places.[8]

All Christians of whatever denomination, theological conviction, or political persuasion suffered. No one was exempt—Christians and non-Christians alike. Leaders in the Three-Self Movement who had tried to cooperate with the government spent time in the work camps the same as those known to be resistant to government policies. The offices of the Three-Self Movement were closed down. The Religious Affairs Bureau of the government ceased to function.

During these years every church in the People's Republic of China was closed. They were either padlocked or else used for some other purpose—as warehouses, factories, or schools. For the first time in more than three hundred years there was no public Christian worship of God in that vast land.

Then in 1972 a tiny crack appeared. Two churches in Beijing began holding services again. How did this happen in the face of the ban of religious worship across the land? A pastor of the Rice Market Street Protestant Church told us the story in 1980. Several Indonesian and African members of the diplomatic community went to government authorities in the capital and asked whether there was freedom of worship in China. They were assured that freedom of religion was guaranteed in the constitution. Then came the petition: "We are Christians, and we have no place to worship! Please permit a church to reopen so that we can worship in accordance with the freedom guaranteed in your constitution!" The request was granted. The Roman Catholic South Cathedral and the Protestant Rice Market Street Church reopened. At the Rice Market Street Church attendance averaged ten to twelve persons, the only Chinese present being three pastors, who took turns officiating, and their wives. The service was in Chinese and English. It consisted of hymns, prayers, and Scripture. There was no preaching, but there was a regular observance of the sacrament of the Lord's Supper. A tiny new beginning happened when some Third World Christians, a long way from home, were not ashamed of their faith and were bold enough to ask for a place to worship!

During the height of the Cultural Revolution other religious bodies were given the same treatment as was given the Christians. Most Buddhist temples were closed, and some priceless art treasures and ancient manuscripts were burned. A writer for the Associated Press tells of seeing a detachment of teen-agers defiling the images of Buddha, armed with paste bucket and brush, slapping notices on the other images. A New China News Agency bulletin of August 25, 1966, speaks of revolutionary students and teachers of the Central Institute of Arts setting a fire to images of Buddha and using "axes, picks, and iron spikes to crush the sculptures to pieces."[9] Adherents of Islam probably fared better than either Buddhists or Christians because of their special ethnic minority status and also because of the importance of preserving good relationships with Pakistan and other Moslem states. But during the Cultural Revolution most mosques were closed, and some were destroyed. In some places study of the Koran was forbidden and Muslim clergy were humiliated by being forced to eat pork and lick the heads of pigs.[10]

The Beginning of "House Congregations"

During these dark, dismal days Christianity was kept alive in the homes of faithful believers. A new expression of Christian life and worship known as the "house congregations" was born. It was new because never since the beginning of the Constantinian Era had Christianity been sustained in such a way for such a time. Yet it was as old as the New Testament, for this was how the church began. Through interviews, conversations, and letters a picture of congregational life in China during the Cultural Revolution can be recreated.

A Christian family, a few relatives, and friends would begin to meet in one of their homes to read the Bible, pray, and share experiences. The passage to be studied would be copied by hand from the few Bibles available and circulated around the group. When study of a book had been completed, each believer would have a hand-written copy for personal use. Often the group would meet at irregular times and in different homes. Sundays were preferred, but any day would do. Sometimes they would gather in the evenings. Sometimes they met during the long noon work break.

Occasionally an itinerant lay preacher from a neighboring village would visit the group and there would be special preaching, Bible teaching, and hymn singing. But care had to be taken with visitors because party cadres were sometimes suspicious of strangers. Many of the itinerant preachers were women. These preachers had developed special skills either from previous instruction in Bible schools or from their own study of the Bible and experience. Great diversity was displayed in the different groups, both in the religious experience and in the lay preachers. Sometimes there would be special prayer for healing, for deliverance from demons, and for rain.

When a group got too big, it would divide into two groups. No provincial or national association linked the groups together, but groups within the same vicinity would know each other. Some groups joined together to go on retreats to some isolated mountain area for several days of preaching, instruction, hymn singing, and Christian fellowship. Party cadres were sometimes sympathetic to the Christians, who were often the hardest-working and best-qualified members of the commune. Sometimes cadres knew about their meetings and did not interfere although they could not be officially condoned.

There is good evidence that not only was the Christian faith kept alive in this way but that it spread like some indigenous plant. Young people were often most responsive. One interview tells of a village where thirty percent of the people were Christians and of one production brigade which was nearly all Christian. Witness to neighbors was predominantly through the character of the Christian community—their honesty, hard work, loving concern, and service to people.

Two vivid descriptions, written by village Christians, capture the spirit of these times:

> Even in the worst hours, we managed to meet every week for prayer and scripture reading. Like in the 1966–1968 period, we persevered by breaking up into groups of three or four, gathering in homes, under a tree in the field, or in the parks praying with our eyes open and mouth smiling as if we were talking and sharing a joke. We have our hymns and scripture portions developed on palm-sized photographic paper, just like a photograph. You know you unwrap the paper in the dark, which is very sensitive to light, you put a positive or transparency with words on top of it, sandwich them between two panes of glass and expose it in the sun for two minutes. . . . It's a bit hard on the eyes for elderly people, but it comes in handy, and it keeps better than ordinary paper. And most important, it is easily duplicated. Up to now, our church has over one hundred different pieces, and enough copies for use in a worship service for about eighty people.
>
> Since 1969, we have been meeting again as a whole group. We have an ideal setting—eight Christian families living in a five-house compound opening up to an inner open court. We meet in one of the houses, utilizing for sitting purposes the house, the covered porch and the open court. In winter, we squeeze all the elderly people inside and the young people pack the porch.
>
> This way, we keep each other warm. The difficulty is getting down on our knees. We are so crowded sitting on the floor with our knees almost touching our breast that every time we set out to pray, there is an inevitable commotion. Rev. Yeong, whom we regard as our pastor, joked that this was good because it woke up those who were falling asleep. Indeed, I can say there are always a few who do.

*****

As the largest and best-organized Christian group in town, we were the first under attack. The local brigade teamed up with a provincial contingent and broke into our meeting, confiscated all our Bibles, hymn books and gospel posters and took my father and two others away. . . . Several days later, we were told to line up in the street, and watched father, our brothers and sisters, several senior party officials and ten or twelve teachers forced to take part in a mock parade. My father died soon after the experience. He was seventy-nine.

Our prayer meetings could not go on. Nobody would show up. We could not even be seen greeting each other in the streets.

Around about 1975 or '76, Christians were meeting in homes again. Pastor Chung of what used to be the Presbyterian Church reappeared and word soon circulated of Christians meeting with him. We took heart and soon revived our meeting. Pastor Chung paid us a visit and gave us his New Testament. We held hands and prayed aloud, thanking the Lord for his Word. . . . As of now, there are over fifty people in our service, about half over sixty, the rest young people in their teens and twenties. We have many needs. But the main thing is we have survived and have not dishonoured the name of Jesus.[11]

Assessment of the Cultural Revolution

How shall we understand the Cultural Revolution? Many questions are still unanswered, and considerable differences of opinion remain. What does it mean? Why did it happen? Did it produce any enduring worthwhile results?

One thing is clear. Today within China the assessment of the Cultural Revolution is almost *totally negative*. Government officials, educators, party cadres, Christians, the media, all say the same thing: it was bad. It was indescribably bad. There were few if any redeeming virtues. These were the "ten lost years." It was a time when millions of young people lost their one chance for an education. It was an opportunity which will not come again, for now the schools are filled with a new generation of students. It was a time of disillusionment; high ideals were shattered. It was a time when incompetence was rewarded, and professional skills were penalized, a time of stagnation in science and industry, a time when there was wholesale mistreatment of large segments of the population. The official indictment against the "Gang of Four," on which the excesses of the Cultural Revolution are blamed, lists the following numbers of people who were falsely charged and humiliated: 142,000 educators, 253,000 scientists, 2,500 artists, writers and actors, 500 physicians. Of these, 34,000 were killed.[12] This number was directly attributed to the "Gang of Four." The total number of others who suffered unjustly during these years would run into the millions.

This is not to say that the Cultural Revolution did not begin with some high egalitarian goals. Noble attempts were made to end special privileges for the elite, to eliminate extreme income differences, and to give those in rural areas a more equitable share of the nation's resources. Young people did respond to the appeals made for sacrificial service. But judging from the results—the excesses of the Red Guards, the brutal treatment given so many, the extremism of the "Gang of Four"—the Chinese people today view this revolution in extremely negative terms.

Admittedly this negative assessment comes from professionals and party cadres who were the "underdogs" during these years and who have now regained control. It would be more difficult to know what the peasants and factory workers would say. Yet there is little reason to believe their opinion would be much different. It would appear that during the Cultural Revolution almost everyone was a loser.

Why then did it happen? An explanation is offered by government spokespersons writing for the *Beijing Review:*

(1) *Comrade Mao's mistakes in leadership.* Although Mao's earlier triumphs outweigh his later mistakes, grievous errors were made in leadership going as far back as 1958 and the beginning of the Great Leap Forward. Two basic errors can be attributed to Mao.

The first of these is ideological. Mao "absolutized class struggle" and advocated "continuous revolution." His theory went like this:

> After the proletariat seizes political power and sets up the socialist system, it is still necessary to carry out the revolution in which one class overthrows another, and revolutions of this kind should be repeated several times. The "cultural revolution," the memory of which is still fresh in people's minds, was precisely the practice of this theory. Now it has become clear that this theory is entirely wrong. . . .[13]

Under the guise of class struggle, attacks were made on loyal citizens and party members, and this kept the whole country in turmoil.

The basic objectives of the revolution had been reached in 1949 in eliminating class distinctions, and it should not be necessary to continue this struggle.

Mao's second error was in cultivating his own personality cult and departing from the principles of collective leadership. He no longer treated his colleagues as equals; he grew conceited; he overestimated the role of a person's subjective will, was impatient for quick results, and smug about his successes. This made it very difficult for his colleagues to restrain him so that no one could prevent the Cultural Revolution from running its course.

(2) *Activity of the "Counterrevolutionary Cliques."* Mao's departure from collective leadership made it easy for some of his close friends to betray him and commit many crimes of which he did not know. Lin Biao and the "Gang of Four," including Mao's own wife, Jiang Qing, took advantage of Mao and hoodwinked him. This brought disaster to the country and the people:

> First, the "cultural revolution" was initiated and led personally by Comrade Mao Zedong, who was highly esteemed for his great contributions to the Chinese revolution. But the esteem gradually developed into a personality cult. Lin Biao . . . had an axe to grind and did all he could to exaggerate Mao Zedong's personal role. As a result, the personality cult spread unchecked until it reached its pinnacle during the "cultural revolution." . . . The broad masses of cadres and people knew very little about the "revolution," but out of their confidence in the Party and Comrade Mao Zedong, they plunged themselves into the movement in their hundreds of millions. . . .[14]

(3) *Complex Social and Historical Causes.* The history of international socialism is not long, and the laws governing the development of socialist societies are not altogether understood. The party was not adequately prepared to know how to deal with the contradictions and problems which appeared. Lessons learned from the Cultural Revolution will enable the leaders of the People's Republic of China not to make the same mistakes again.[15]

According to this explanation, the terror of these years is readily acknowledged, but the Cultural Revolution itself is considered an aberration. The system itself is not at fault. Mao, because of his enormous prestige, was able to lead the country in a direction which deviated from the norm. This has now been corrected, and the correct line, which had been followed prior to the Cultural Revolution, has been reestablished.

So much for the official explanation. Some unanswered questions remain. What assurance is there that the same problems could not recur? What checks and balances are there to protect the country and the people from recurring personality cults? Why did it take ten years for the error to be discovered and for the ship of state to be returned to its correct course?

A "New Maoist Man"?

A very different assessment of the Cultural Revolution was made at two ecumenical conferences held at Bastad, Sweden, and Louvain, Belgium, in 1974. Most of the papers presented and the reports of the conferences, attended by more than ninety Roman Catholic and Protestant China scholars and theologians, alluded to the excesses of the Cultural Revolution but emphasized what they thought were its positive and lasting contributions. The conference reports refer to the development of a "new Maoist Man" through this revolutionary experience — a new breed of human beings who were freed from selfishness and motivated for self-sacrificing service. Some of the papers refer to this new ideal in terms of the egalitarian ideals, goals, and values which were being set forth at that time. They did not assume that the goal had been reached or that such an ideal had actually been achieved.[16] But others seemed to indicate that a transformation of human nature had actually taken place through Maoist thought and the revolutionary experience. One paper spoke of

> ways in which Chinese have been re-made in the course of a revolutionary experience into men who live not for themselves but for others to the point that they can face even death with a spirit of hope—and to indicate the way in which this revolutionary experience might be seen by Christian theology to be an eruption into history of the salvation of God.[17]

China, under the guidance of Mao Zedong's thought, has formed a kind of society pointing toward the reign of God, according to another report:

> The social and political transformations brought about in China through the application of the Thought of Mao Tse-tung have unified and consolidated a quarter of the world population into a form of society and life-style at once pointing to some of the basic characteristics of the kingdom of God and yet consciously rejecting God as the source of man's real hope and strength.[18]

Some dissenting voices were heard. An unsigned paper, written by a Chinese Christian observer who had lived in the People's Republic, states that the "New Maoist Man" is more of a myth than a reality:

> In recent years, some Western scholars have tended to describe people in Communist China as a kind of "New Man," with newly acquired qualities of devoted service and self-sacrifice, faithfully following Chairman Mao's moral exhortations in pursuit of lofty social goals. *This, however, is mainly the view of deluded observers from outside.*[19]

What had been mainly "required conformity" had been misinterpreted by many foreign well-wishers as no less than "rebirth."[20]

Charles West of Princeton Seminary, in reacting to this theologizing which equated the transformation of China by the Communist party with the redeeming work of Christ, has this final word: "There is only one thing wrong with this: it is idolatry, not theology."[21]

One crucial, decisive difference exists between the "New Man" according to Mao and according to Christ. In Mao's thought there is no forgiveness, no reconciliation, no *agape* love:

> As for the so-called love of humanity, there has been no such all-inclusive love since humanity was divided into classes . . . it is impossible in a class society. There will be a genuine love of humanity—after classes are eliminated all over the world. Classes have split society into many antagonistic groupings; there will be love of all humanity when classes are eliminated but not now. We cannot love enemies, we cannot love social evils, our aim is to destroy them. This is common sense.[22]

Self-sacrifice and service? Yes, but only for those of the right class. Since class struggle is continuous, and since at any time the lines can be arbitrarily redrawn between friend and foe, party and antiparty, rightists and leftists, reactionaries and revisionists, violence and struggle would be the norm. This is the good news according to Mao.

A Chinese visitor to the People's Republic shared with a Christian leader a description of China's "New Man" as perceived by some Western theologians. The reaction was peals of laughter:

> If I understood him aright, he laughed because he felt that the western China experts were far too naive. He laughed because the description of the "New Man" under the Chinese Communists came just at the time when China was undergoing its most unprincipled period, the Cultural Revolution, when throughout the land there was "no law and no heaven." He laughed because in the face of political fantasies these people had forgotten the biblical truth that only in Christ can there be a "New Man."[23]

Open market scene in Xuzhou

Students in English language laboratory at Fudan University in Shanghai

Bishop K. H. Ting, President of China Christian Council

Roman Catholic Bishop of Beijing, Michael Fu Tieshan

Protestant worship service in Chendu, Sichuan in China's far West

8

The Post-Mao Era

To Cyrus the LORD says,
"I myself will prepare your way,
  leveling mountains and hills.
I will break down bronze gates
  and smash their iron bars. . . .
I appoint you to help my servant Israel,
  the people that I have chosen.
I have given you great honor,
  although you do not know me."
                    (Isaiah 45:1–2, 4 TEV)

The Year 1976

The year 1976 was a momentous year for the Chinese people. It is hard to recall when so many significant events have been packed into so short a space of time. As a giant ocean liner turns in an arc to make a change of course, so the country of one billion turned full circle.

The Death of Zhou Enlai (January 8). The year began with the death of Zhou Enlai after a long bout with cancer. Although not unexpected, his death created a crisis in the affairs of government. Zhou had been a steady, constructive force behind the meteoric Mao. He had worked in Mao's shadow—behind the scenes as negotiator, diplomat, compromiser, and as the architect of *rapprochement* with the United States. Zhou had the quality to bend with the wind, to accept patiently temporary reversals in order to achieve long-term results. He was the only senior official among Mao's contemporaries with whom Mao never broke. Zhou had held the post of premier since the founding of the PRC, and his death immediately precipitated a struggle as to who would succeed him. The vice-premier was Deng Xiaoping, Zhou's protégé, who had been taking over more and more of the administration of government during Zhou's illness. But Deng had been ousted once by Mao at the height of the Cultural Revolution and had only recently been quietly rehabilitated by Zhou. Deng was bitterly opposed by the ultraleftist Shanghai faction whose candidate was Zhang Chunqiao, a former Shanghai journalist, later to be tried as a member of the "Gang of Four."

At the meeting of the Politburo, someone nominated Deng. Jiang Qing countered by nominating Zhang. The ultraleftists flatly said they would not serve under Deng. The PLA generals blocked Zhang's appointment. Mao, who had apparently been silent up to this point, proposed Hua Guofeng, a political unknown who had come from Mao's own province and had never caused him or the others any trouble. He was obviously a compromise choice that might hold until either of the two factions could command the votes to push through their own candidate. He was named acting premier. Deng remained vice-premier.[1]

The Ouster of Deng Xiaoping (April 6). In the months following Zhou's death, both factions continued their indirect sniping at each other. This came to a climax at the time of the Spring Festival when it was customary to honor the dead. A large crowd of people began to assemble before the Monument to the People's Heroes in Tiananmen Square, bearing wreaths, reciting poems, and placing memorials on the steps of the monument in memory of Zhou. It all started innocently enough, but the crowds began to swell and in their eulogizing of the dead premier, it began to appear that they were expressing their discontent with the present direction of the government. The poems were full of double meanings ridiculing Jiang Qing and the Shanghai faction. The verse of one memorial proclaimed, "The day of Qin Shihuang is done." The barb was aimed at Mao for Qin Shihuang was the despotic first emperor of China and one of Mao's favorite heroes.

The news of what was happening in the square was carried to Mao, who acted quickly. He ordered the city authorities to remove the wreaths from the monument. This precipitated a riot, and for fourteen hours 100,000 people struck back at the militia. Vehicles were burned. Several hundred people were injured. Some died. It was the worst show of violence since the Cultural Revolution.

The Politburo met hastily. Somebody had to be the scapegoat for the disturbance. Deng Xiaoping was thought to have been behind the demonstrations, for the sentiments expressed were those of his sympathizers. Mao had once said of Deng in an outburst of anger, "He has never been a Marxist." His suspicions returned. On April 6 Deng was dismissed from all his posts. Hua's appointment as premier was made permanent, and in addition he was named Mao's heir. Mao is reported to have said to Hua, "With you in charge, I am at ease." It was a remark used effectively to bolster Hua's rather shaky position.[2]

Mao's Death (September 9). The actions taken to remove Deng and to establish Hua as successor were probably Mao's last decisions of any significance. He was 82 and thought to have Parkinson's disease. After April he saw no more foreign visitors. For all practical purposes the Mao era had ended. The country and the party were waiting for him to die. While he lived, the Politburo was paralyzed and incapable of decision. Those close to him were jockeying for position. For a while it seemed that his wife, Jiang Qing, had the inside track because of her proximity to Mao and the sources of power.

For some time before his death, Mao had expressed forebodings and doubts as to the future of the revolution after he was gone. In a poem written to Zhou Enlai before Zhou's death, he wrote these poignant lines:

> Loyal parents who sacrificed so much for the nation
> Never feared the ultimate fate.
> Now that the country has become red,
> Who will be its guardians?

> Our mission unfinished may take a thousand years.
> The struggle tires us, and our hair is gray.
> You and I, old friends,
> Can we just watch our efforts be washed away?[3]

On September 9 the death announcement came:

> The Central Committee . . . announce with deepest grief to the whole party, the whole army and the people of all nationalities throughout the country:
> Comrade Mao Tse-tung, . . . passed away at 00:10 hours, Sept. 9, 1976, in Peking because of the worsening of his illness and despite all treatment, although meticulous medical care was given him in every way after he fell ill. . . . The Chinese people and the revolutionary people the world over love him from the bottom of their hearts.[4]

To use his own phrase, Mao had gone to "see Marx."

Cables of condolence arrived from 123 foreign governments. In New York the United Nations' flag was flown at half mast. In Hong Kong the stock market fell. In Moscow *Izvestia* carried the news in two lines at the bottom of its next-to-last page.

In China a million people came to the Square of the Gate of Heavenly Peace for a funeral rally at the end of a week of mourning. For three minutes 900 million Chinese stood at attention while every siren in the country, on trains, factories, and ships sounded.

In China ancient belief held that the passing of a dynasty would be marked by earth tremors and celestial phenomena. Earlier in August 1976 an earthquake had leveled the city of Tangshan killing 250,000 people. The Maoist era had ended.

The Arrest of the "Gang of Four" (October 6).   The month following the death of Mao is shrouded in mystery. Hua was confirmed as both premier and chairman of the party, but he lacked the political support or skill to consolidate his base of power. Undoubtedly, the struggle between the two factions continued, but it is not clear what happened to tip the balance against the ultraradicals who seemed to have held the edge at the time of Mao's death.

In all probability they had become isolated from the mainstream of Chinese public opinion. The people were weary with the rhetoric of class struggle and the campaigns for ideological purity. The disturbance at the time of the Spring Festival had revealed a deep level of popular support for Zhou, who exemplified stability and moderation. Deng's dismissal was not a popular one. He had the support of party cadres due to his years as the chief administrator. The People's Liberation Army (PLA) was biding its time to intervene.

Then on October 22 a terse announcement was made by the New China News Agency: "Jiang Qing, Wang Hongwen, Zhang Chunqiao, and Yao Wenyuan were arrested on October 6." That was all. No explanation. All were members of the Politburo at the time of their arrest. All would be tried later as the "Gang of Four." Their indictment, which was not announced until much later, stated that the four were guilty of persecuting many loyal party members and citizens during the Cultural Revolution and of plotting to seize control of the government.

These arrests touched off a campaign to "Smash the 'Gang of

Four!' '' and their cohorts and to rid the country of their influence. A new regime needed to dissociate itself from the fiascos of the past. Everything which had gone wrong in China in the past ten years could conveniently be blamed on the "Gang." It was a time of national catharsis. A new alignment of the party was being formed, a new power base was being forged, and a new direction for the country was being charted.

Deng Xiaoping and the Four Modernizations

In early 1977 wall posters began appearing in Beijing calling for the return of ousted Deng Xiaoping. With the solid support of senior army generals, party technocrats, and intellectuals, the movement gathered force. With his old enemies, the "Gang of Four," in jail, there was no effective opposition. In July he was reappointed to his position of vice-premier. At the age of 72 he said he did not aspire to the position of either chairman or premier—perhaps signaling the fact that had he wanted either or both positions, he could have had them. Quickly he became known as the new strong man of China. Tough, abrasive, diminutive, pragmatic, and resilient were the words used to describe him. Quickly he began to consolidate his position, placing his supporters in key positions and weeding out those who had opposed him.

A new administration required a new national campaign which would rally the people and signal a new direction. Deng's watchword was the Four Modernizations: modernization of agriculture, industry, science and technology, and national defense. Although not stated as such, it was a subtle reversal of Mao's doctrine. Mao's memory needed to be desanctified without being repudiated entirely.

Ever since 1949 the People's Republic had had twin goals of *communization* and *modernization*. The first was the Marxist goal of establishing a classless egalitarian society with minimum pay incentives and heavy doses of ideology and continuing class struggle. The second goal was building a modern industrial state out of a backward underdeveloped one.

As long as there was no conflict between the two goals, there was no problem. Both required increased food production, a degree of industrial growth, minimal education, and health benefits. When the two goals coincided, the People's Republic took giant strides forward. This was the case in the mid-1950s. But when the goals came into conflict, there was trouble. Increasingly the history of the People's Republic showed that often the goals were mutually exclusive. It could be either "red" or "expert" but not both. An emphasis on technology and the concentration of industrial power inevitably demanded pay incentives and a repudiation of egalitarianism. Mao had sought to "eliminate the three differences"—between manual and mental labor, between peasant and factory worker, between rural and urban life. But this had brought a halt to the intellectual vitality of the country and stagnation to industrial development.

When the two goals came in conflict, Mao invariably swung to the left, toward the goal of communization. This is what happened during the Great Leap Forward and the Cultural Revolution. With the emergence of Deng Xiaoping as the new leader, the swing was back to the right. The contrast between the two lines can be seen below:

Mao	Deng
leftist	rightist
"red"	"expert"
ideology	pragmatism
continuous revolution	stability
egalitarian	pay differentials
self-reliance	foreign trade
mass education	higher education
rigid thought control	relaxation of controls

In February 1978 a new ten-year plan was unveiled which laid the groundwork for bringing about the Four Modernizations. The plan focused on heavy industry and the establishment of 120 new industrial projects throughout the country. A new feature of the plan was the willingness to use massive importation of Western equipment and technology, which would be paid for in foreign loans. Initial estimates of the cost ran as high as $200 billion. The plan was probably more of a rallying cry for a new economic drive than it was a reflection of careful economic planning.

By December the economic planners had come to the sober realization that the size, complexity, and expense of the program made it unrealistic. The gap between China's existing capabilities and its ambitious projections for the future was just too great. The decision was made to shelve the plan and in its stead embark on a more modest three-year readjustment period. The emphasis on heavy industry was cut back and replaced with an emphasis on agriculture and light industry. This did not require such massive doses of capital and foreign technology, and was more responsive to the clamor of the people for consumer goods which they had long been denied. The fourth modernization—national defense—was given last priority on the shopping list.

The new leaders were also coming to realize that there would have to be certain attitudinal changes for economic modernization to go forward. Some called this the "fifth modernization" which was in the realm of "spirit"—a strange new word for dialectical materialists! Deng Xiaoping spoke of "a secular spiritual civilization," by which he meant thought, ideals, beliefs, and moral concepts.[5]

Into the '80s

A new climate was needed in which the Four Modernizations could flourish. Creating such an environment has been the motivating force as China moved into the 1980s. This explains the sweeping changes which have now appeared on the China landscape.

Opening to the West. With dramatic suddenness on December 15, 1978, President Jimmy Carter made a historic announcement to the American people:

> The United States of America and the People's Republic of China have agreed to recognize each other and to establish diplomatic relations as of January 1, 1979.
> The United States of America recognizes the Government of the People's Republic of China as the sole legal Government of China. Within this context, the people of the United States will maintain cultural, commercial, and other unofficial relations with the people of Taiwan.[6]

For both the United States and China, two pragmatic considerations were behind the breakthrough: trade and the Soviet Union. Both nations recognized that the advantages of establishing trading relationships and of building a deterrent against a possible common enemy far outweighed the sticky problem of Taiwan.

China and the West have long been natural trading partners, and so when relationships became normalized, there was a rush to get in on the action. The lure of one billion new customers was all but irresistible for Japanese and U.S. trade commissions, manufacturers, and traders. China was eager to sign contracts that would bring in new technology and build new plants. There was great impatience to make up for the "ten lost years" of the Cultural Revolution.

But it was not all that simple. Bureaucracy, red tape, and unfamiliarity with Western ways of doing business produced considerable frustration. In some cases China proceeded too rapidly in signing contracts with little coordination, only to realize that if the pace kept up, foreign exchange reserves and developmental loans would be depleted. For example, a $4 billion contract with Nippon Steel for building the giant Baoshan steel mill on the outskirts of Shanghai had to be partially canceled. This made other trading partners wary of plunging in.

Nevertheless, trade has increased phenomenally. Trade with the U.S. was $377 million in 1977 and increased to $4 billion in 1980. The United States is now China's third largest trading partner, after Japan and Hong Kong.

Normalization of relationships has also opened the floodgates for all kinds of other exchanges. Deng Xiaoping visited the U.S. on something of a whirlwind, triumphal tour in January 1978. Three U.S. presidents and ex-presidents have visited the People's Republic along with senators, representatives, high government officials, and generals. In 1981, 7,000,000 tourists visited the People's Republic. Of these, 6,000,000 were Chinese from Hong Kong and Macau; 100,000 were Americans. Tourism earned for China $700 million in 1981.

In this same year approximately 10,000 Chinese visited the United States. Most of these were scholars, scientists, and technicians who came for research and study. One remarkable thing about this number was the large number—fifty percent of the total—who came under private auspices of one kind or another. Streams of Chinese commercial and scientific delegations, averaging about 130 per month, have been coming to the United States since 1981. The United States has placed 106 American scholars at universities in China for study in science and the humanities. More than thirty American universities have signed exchange agreements with Chinese universities.

The list of people-to-people exchanges, most of them under private sponsorship, is long and varied. It includes track coaches, dancers, librarians, artists, diving teams, museum administrators, symphony orchestras, acrobats, medical doctors, and violin teachers. The rapidity with which these exchanges have grown, the spontaneous way in which they have developed, and the enthusiasm with which they have been welcomed is certainly evidence of the deep-rooted friendship between the Chinese and American peoples which was tragically interrupted for a season but now is blooming again.

Most all American visitors to China have been impressed by the spontaneous friendship of the people. When asked how the attitude could change so quickly and completely, a professor at Nanjing University replied that there were three reasons for the renewed friendship. First, a natural affinity exists between the Chinese and American people. Both are pragmatic. Both have the same sense of humor. Second is the matter of distance! The United States is on the other side of the ocean. No long common border, such as exists with the Soviet Union, troubles relations. Third is mission work in the past. A great reservoir of good will was created by the humanitarian service of missionaries.

Profit Incentives. The break with the Mao tradition was most radical in the reintroduction of profit-making incentives. The goal of abundance for all in a classless society was unchanged. But some would arrive at the promised land sooner than others.

This was not a return to capitalism. The means of production was still tightly controlled by the state. Land was still owned and controlled by the communes. But through a number of modifications, changes were made in the socialist system. Wages of key personnel were raised. Price controls were removed except for rice, cooking oil, and cotton cloth. Farmers were permitted to keep five percent of the land in private plots. Farmers' markets appeared in the cities where peasants could sell their produce, often at prices a little higher but with better quality than that at the state-controlled markets. Plant managers were freed to make production and pricing decisions on the basis of market considerations. In the city small family-owned shops and home industries were encouraged. In the country peasants were permitted to own their own homes and even to build new ones with savings invested and drawing interest in state banks. Billboards with advertisements for Coca-Cola and Canon cameras appeared where previously there had been ideological slogans.

The story is told in headlines from *The New York Times* during 1980 and 1981:[7]

"CHINESE ARGUE HEATEDLY
OVER WHO WILL GET RAISES"
(May 14, 1980).

A forty percent pay increase was announced, but in a sharp break with the egalitarian past, it would go to those who were the most skilled and those who worked the hardest.

"CHINA TRIES CAPITALISM, AND IT WORKS"
(August 14, 1980).

Sichuan Province, devastated during the Cultural Revolution, has been turned into one vast laboratory for economic recovery. Factories are experimenting in competing for customers, producing and advertising new products, cutting costs. Production has been dramatically increased, profits have risen, prices paid by consumers have fallen.

"NEW CHINESE POLICY EMPHASIZES
PROFITS AND LOCAL CONTROL"
(September 1, 1980).

Plant managers have been turned loose to make their own decisions based on market considerations. The drudgery of fulfilling arbitrary state quotas has been relaxed by a system that rewards quality and penalizes incompetence.

"CHINA'S NEW PRAGMATISM"
(September 1, 1980).

A young plant manager, with the enthusiasm of a convert, speaks of decentralization, market forces, price incentives, private farm plots, and small-scale enterprises. The slogan has been changed to "from each according to his ability, to each according to his worth"—not "needs."

"CHINA'S PRAGMATIC FARM RULES PAY OFF
IN MORE FOOD AND MONEY FOR PEASANTS"
(November 5, 1980).

Average annual per capita income for a commune of 27,000 increased from $57 to $87 in 1979 because of incentives which had been introduced in assigning land to smaller work teams and families. The all-important "work points" were granted on the basis of each peasant's actual work production. Some peasants were allowed to keep whatever they grew beyond the assigned quotas. Private plots had greatly increased the standard of living within the commune.

"CHINA, TO RELIEVE UNEMPLOYMENT, GIVES PRIVATE SECTOR MORE LEEWAY" (November 24, 1981).

China has moved closer to becoming a mixed economy by encouraging the development of private enterprise. Small-time entrepreneurs are permitted to employ two helpers and five apprentices. Unemployed youth are encouraged to find jobs by forming cooperatives and providing services such as repairing bicycles, tailoring, taking photographs.

Educational Reforms. Higher education had been devastated during the Cultural Revolution. During much of the time universities and medical schools had been closed. The course of study for primary and middle school was cut from twelve to ten years. The curriculum included large doses of Mao Zedong's thought and manual labor. Entrance examinations to universities were eliminated, and students were chosen from factory worker and peasant classes on the basis of their ideology. Senior professors, presidents, and administrators were sent to work camps in the countryside. A comment heard on a university campus in 1980 is the most revealing: "Before the Cultural Revolution, we studied Russian. After the Cultural Revolution, we study English. During the Cultural Revolution we studied nothing at all!"

Drastic shifts in policy were introduced in 1978. The years spent in primary and middle school were lengthened again to twelve years. Entrance examinations returned. Qualified faculty and administrators returned to their posts. Time spent in indoctrination and labor was reduced. The Chinese Academy of Science resumed its research work. Four times as many students were enrolled in middle schools in 1978 as there were in 1966.[8]

A report given by the ministry of education in 1980 indicates the magnitude of China's education program and the achievements which have been made. Statistics reported 210,000,000 students enrolled in 164,000 kindergartens, 900,000 primary schools, 160,000 middle schools, and 633 universities and colleges. China's school population almost equals the entire population of the United States!

In the past thirty years China has unquestionably taken gigantic strides in putting at least primary schooling within reach of most of the populace. Ninety-four percent of China's youngsters are said to have some primary school education. The government has developed a much simplified method of writing the Chinese characters and the standard Beijing dialect (Mandarin) is universally spoken throughout the provinces.

There are bottlenecks in the system once one moves beyond primary school. Less than half the number who finish primary school can go on to middle school. Of all of China's university-age youth, only two or three percent get to enter college. For example, out of 4.6 million students who took the 1979 university entrance examinations, only 370,000 or 5.8% were enrolled. The university enrollment in 1980 was about 1,200,000. In 1981, 270,000 students graduated from universities and technical schools, an all-time high.

What to do with the students who finish middle school and are not able to go on to university has been a very serious problem. In the past they were sent to work in the rural areas, but this produced great discontent. The state is in the process of developing technical schools which will teach a trade, but this has not yet been widely put into effect. Droves of unemployed youth have become a serious social problem in the large cities.

Conversations with students at Nanjing University revealed much about college life. Once a student has passed the entrance examination, he or she is enrolled at the university to which the student has been assigned by the state. Tuition fees are minimal, but each student is expected to pay food costs. Most students live in very crowded dormitories. Each is assigned to a department of study on the basis of the state needs, although the student may express a preference which is taken into consideration. When students graduate, jobs are waiting at the position to which they have been assigned. Again, students are asked their preferences and are usually assigned to locations near their homes, but the needs of the state are decisive.

The "Christian colleges" were merged into the state university system in 1952. Today some of the key universities of China are built around the campuses and facilities of those college. For example, Yenching is now a part of the Beijing University complex, and St. John's campus in Shanghai is used by the East China Political Law Institute. University administrators, in some cases somewhat reluctantly, acknowledge the contribution that the former "Christian colleges" have made both in buildings and facilities and in the training of many of the present senior faculty members.

Due Process. Advancement of the Four Modernizations will depend on a stable government and a predictable legal system. The new leaders, some of whom have themselves suffered from arbitrary arrest, clearly understand that no progress can be made under a system like that of the Cultural Revolution when any group could arbitrarily denounce other groups, punish so-called enemies of the state on the basis of rumor, and seize control of institutions without legal process. At least managers, government officials, and intellectuals have to know what to expect. Will contracts be enforced, disputes settled according to some fair legal basis, and the power of police and bureaucracy curbed? Without some such assurances, even with the best technology, the modernization program will flounder.

It is not surprising, then, that the new PRC constitution of 1978 included a number of basic judicial reforms. It reestablished the position of procurator, which supervises and controls police activity, ending their unfettered power to make arrests. The accused now has the right of defense. Cases are to be tried in public. Torture is prohibited. Rules of evidence have been established.

Equally important, in 1979 a new criminal code was promulgated which went into effect in 1980. The code defines numerous offenses and prescribes the punishment to be meted out on each. The law protects the legitimate private property of citizens and provides for heavy penalties against public officials who violate the rights of citizens. Unlawful imprisonment is strictly prohibited.[9]

How are we to assess the practical effect of these changes? Jerome A. Cohen, legal expert on China at Harvard Law School, writes that "events since the downfall of the Gang of Four have, on the whole, been rather encouraging," but also advises an attitude of "healthy skepticism." Some skepticism is warranted says Cohen, because as yet these are but "paper reforms." Another caveat is due because there is no independent court system free from coercion from other state agencies. Mao's distinction between the two kinds of contradictions—"between the enemy and ourselves" and "within the people"—means that those of the wrong class background ("the enemy") may not be considered "equal before the law." Class labels, still in effect even thirty years after the revolution, can still be used to discriminate against children and grandchildren of former landlords and capitalists. Also, it is not clear whether the new criminal code will apply in "noncriminal" cases, where severe punitive sanctions were applied under the guise of "rehabilitation through labor." Although charged with no criminal offense and technically not criminals, millions were previously deprived of liberty and jobs completely outside the judicial system.

Nevertheless, writes Cohen, "some progress is taking place and more seems on the way." It appears that China will introduce the practice of "people's lawyers." Great attention is being given the legal profession. Provisions have been made for disciplining Party members and functionaries. The attention given to the trial of the "Gang of Four" will serve both as a model and a deterrent. China is now a member of the United Nations and eager to assume leadership among Third World countries. Although China has never adopted the United Nations Declaration of Human Rights, it is bound to be influenced by this document.[10]

Relaxation of Controls. In order to establish a climate for modernization, it has been necessary to relax some of the controls affecting freedom of expression, of thought, and of religion. This was a chance that had to be taken. The new relationship with the West and the necessity for regaining the support of the intellectuals made this move necessary. In the words of a Chinese university professor, "It was part of the package."

The first step came with the rehabilitation of one-half million intellectuals, party cadres, professors, artists, and pastors who had been accused of "rightist tendencies" and had been sent to the countryside to be reformed in work camps. Full rights of citizenship were restored.

In some cases compensation was made for property that was lost. Positions and jobs were returned.

The dilemma faced by China's new leaders in their attempt to relax controls—giving some freedom of speech but not too much—is illustrated in the incidents which took place around the Xidan Wall, nicknamed "Freedom Wall," in the winter of 1978. John Fraser, reporter of the *Toronto Globe and Mail*, who became a participant in the events, tells the story in a graphic way.[11]

In mid-November 1978 big character posters (*dazibao*) began to appear on a wall near a busy intersection and bus stop in downtown Beijing. At first the posters attacked the deposed mayor of Beijing, Wu De, for his responsibility in the suppression of the demonstrations in honor of the late premier, Zhou Enlai, at the time of the Spring Festival. Since this was in support of the new government policy, it was nothing unusual.

By the third week of November, however, the campaign of *dazibao* had exploded into a full scale demand for complete freedom of speech and democratic government. Thousands would appear before the Xidan Wall each evening to read the posters and discuss what had been written. Fraser compared the experience of being in a *dazibao* gathering to the "lot of a sardine in a tin"! It turned into a "non-stop mayhem caused by people at the back trying to get to the front and the people at the front trying to get to the back" without losing life or limb. It became a cross between London's Hyde Park, and a New England townhall meeting. The masses had found their voice.

Correspondents John Fraser and Robert Novak were beseiged by the crowds one evening and showered with questions about democracy in Western countries. Fraser proposed that the group give their complaints and concerns to Novak who could share them with Deng, with whom he had an appointment the next day. The response was an electric, spontaneous outburst of applause. Then they began raising issues and questions. While supportive of the current leaders and the new freedom, they wanted more of the same thing. They raised questions about Mao's responsibility for the Gang of Four, the mind-boggling shifts in ideology, and asked for the right to criticize their leaders and have free elections with secret ballots.

Fraser returned to the Wall the next evening and faced a crowd of more than 20,000 people waiting to hear what Deng had said. Six "trumpeter voices" relayed Fraser's words after they had been translated by an interpreter. Deng had reported to Novak that the Xidan Wall was a good thing and could go on forever. The crowds were ecstatic. Deng had also said that not all of the things the masses had said were correct. The crowds were silent. Other words followed. But the amazing thing was that they had gotten through to their chief of state in a press conference relayed through a foreign correspondent!

For the next week there were new posters every evening, large crowds, and free discussion—then an abrupt change. There was an official announcement deploring the gatherings. Police "bully boys" began to infiltrate the crowds, intimidating and threatening foreign visitors. But the movement was not all that easy to turn off. Posters continued to appear, and the crowds continued to gather before the wall until April 1979. Then, with the arrest of the human rights leader Ren Wanding for posting two *dazibao*, the movement came to an end.

In the field of the arts, there has been this same limited relaxation of control. Under Mao the arts existed only to serve the political ends of the revolution. The party, not the artists, set the agenda and prescribed the form and content the artistic work should take. In the early days of the revolution, folk operas and short stories had been a powerful and creative tool in mobilizing peasant support, but with the revolutionaries firmly in control, the artists were caught in a dilemma. They knew how to attack the known villains of the past—the KMT, the Japanese, and oppressive landlords—but they were at a loss as to how they could safely deal with the issues of the present. Heroes and villains were constantly shifting places!

Under the cultural dictatorship of the "Gang of Four," the role of the creative artist became intolerable. China's rich classical heritage was banned. Western music and literature were proscribed. Artists were hounded to death. Only the six approved revolutionary operas could be shown. What emerged was poster art—the faces too bright, the grins too forced, the personalities stereotyped, the dialogue reduced to pep talks, and all the plots about class struggle.

With Jiang Qing and her cronies safely behind bars, long banned books—both foreign and Chinese—have reappeared. Uncensored versions of favorite classical operas and stage plays are again being produced. Romantic themes are again being featured in fiction. Zhou Enlai has replaced Mao as the symbol to be revered and honored.

What of the future for the arts? The new leadership has never repudiated the right of the party to have the final authority in setting controls for the artist. The present official emphasis has been to return to the pre-Cultural Revolution period when restraints were exercised but not so blatantly. In 1982 there have been signs that controls over literature and the arts are again being tightened..[12]

For Christians, religious freedom is a matter of primary consideration. The unexpected developments of this dramatic story will be told in the next chapter.

Population Control.[13]   Not until after the Cultural Revolution did China's leaders realize the magnitude of the problem of population growth. All the progress achieved in food production and technology could be wiped out by an uncontrolled increase in the number of mouths that needed to be fed. In an address to the National People's Congress in September 1980, President Hua Guofeng launched a crash program to bring population growth under control. The state called on each couple to have but a *single child* with the aim of keeping the population to a maximum of 1.2 billion people by the end of the century.

The program is spelled out in the planned parenthood regulations for Guangdong Province:

(1) Late marriages are encouraged. The minimum marriage age for men is 25 and for women 23. Educational institutions are permitted to admit only unmarried students. Students having children while in school will be expelled.

(2) Economic incentives are provided for one-child families. This reverses the age-old tradition that having large families has social and economic advantages. Instead of providing grain allocations on the basis of family number, (''more pay for more births''), the state provides ''one-child preferential treatment certificates.'' One-child families receive the same foodstuff allocations as those with more children, and they also receive priority in housing and jobs. Penalties are to be levied on parents if the wife becomes pregnant with a third child, or a second child if this is less than four years after the first. Medical costs for

pregnancies of second or third children will be borne by the family, not the state.

(3) A wide range of contraceptives is provided free of charge. Each health center has been instructed to give first priority to family planning education.

(4) Abortions are encouraged in the case of second or third pregnancies. These are provided free of charge. In extreme cases, sterilization seems to be required.

It is not clear how widespread or how strictly enforced planned parenthood regulations are. It seems that coercion at times has been used, but for the most part, peer pressure suffices. Whatever the case, the results have been impressive already. Sichuan, a province of nearly 100 million, has reported what may be one of the most drastic drops in the growth rate ever recorded—from 31 births per thousand in 1970 to 6.7 births per thousand in 1979. The reliability of such statistics is subject to question, but population experts at the United States Public Health Center for Disease Control (CDC) in Atlanta, Georgia, have been extremely impressed with the results of their investigations and interviews with public health physicians from the People's Republic. In fact they believe that it has been so successful that two concerns have been raised: (1) the frequency of abortions is alarming and may become a serious health hazard; and (2) the norm of the one-child family may lead to such a sharp downward population curve that it will make it extremely difficult for the next generation of workers to support the large number of old and retired people.

A Middle Way?

The PRC is now moving into its fourth decade. In comparison to China's long history and many dynastic changes, this has been a very short time. But in these years it has brought about cataclysmic changes and weathered many storms. Today its people are enjoying a degree of peace and stability unknown for at least the past hundred years.

Under Deng, China has chosen a middle way—retaining in large part the socialistic pattern of the Mao era but rejecting the radicalism of the extreme left. This approach has a distinct Chinese flavor, for during their long years of history and many dynastic changes, they have learned to choose the moderation of a middle way. The approach is as old as Confucius who venerated a "golden mean"—searching for the path that would avoid excesses and extremes. After periods of violence and change, the Chinese people have sought return to the norm of law and order. They have absorbed the periodic invasions of their barbaric neighbors and assimilated and civilized the ideas and changes that they introduced. Can they do the same for Marxist communism?

There are pitfalls on either side of the middle way, and mountains of difficulties stand in the future. The campaign for modernization is having far more difficulty in making progress than was previously imagined. China is still a very poor country on a subsistence economy. The government ran large budget deficits for both 1979 ($11.3 billion) and for 1980 ($7.4 billion). These are minuscule in comparison to budget deficits in the United States, but give serious concern to China's economic planners, given their much smaller economic base and gross national product. Inflation has become a nagging problem, officially pegged at 6.5%, but unofficially estimated at 20% in urban areas. China must still import grain to feed its one billion. In 1980 the United States supplied China with $1 billion worth of wheat. The plans for industrialization and plant construction have been sharply cut back. China lacked the infrastructure—transportation, electric power, communication—on which to build. The Communist party's ideological journal suggests that ten million Chinese were unemployed, out of an urban work force of 115 million at the end of 1980.[14]

A more serious problem has been what the *People's Daily* has termed "a crisis of faith in Marxism." According to a *New York Times* article entitled "Apathy Replaces Marxist Idealism Among Chinese":

> Three decades after the triumph of the Communist revolution, there is widespread disillusionment among the people of China with both the Communist Party and its Marxist ideology. The idealism, the drive, the almost religious ideological fervor that marked Communism's early years and lasted until the Cultural Revolution, have largely vanished.[15]

Skepticism has undoubtedly been created by the many twists and turns that have been taken in defining the party line. Deng Xiaoping has understood this mood and answered it by substituting pragmatism for ideology. As Fairbank puts it, "The initial enthusiasm of the revolution had been spent."[16] The question now is what will take the place of the zeal and the fervor that kept the engines running?

An acute problem has been the frustration and disillusionment of youth. Some were leaders of the Red Guards who do not know what to believe now that their former heroes have been discredited and the ideological "line" has shifted back and forth. Other young people were caught up in the massive attempts to relieve the population pressure in the cities and were transported against their will to the rural communes. Still others lost their opportunity for a normal education or a chance to learn a trade during the ten chaotic years of the Cultural Revolution. Through no fault of their own, they find themselves unfitted for the present emphasis on modernization.

In a poll taken at Fudan University in Shanghai in 1980, only a third said they believed in communism. Nearly twenty-five percent said they believed in "fate," and a few believed in Christianity. Twenty-five percent believed in "nothing at all."[17]

Some of those who were sent to the rural communes have now drifted back to the cities. In 1981 an estimated 300,000 of these illegal "returnees" were living in Shanghai. Some have organized legitimate business ventures such as repair centers and handicraft shops. But others roam the streets in gangs engaged in petty crimes. Others are fond of imitating everything that comes from outside China—queuing up at movie theaters, scalping tickets, engaging in the black market sale of everything from record albums to blue jeans. Newspapers in China have recently referred to the growing problem of juvenile delinquency and the need for harsher measures to maintain order. Yet there is considerable sympathy for the young people, realizing that in many cases they are the victims of circumstance.

China Notes has reported a remarkable letter written by a young woman in the national publication *Chinese Youth* in May 1980, which has produced something of a sensation since she spoke for many:

> Her name is Pan Xiao, 23 years of age. In the letter she frankly told the journal that "life for me has lost all its mystery and attraction. I have come almost to its end. I have traveled the path from hope to disappointment and despair. What began with selflessness now ends with egotism."

> She said that since childhood her aim had been to make life
> more beautiful for others and to dedicate herself to the Communist
> Party and the people.
> But the facts of life had disillusioned her. . . . Revolution no
> longer seemed such a lofty ideal, and yet a life lived for mere enjoy-
> ment was meaningless. "I cannot live for living's sake," she
> wrote.[18]

The letter produced an immediate response from its readers. More than
40,000 letters flooded the editorial department of the journal in the next
three months. Reader reaction ranged from complete sympathy to complete disapproval. Many readers offered advice. The *People's Daily*
and other influential newspapers took up the debate. Young people of
China are searching for a deeper meaning to life and more adequate
answers to its problems. The debate goes on.

In passing it must be noted how similar China's list of problems is
to that of the United States—budget deficits, inflation, unemployment,
a faith crisis, the younger generation, juvenile delinquency! Americans
can hardly claim to have solved them either. In spite of our different
systems and different cultures, perhaps the problems we face are not all
that different!

Another problem the United States and China have in common is
the question of Taiwan. During 1982 the two nations engaged in what
were described as "extremely sensitive discussions" relating to continued arms sales to Taiwan. The United States canceled plans for the sale
of advanced fighter aircraft but wanted to go ahead with plans for sale
of spare parts for planes which Taiwan now possesses. China believed
this would be a violation of the spirit of the 1979 agreement by which
the United States recognized the People's Republic of China and sev-
ered official relationships with Taiwan. In August 1982 a compromise
was worked out which may settle this sensitive issue at least for a time.
The United States and China signed an accord in which China pledges
to seek reunification with Taiwan by peaceful means, and the United
States promises not to exceed present levels of arms sales to Taiwan
and to reduce these sales gradually.

Deng Xiaoping is approaching 80. He has moved to place younger
men in the top echelons of party and government. In 1981 Deng's
protégé, Hu Yaobang, aged 66, replaced Hua Guofeng as party chair-

man. Zhao Ziyang, 62 years old, is premier. Deng, like Mao before him, has had his own problems with China's massive unyielding bureaucracy. Older men have been forced into retirement. Those who are deemed incompetent and those unwilling to accept Deng's changes are being weeded out. China seems to be undergoing an extensive overhaul of the government ministries, cutting back sharply on the number of functionaries.

In the draft of the new constitution presented to the National Party Congress in the fall of 1982, a major change was proposed in the administration of the people's commune system. The commune will be retained as the basic economic organization to manage farmlands and for production, but it will no longer function as the political organization to handle government administration. This will be administered by newly re-established township governments. It was felt that abuses of power occurred when both economic and political power were retained in the same organization. This basic change in the Communist system again illustrates the willingness of Deng Xiaoping to sacrifice ideology for pragmatic solutions that work.

Deng seems to be firmly in control, although in the spring of 1982 there was a flurry of rumors that he had been downgraded to a position of lesser rank because of a long absence from the capital. Now it seems he was on an inspection tour, dealing with intransigent members of the bureaucracy.

Many observers believe that whatever changes in the leadership appear after Deng's death, the changes which he has introduced will be irreversible. Barring some worldwide upheaval, it appears that the middle course of pragmatic socialism Deng has charted will continue.

China has chosen the socialist option. Today there is little reason to think that this does not have the support of the great majority of China's one billion. It is the socialist option, but the Chinese people have and will continue to put their own distinctive stamp upon it. It is difficult to know what they will come up with, but one thing is certain. They will seek to solve Chinese problems with Chinese solutions in Chinese ways.

What is the future for the Christian church in this middle way of pragmatic socialism? This is the subject to which we must turn in the next chapter.

9

The Church
Alive and Well!

*. . . unless a grain of wheat falls into the earth and dies, it
remains alone; but if it dies, it bears much fruit.*

(John 12:24)

The reopening of the churches in China cannot be described
without the use of the word "miraculous." Western theologians who
were not used to using this word find in visiting China that it is the only
way to explain the phenomena they observe. By "miraculous" one
means events which cannot be explained by the historical events which
preceded them. The government relaxation of religious controls can be
understood since it is in line with the political exigencies of political
life in the post-Mao era. But *what happened* when the controls were
lifted defies a strictly historical explanation. The vitality of the Christian community was something nobody expected. The church was
thought to have died. As late as the summer of 1979, a Protestant mission executive wrote that "organized Christianity in the People's Republic of China, has, as far as we can see, disappeared."[1]

The extent to which the Christian movement had been kept alive
and had grown through small group meetings in homes was a total surprise even to Chinese Christians nearest the scene of the action. Chinese Christians, isolated from one another in very small groups, did not
know that similar Christian groups had been meeting all over China.
When the curtain of silence was lifted, there was amazement at what
had been taking place. Asked to explain what had happened, Chinese
Christians have simply replied, "The Holy Spirit has been at work."

In the early 1950s the missionary movement had come to an end.
For twenty-five years there had been no foreign missionary activity.
There was every reason to think that the results which had been
achieved through 150 years of effort would be lost—that like the efforts
of the Nestorians in the seventh century and the Franciscans in the thir-

teenth, all significant traces of the Christian faith would vanish from Chinese soil. Yet in spite of the limitations of the missionaries—their foreignness and their connection with the colonial system—the seed of the Christian gospel had been buried deep in the soil of China. And when springtime finally came, new shoots full of vitality and life began to emerge. But it was not the same as what had been planted. Christianity had taken a form and shape which the missionary could not have planned or predicted or understood. What finally came up, after the long winter years of the Cultural Revolution, was distinctively and thoroughly Chinese! Nevertheless, it was the same gospel, the same Lord, the same faith, and the same church. The explanation comes from John 12:24: ". . . unless a grain of wheat falls into the earth and dies, it remains alone; but if it dies, it bears much fruit."

The Year 1979

The break came in the year 1979. As 1976 had been a momentous year for the political life of the People's Republic, so the year 1979 marked the beginning of new life for the Christian community. At least for a season, the long winter was over. There were many signs that a thaw had begun.

In January the Bureau of Religious Affairs reopened its doors after having been dormant since before the Cultural Revolution. This was tacit acknowledgement that the government recognized the existence of religious bodies and felt the need to have some agency deal with them. An editorial in *The People's Daily* proclaimed that China's government would "staunchly and consistently uphold Article 46 of the [1978] Constitution" which guarantees that people have "freedom to believe in religion, and freedom not to believe in religion."

In Beijing the Institute for the Study of World Religions was activated again after having been closed since 1966. A prominent Buddhist scholar, Jen Chiyu, was made director, and an influential Protestant Christian, Zhao Fusan, deputy director. Zhao was the first Chinese Christian minister to visit the United States in thirty years. In 1982 he became director of the institute. In Nanjing a Research Institute on Religion was opened at the university with Bishop K. H. Ting appointed as director. It was the first step leading toward the formation of a seminary.

Christian pastors, who had been arrested or sent to the rural work camps for reeducation along with other intellectuals, were released and their citizenship rights were restored. Prominent among these was the popular Protestant pastor, Wang Mingdao, who had served a prison sentence of twenty-two years.

In March a delegation of Chinese Protestant ministers from Hong Kong was invited to visit China. They were escorted by members of the Three-Self Committee and the newly activated Bureau of Religious Affairs. The Chinese Christians on both sides were overwhelmed with emotion as old friends met. They worshiped with Chinese Christians in Hangzhou in a special church service arranged for the occasion. They were given a reception in Shanghai and met with Religious Affairs officers in Beijing. They observed churches being prepared for return to the Christian congregations and engaged in free and spirited discussions late into the nights.

Then in September an official Chinese delegation attended the Third Assembly of the World Conference on Religion and Peace in Princeton, New Jersey. The group consisted of eight religious leaders—Protestants, Muslims, and Buddhists. Significantly, no Roman Catholics were included.

For the Protestants the most significant meeting took place at the Inter-Church Center in New York city. Although billed as an unofficial visit, it was the first contact between Chinese Christians and the United States' National Council of Churches since relationships were broken in 1950. This was a historic occasion. Bishop K. H. Ting, leader of the Protestant group, brought warm greetings from Christians in China and answered questions freely and frankly. Later the Protestant delegation visited the office of the Presbyterian, U.S., General Assembly in Atlanta, as well as church headquarters in other cities. While in Atlanta, the group spoke in Protestant churches, engaged in discussions with church leaders, and addressed a public meeting held at the Presbyterian General Assembly Mission Board.

On September 2 a congregation of 5,000 people jammed into the Mo En Church (formerly Moore Memorial Methodist Church) in downtown Shanghai for two historic services, the first public worship in the People's Republic since the Red Guards went on their rampage in the summer of 1966. In quick succession, other churches began to open. The East Mountain District Christian Church in Guangzhou opened on September 30, 1979, with an overflow congregation of 800. The Drum Tower Union Church in Hangzhou opened on September 23, 1979, with 1,000 in attendance.

Why the Change in Government Policy?

The long closed door had been opened. There were still some misgivings, considerable suspicion, and much uncertainty. But still the door had been opened. Why had the government changed its policy?

Government officials have said that there has been no change in the Communist party's position on religion. The position of the party remains that of atheism. But the party has now returned to its pre–Cultural Revolution position when religious freedom, guaranteed by the constitution, was respected. The Gang of Four had destroyed this freedom, as well as many other things. Now that they have been eliminated, things are back to normal. The government position is clearly stated in an article in the June 14, 1980, edition of the *People's Daily (Renmin Ribao):*

> Our policy of freedom of religious belief is interpreted as follows: Every citizen has the freedom of religious belief and the freedom of nonbelief. He has the freedom to be a religious believer today and a nonbeliever tomorrow, and the freedom to be a nonbeliever today and a believer tomorrow. He has the freedom to observe this faith or that faith. Every citizen with or without a religion enjoys the same social and political status in our country. Religions with many or few followers rank equally.

And yet comparison with the pre–Cultural Revolution period reveals that there has been a change. The government of Deng Xiaoping has been more open to religion than that of the People's Republic prior to 1966. Chinese Christians are now attending Christian gatherings and events abroad. Church representatives from abroad have been invited to China. Prior to 1966 these things did not happen. Before that date government pressure worked to reduce the number of open congregations. Now the Religious Affairs Bureau has been actively assisting in negotiating the return of churches, securing the payment of back rents, and in the printing of Islamic and Christian Scriptures.

So there has been a change in policy which has gone beyond a mere return to the position in effect before the notorious "Gang of Four." Why? We must recognize the work of the Holy Spirit in all of this, as the Chinese Christians do, but from a human standpoint several reasons might be suggested.

(1) Deng's new opening to the West requires a return, in some degree, to an open society at home. Freedom of religion is a part—a small part—of a much bigger picture. It is simply one of the risks that has to be taken in order to gain the international support which China needs.

(2) Deng is attempting to forge a new alliance which includes all segments of the Chinese people. This is necessary to carry out the massive effort for the Four Modernizations. Of great importance are the thirty million people of the Islamic ethnic minority in the far west. Buddhist influence is still strong among the peasants. Included are the Christians who are a very small group that poses no threat to the regime but has high symbolic value in Western and Third World relations.

(3) One might conjecture that the previous repressive policies failed. The persecutions had created thousands of small, self-contained Christian communities operating for the most part in secret. These groups were growing and control of them was virtually impossible. It would be far better to permit them to come out in the open and receive some kind of tacit recognition rather than continue underground as potentially divisive, secret societies.

(4) Christians of all persuasions suffered during the Cultural Revolution along with intellectuals, artists, rightists, and senior party members. Through the fires of common suffering, a new solidarity with the Chinese people had been wrought. Through the deep waters of the Cultural Revolution, the stains of colonialism have been washed away. At least for Protestants, the suspicion of foreign loyalty has been removed. What Christian missionaries could not do, the Red Guard have accomplished!

(5) Some have raised the possibility that the treatment of religious groups today may parallel the treatment given the intellectuals at the time of the "Hundred Flowers" episode in 1957. Is the government encouraging Christian leaders and followers to come out into the open so that they can be identified and cut down at a later time? No doubt some Chinese Christians have reservations about the change and share

these fears about the future. Yet there seems to be much evidence that the present circumstances cannot be compared with that of the "Hundred Flowers." That "blooming and contending" episode lasted a scant six months. The present period of limited religious freedom is now extending into its fourth year. Also, there is no reason to think that the churches have become a refuge or a bastion for dissidents who are interested in attacking the government. Christian congregations, whether they worship in homes or in public, have not become hotbeds for counterrevolutionary activity. Worship services have been nonpolitical in nature.

This new policy of religious freedom is not carried out consistently throughout all of China. In certain areas officials have continued the antireligious bias of the Cultural Revolution. Sometimes Bibles and Christian literature have been confiscated in the mails. In some places young people under the age of eighteen have been denied the right to attend church services. Party members and soldiers are prohibited from becoming Christians.

Representatives of the five officially recognized religious groups (Buddhism, Taoism, Islam, Catholicism, and Protestantism) in the Chinese People's Political Consultative Conference petitioned a change in the 1978 constitution which stated: "Citizens enjoy freedom to believe in religion and the freedom not to believe in religion and to propagate atheism." The implication was that only atheism has the right to be propagated.

The new constitution approved in the fall of 1982 does remove the offending clause but adds much more:

> Citizens of the People's Republic of China enjoy freedom of religious belief.
>
> No organ of state, mass organization or person is allowed to force any citizen to believe or not to believe in religion. It is impermissible to discriminate against any citizen who believes or does not believe in religion.
>
> The state protects legitimate religious activities. No person is permitted to conduct counterrevolutionary activities or activities of disrupting social order, harming people's health or obstructing the educational system of the country.
>
> Religion is not subject to the control of foreign countries.[2]

Postdenominational Christianity

During 1980 churches across the length and breadth of the land continued to open. What is more remarkable, when they were opened, they were filled to overflowing with people! By midyear, thirty-five churches were known to have been opened. By the end of the year there were at least one hundred. More were on the way. There was a growing need to reestablish a national organization which could give some leadership to the movement and represent the Christian Protestant constituency before the government.

On March 1, 1980, the standing committee of the national Three-Self Movement held an enlarged meeting in Shanghai. It was the first national gathering of Christians in more than ten years. The former president of the Three-Self Committee, Y. T. Wu, had died a few months earlier and the committee was in new hands. The major work of the committee was the preparation of an "Open Letter" which was addressed to "brothers and sisters in Christ of all China." It was mailed to known Protestant groups. Significantly, no denominations were mentioned. The church in China had moved into what its leaders now are calling a "postdenominational era." In setting the stage for this new period of history, the letter gave thanks to God that such a letter could now be written openly, and that "His rod and His staff were never far from us as we moved through the valley of the shadow of death."

The writers rejoiced to hear of the large number of Christians who had persisted in their faith and had continued to witness in spite of persecution and trial. They cited the achievements of the Three-Self Movement which had brought Christians closer to the people of China and had heightened their sense of national pride with the result that non-Christians and party cadres had changed their attitude toward Christianity, no longer considering it a foreign religion.

They agreed on priorities for the future: publication of the Bible, printing of Christian literature, preparation of young men and women for the ministry, correcting government policy in areas where freedom of religion had not been well implemented, elevating the consciousness of Christians in love for the homeland, strengthening the pastoral work of the churches. They also laid plans for the organization of a new

"Christian national structure" which would be a service organization but would respect differences of faith and would not "interfere with or make uniform our beliefs."

The letter issued a warning against those who sought to disrupt and divide:

> We are aware that in churches abroad there is a small number of people still hostile to New China today. They attack our principled stand on Three-Self and put their hands into our church life in the name of "evangelism" and "research." Regardless of the colour of their skin, they are trying in reality to push Chinese Christianity back to the colonial past and earn for it again the onus of a foreign religion taking its stand against the Chinese people.

It also extended an invitation:

> As to those Christians abroad who assume an attitude of equality towards us and respect our principled stand on independence and self-government, we are ready to enter into friendly relations and fellowship with them.

The letter expressed a hope for the return of their beloved brothers and sisters of Taiwan to the "bosom of the mainland" within the decade.[3]

The "Open Letter" marked a new beginning for the Three-Self Movement. Undoubtedly there were those who remembered the harsh things said and done by the leaders of the movement in earlier days and who continued to view it with suspicion. But *all Christians*—those who had opposed the movement as well as those who had supported it—had suffered during the Cultural Revolution. It was time to start over, and the tone of the letter was conciliatory, aimed at forging a new unity of purpose and understanding. A call was made for patriotic support of the homeland, but the political rhetoric was restrained in contrast with earlier Three-Self epistles. There was a warning, but it was meant for a small number abroad who might be divisive. The one reference to the "colonial past" was muted and a readiness was expressed to enter into new friendly relationships with Christians in other lands. For those suspicious of some central body dictating a unified theology, there were assurances that differences of faith would be respected and that no interference would be made with long-cherished beliefs and practices.

There is reason to believe that the letter was well received. Groups of Christians held special meetings at which the letter was read and reread. Hopefully, it signaled the beginning of a better day.

The long-awaited organization of the "new national structure" referred to in the "Open Letter" took place in Nanjing in October 1980. One hundred seventy-six delegates attended the meeting from the various provinces, municipalities, and autonomous regions. Nine delegates from five other nationalities (Korean, and other minority tribal or linguistic groups) were included. The name selected for the new organization was the "China Christian Council." Bishop K. H. Ting was elected president. The message announcing the formation of the Council was sent to all Protestant groups and again was conciliatory in nature, appealing for the "unity which the Spirit gives." The message welcomed those who worshiped in homes, alleviating the fears that the new body would move to restrict worship to government-sanctioned churches:

> All those obedient to Christ who worship in spirit and in truth, whether in church-buildings or in homes, pledge to be of one mind in looking up to Jesus on whom our faith depends from start to finish.

The Council expressed a desire to establish relationships with overseas churches under certain conditions:

> While holding fast to the Three-Self principle, we are open to friendly relations with churches and Christians abroad on the basis of equality and mutual respect, thus witnessing to our common fellowship in Christ. But we are strongly opposed to the small number of people abroad who take a hostile attitude towards New China, disregard the authority of the Chinese Church and our Three-Self principle, make efforts to split up the Chinese Christians communities and even to engage in anti-China subversive activities under the guise of spreading the gospel.

The Council celebrated its new freedom and unity:

> Throughout the conference we felt we were bathing in the grace of God. The Spirit was indeed moving in our midst. Owing to the fact that during these years we have been throwing off denominational prejudices that divided us, we were able to enjoy deeply the goodness and pleasantness of brothers and sisters dwelling together in unity and the felicities of the communion of saints.[4]

The Council is not a united church. Matters of creed, sacraments, and polity have been put off so that more immediate matters could be dealt with. It is understood that these decisions will have to be made later, but this will take time, great care, and much study. Although government influence had some effect on creating the present unity, there seems little desire to return to Western denominations. If divisions occur, at least they will be Chinese in origin!

The message to the churches speaks of the "division of labor" between the Council and the continuing Three-Self Movement. The Council will give major attention to pastoral care, training of church workers, publication of the Bible, and producing Christian literature. The responsibilities of the Movement are not so clearly spelled out, but one might assume that they would include the formulation of policy in support of the Three-Self principles, the promotion of patriotism, and government relationships through the Religious Affairs Bureau. Actually there is a great deal of overlapping between the officers of the two organizations.

Open Churches and House Congregations

Protestant Christianity has emerged in the post-Mao era with two different forms of expression. First are the churches which have been returned to the Christians and are open for public worship. There has been a steady growth in the number of these congregations since the Mo En Church opened in September 1979. In July 1982 there were at least five hundred such congregations in the cities of China. This has taken a considerable amount of complex negotiation between the Three-Self Movement, the Religious Affairs Bureau, and the former occupants of the property. For example, the Community Church in Shanghai had been occupied by a troup of opera singers; the Mo En Church was being used by a middle school; the church in Suzhou had been a factory. Other facilities had to be found for the people being forced to move. In a land where every available building space is in use, this was no mean achievement. Many church buildings had been damaged by the Red Guards or by the misuse of the former occupants. Incredibly funds were often provided by the Religious Affairs Bureau from rents that had been received! The former West Gate Presbyterian Church in Xuzhou reported that it had received the equivalent of $14,000 to rehabilitate the church and provide for pews.

These churches all seem to be well attended and many of them are packed for services. Two or more services are held on a Sunday, and some are open on Saturday for Seventh-Day Adventist worshipers or others unable to come on Sunday. It is reported that between 15,000 and 20,000 worshipers attend the seven Protestant churches in Shanghai in an average week. These churches are so crowded that there are plans to open three additional churches by the end of 1982. At times pastors have had to urge worshipers at one service to "please leave" in order to make room for those waiting outside who have come for the next service! One must come an hour early to be assured a seat. Those unable to crowd in listen to the service broadcast over a public address system in the church courtyard and peer through the open windows. Many of the worshipers are older people, but the congregations include a number of young adults, and youths often fill the choirs.

The worship service tends to follow the same forms used by that particular congregation prior to 1949. There are hymns, prayers, Scripture readings, but the main feature is always the sermon—usually a lengthy one. An American teacher residing in China tells of the church service he frequently attends:

> The old church building, some say, is now 100 years old. It is crowded with worshipers of all ages, extra wooden benches of unknown vintage being carried into the sanctuary as latecomers arrive by bicycle and bus from every district of the city. Pastor Sun's order of worship is simple, functional, with opening hymn followed by prayer, then straightway into the sermon. Bible verses are interspersed in his sermon as required, with all worshipers reading aloud, or following along in their own books, some old, some very new.
>
> The old pastor has no doubt survived many battles, conflicts, struggles, the devastation of the old order, to be replaced by a newer one, the chaos of the Great Leap Forward, the catastrophy of the Great Proletariat Cultural Revolution. . . . But his word remains stable, yet never dated, tested by perhaps time and eternity, that God loves mankind and individuals, that Jesus arrived to forgive even the most gross sinner, that health, strength, courage, and life itself are derived from above, and that grace and salvation are freely given despite individual and collective unworthiness. His language was simple, yet profound, that God is our Leader and Comforter, despite

all contradictions, all catastrophies, all wrenches in the world
order. . . .

There were no announcements, no offering, no musical inter-
ludes, no choir, no ushers, no bulletins. A spartan order perhaps, but
never devoid of meaning, reassurance, and anticipation. Pastor Sun's
sermon was followed by a closing hymn, begun by the old pastor
himself, then spreading spontaneously through the congregation.
Then a short period of prayer by worshipers, a brief benediction, and
it was over.[5]

In many cases, pastoral teams serve these congregations. Usually
these are elderly men, although ordination of women is recognized.
Often the pastors for one congregation represent different communions—the Rice Market Church in Beijing is served by one former
Presbyterian, one former Anglican, and one former Methodist. When a
church is to be reopened, it seems that an informal consensus is
reached among the Christians in the city as to the pastor to be called.
Then a nomination is made to the Religious Affairs Bureau for approval. Christians in one city strongly affirmed that the government officials approved whoever the Christians wanted and did not interfere in
ecclesiastical matters. Nevertheless, Religious Affairs Bureau approval
does mean that dissidents or potential troublemakers can be eliminated
from consideration.

Pastors take turns preaching and presiding at worship services.
Much time is spent in visiting and in talking with Christians and others
who come to the church office. Christian nurture is a top priority. Pastors arrange special classes for those seeking baptism and have prayer
meetings and Bible studies during the week. There is no Sunday school
and apparently some hesitancy about working with youth under the age
of 18. Churches are not involved in any form of community service or
social activity. This goes beyond the limits of what is included under
religious freedom. There have been a few church weddings. In the
Beijing churches communion is observed once a month and is well attended. In the fall of 1981 an American National Council of Churches
delegation attended a service at the Mo En Church where more than
sixty adults confessed their faith in Jesus Christ and were baptized by
sprinkling. Others have been baptized by immersion. Apparently it is a
matter of personal preference on the part of the believer.

As yet congregations have no formal mode of church government. When decisions must be made, there is informal discussion and a consensus is reached. There are no church officers although Christians in Xuzhou spoke of their "elders" since this is what they were used to. Membership rolls have not been kept by the churches in Beijing because there is still some apprehension about having one's name identified on a public list as a "believer." Pastors are paid a stipend which averages somewhat higher than that of a manual laborer. Funds come from rental income received from church property still being used by secular organizations. As one church leader put it, "The church is the only capitalistic organization in a socialistic society—receiving income from its property holdings!" The churches also take offerings. In most cases these are taken not by "passing the plate" but by placing an offering box in the rear of the sanctuary into which worshipers can put their contributions as they wish. Offerings, including rice rations, and other nonmonetary gifts have been very liberal considering the overall level of poverty. The church has very limited needs and takes pride in its ability to provide adequately for them.

The other form of church life which has emerged in China has been the house congregations. The open churches are but the tip of an iceberg. Many, many more Christians meet for worship in their homes. In this they are similar to the churches of the New Testament.

It began during the bleak and lonely days of the Cultural Revolution when public worship was banned. In order to keep alive their faith and to nourish each other, they began to worship in homes. In Shanghai a young woman told the NCC delegation from America about how her mother and father would take her and her brother into the darkness of their bedroom each night. Very quietly so that no one outside could hear, they repeated the hymns and prayers of the church. This they did for ten years! A couple tells of taking their child every Christmas Eve for a vigil in front of a warehouse unlit and locked up for the night. There, before what had once been their church, the Christmas story was told and retold—for ten long years.[6] In the Christian homes of China, Christianity was kept alive.

Now that worship in churches has been resumed, many Christians continue their habit of home worship. There are nowhere near enough open churches to accommodate the number of believers. Worship in homes is the only form of Christian community in most country areas and small villages where there are no church buildings. Some Christians worship both at home and in the churches, rejoicing in the Christian fellowship and preaching of the larger congregations as well as the family intimacy of the house gatherings.

Some house congregation people undoubtedly have continuing suspicions about the leadership of the Three-Self Movement. Some suffered during the time of the denunciation meetings of the 1950s and remember with bitterness those experiences which they blame on the Three-Self leaders. Yet some Hong Kong and United States observers overemphasize the differences between these two groups when they speak of an "official apostate church" recognized and used by the Communist hierarchy and a "true underground" church made up of house congregations. This analogy seems to be a gross exaggeration. In some areas differences are real and acute. Some house church people have reported harassment by local Three-Self leaders. Suspicion continues that the Three-Self Movement is a government instrument for the control of the churches. On the other hand, some of the differences probably go back to the "modernist-fundamentalist" debates of earlier years.

In other areas, however, distrust seems to be disappearing. House congregations in some places have received the full support and encouragement of Three-Self leaders. Whatever excesses may have been associated with the Three-Self Movement in the 1950s, genuine efforts have been made for reconciliation and a new beginning. Open church congregations are made up of many different denominational backgrounds including the Jesus Family and the Little Flock, who were strongest in their opposition to the Three-Self Movement in the 1950s. Worship services in open churches are not used for political propaganda. Preaching is biblical and theologically conservative.

The house congregation movement continues to grow rapidly and to show remarkable vitality. It is strongest in the southern provinces where Christianity has deeper roots. There is great diversity of doctrine and practice. Leaders are mostly laypeople and part-time evangelists who hold other jobs. Many are women. Many lack formal Christian training. The Chinese Church Research Center in Hong Kong reports fantastic growth with some accompanying problems:

The church in Henan has spread like wild grass, beyond the belief of those who sowed the first seeds. Since Liberation, the number of believers has increased at least ten times. Reports to this center tell of the faith that is moving mountains of hardship and suffering. . . .

Yet this wild growth has brought problems. Few believers have Bibles, still fewer are grounded in the truths of Scripture. In some areas, belief in Christ has been merely synthesized into the folk religion of the area.[7]

The report which follows tells of gross superstitious practices, Buddhist influences, untrained leaders, and factionalism. Desparately needed are Bibles, Christian literature, and training classes for the lay leaders.

Bible Publication and Distribution

Bibles are a precious commodity in China. They are precious both because they are honored by Christians and because they are scarce. No Bibles or Testaments had been printed in China since the late 1950s. Many Bibles were destroyed by the Red Guards in their rampage during 1966 and 1967. For a dozen years there was a "famine on the land," not of bread or water, but of "hearing of the words of the LORD" (Amos 8:11). As Christian worship was resumed and groups began to meet more openly, there has been a tremendous clamor for Bibles. Stories are told of the great lengths to which Christians would go to get a copy of Scripture. Whole books of the Bible have been laboriously copied by hand and circulated from person to person. A pastor appeared at the headquarters of the Three-Self Movement in Nanjing, having come all the way from the Northeast Provinces (Manchuria) to ask for a Bible. He had not seen one in ten years! There has been an overwhelming response to radio broadcasting beamed into China which read at dictation speed passages from the Bible night after night. Clearly, the printing of the Scriptures in China had to be a top priority.

In October 1980 the China Christian Council was able to print 135,000 copies of the Bible and New Testament with the help of the Religious Affairs Bureau, which secured paper and arranged for use of government presses. A subsequent printing of 270,000 was made in 1981 and there were plans to print 650,000 copies during 1982. All cost of these printings are borne by Chinese Christians, many of whom purchased copies in advance. The 1911 Union Version was used in this printing without change. This does present difficulties for the general public and for new believers due to the new, simplified way of writing the Chinese characters which has been put into practice. However, this is the version known and loved by older Christians and the version which sustained their faith during the long difficult years. In 1982 a Korean version of the Bible was also printed in Shanghai to meet the needs of the Korean ethnic minority, many of whom are Christians.

Three-Self leaders and others deeply resent the smuggling of Bibles into China which is done by some religious groups. They believe that these activities are flagrant violations of the sovereignty of their nation and church. The United Bible Societies and Protestant denominations in the West have opposed such smuggling practices, but they are being continued by some independent groups.

Time magazine, in its October 19, 1981, edition, carried the story of an attempt to smuggle a million copies of the Bible into China by two organizations known as Open Doors and Brother Andrew International. The operation, dubbed "Project Pearl," was carried out with military precision and practice landings in the Philippines. Several hundred one-ton crates, each containing forty-eight waterproof boxes with ninety Bibles each were loaded aboard a specially built one-hundred-foot barge in Hong Kong. The cost of the venture was $6 million, contributed for the most part through the solicitation of Christians in the United States and Canada. The landing was made on the night of June 18 on the South China coast near the port of Shantou (Swatow). The unloading process went smoothly until an army patrol turned up unexpectedly and stormed the beach where the unloading was going on. Hundreds of villagers were arrested as they were repacking the illicit cargo. It was later reported that most of those arrested were released. Open Doors estimates that sixty to eighty percent of the shipment got through. Other sources from within China have reported that half the shipment was lost in the tide during unloading and that most of the remainder was confiscated. Such attempts at Bible smuggling is deeply resented by patriotic Christians in China because it casts the Christian faith as a foreign subversive religion, reflects on the integrity of the church in China, is dangerous for Christians in any way involved, and is sure to increase the survcillance of the government over all Christian groups.

The problem of Bible publication and distribution in China remains a critical one. China Christian Council leaders believe that they are doing everything possible to provide for this need under some rather difficult circumstances. For them this is a matter of their own self-reliance and respect. They believe that although there continues to be a shortage of Bibles, this has been exaggerated by the agencies engaged in Bible smuggling who do not mention in their appeals for funds the fact that Bibles are being published quite legally within China. There has been some discussion as to how Bibles, printed in Hong Kong or the West under the auspices of the Three-Self Movement, could be distributed legally within China. But so far nothing has been worked out. This would certainly be the best solution.

Nanjing Union Theological Seminary

Another critical problem facing the church is the training of future pastors. Although churches open at present seem well supplied with teams of two or more pastors, all are older men and a few women. Most of them received their theological education in denominational seminaries prior to 1949 although the old Nanjing Seminary did graduate a few students as late as 1966 before it was closed by the Red Guards during the Cultural Revolution.

What kind of pastor and what kind of pastoral education would be appropriate for the church in the New China? Initially some felt that the only viable form of ministry would be a voluntary, part-time clergy, serving a de-institutionalized church. But with the reopening of the churches and the flood of people attending the worship services, it soon became apparent that pastors would be needed for more traditional patterns of pastoral service.

A decision was made to reopen the Nanjing Seminary and to offer a four-year course of study. A request was sent to church groups asking for applications from prospective students. More than seven hundred replies were received! In December 1980 competitive examinations were given to 380 of these candidates, and from these the first class of fifty-one was accepted. The seminary opened its doors in March 1981. Students came from the twenty-two provinces, municipalities, and autonomous regions of China. Twenty-nine were men. Twenty-two were women. The youngest was 19; the oldest 35. All were middle-school graduates, and most came from Christian families. All were baptized Christians. All were committed to serving as pastors in the uncertain circumstances of the New China.

The faculty consists of a small group of overworked men and women. Bishop K. H. Ting is the president; the administration of the school is handled by Vice-president Chen Zeming. Students and faculty share a close-knit life together on the small pre-1949 campus, whose facilities include five classrooms, a chapel, a library, and a dormitory. Students pay no tuition but are expected to pay for their food. Local churches provide scholarships. The seminary is partially financed through the payment of rental fees by the government on former church buildings and property.

The four-year course of study is surprisingly like that of seminaries the world over except that it includes some liberal arts subjects one would expect in an undergraduate college course. A three-year graduate course for college graduates was added in 1981 with several students enrolled. A new class for the four-year course enrolled in the fall of 1982. The seminary curriculum is rather traditional with a heavy emphasis on Bible study, doctrine, church history, and pastoral subjects. All students are required to give several hours a week to the study of politics as is true of all other schools in China. The students come from a wide range of denominational backgrounds but from a generally conservative theological perspective.

Seminary faculty have said that they are now just beginning the task of formulating a more indigenous mode of theological education. It was more important in the beginning just to get started, and this they have done. But for the future two major theological questions must be faced: (1) How does Christianity relate to Chinese culture? (2) What are authentic Chinese expressions of the faith?[8]

The influence of the seminary goes beyond its own campus. In 1981 the faculty were invited to give five lectures on Christianity at nearby Nanjing University. They were amazed at the response when 1,000 students showed up! As a result of this experience, Dean Chen Zeming offered an elective at the university on Christian doctrine, and plans were made for forty students. When 180 applied for the course, it had to be moved to a larger lecture room. Such is the interest of students in the long-taboo subject of religion.

Seminary faculty are also engaged in the preparation of a correspondence course for lay people and house congregation leaders. This has been a great success and is one answer to poorly trained leaders. The course provides Bible studies, church history, sermon outlines, hymns, devotional helps, and a question-and-answer column on theological issues. The first edition of 10,000 copies was immediately used up. The number of copies produced has now been increased to 30,000. The course is mailed to individuals and groups all over the country. The seminary also produces the bimonthly journal, *Tian Feng* (Divine Wind), which is sent to subscribers both inside and outside China.

The seminary is in need of building up its library, which was largely destroyed by the Red Guards in 1966. An ecumenical effort from abroad is being made to do this. Plans are projected for three new buildings—a library, an apartment building for faculty housing, and a student dormitory. Money would come from rental funds in an agreement to be worked out with the Religious Affairs Bureau.

As church leaders look to the future, it is becoming obvious that the one seminary in Nanjing will not be able to meet the needs of the Christian community, due to the increasing number of churches that are being opened, the advanced age of many of the pastors, and the great distances involved. A second seminary was to open in Shenyang (Mukden) in the Northeast (Manchuria) in the fall of 1982. A third seminary is being planned for Guangzhou (Canton). In other regional centers short-term seminaries or Bible schools are being talked about for training lay leaders and for seminary preparation.

Why Do They Come?

There is no doubt that Christianity has gained a receptive ear in post-Mao China. The evidence for this is overwhelming: the crowded churches on Sunday, the house congregation phenomenon, the thirst for the Scriptures, the number of young men and women seeking to enter the seminary. People have become believers from all walks of life—including those who are members of the Communist party. The following incident is told by *The New York Times* correspondent, Fox Butterfield, in his new book:

> I was not prepared for an energetic, candid, middle-aged Party mem-
> ber who was chairman of her local street committee, the lowest level
> of government organization. One evening when I stopped by her
> fifth-floor walk-up apartment, I found she was reading the Bible. I
> was incredulous. . . . She explained that recently a forty-five-year-
> old man had knocked on her door, claiming to be a friend of a wom-
> an she knew. He wondered if she believed in God or had read the
> Bible. . . .
>
> In the end, my friend accepted his offering of a Chinese-language
> Bible. . . . She was reading it with evident interest. "You don't
> know it," she advised me. "But Christianity is spreading rapidly in
> China because people are so disillusioned with communism." If she
> had been a political dissident, I would have been doubtful. But she
> was the neighborhood Party boss.[9]

As to the number of Christians now in China, there has been a wide
disparity in the estimates given. All are agreed that there are more
Christians in China today than in 1949. In the summer of 1982 the
Religious Affairs Bureau estimated that there are 3,500,000 practicing
Protestants. This is probably a rock-bottom figure. Other estimates run
much higher. The Chinese Church Research Center in Hong Kong estimates that the number is more like 25,000,000. This is based on very
rough estimates of the number and size of house gatherings and seems
highly inflated. The truth is that nobody knows, and there is no way of
arriving at accurate statistics.

Whatever the case, the growth has been phenomenal. And since a
large number of people would have died during the past thirty-two
years, a large percentage of these Christians are those who have come
into the fold since the 1949 Revolution. A remarkable study made of
the Drum Tower Church in Hangzhou revealed that of its 1,500 worshipers, only 500 were baptized prior to the Cultural Revolution! Most
of them are new believers.[10]

Why have they come? Christians in China, when asked this question, give many different answers. But they agree that the growth is *not*
because of great preaching, *not* because of some great evangelist, *not*
because of mass meetings, *not* because of organization or a carefully
orchestrated movement. Many say simply, "It has been the work of the
Holy Spirit."

When pressed further for reasons, various answers are given.

(1) Some come because they are curious. There is great interest and fascination with a subject long regarded as taboo. Some are interested in all things Western—blue jeans and rock music—so they are interested in learning about the Westerner's religion.

(2) Some Chinese have become disillusioned and cynical with Communist ideology and are looking for something else. The Cultural Revolution was devastating to the idealism of those who genuinely and conscientiously wanted to "serve the people." The party line has shifted too many times, producing a "faith crisis" for the faithful. Christian worship gives an opportunity to participate in one thing not controlled by the state, as a mild and permissible form of dissent.

(3) Another answer given many times is that people come because they are "seekers of the truth." They yearn for answers to the meaning of existence, the ultimate issues of life and death. They want something more than a full rice bowl and a tedious, monotonous job.

(4) Some are attracted by the warmth and companionship of the Christian community. In recent years, there has been much dislocation in society. People have been uprooted. People are lonely. Husbands have been separated from wives, young people sent to school far from home, workers assigned to production teams in some distant part of the country.

(5) The character of individual Christians has had a high appeal for their non-Christian associates. The only form of Christian witness and evangelism permitted outside the halls of worship is the personal testimony of friend to friend. The Christian virtues of love, mercy, forgiveness, and patience have won the respect and the hearts of many.

(6) Some come who in an earlier year would have rejected Christianity because of the taint of imperialism and colonialism. Today, however, Christianity is not perceived as something alien to Chinese life and loyalty, but as something of and for the Chinese. The major stumbling block of foreignness has been removed.

Christians have noted one difference between the growth of the Christian movement today and that before 1949. A retired teacher in a former mission school said with some excitement: "Before we had to go to our non-Christian friends and urge them to become Christians. Today our non-Christian friends come to us and ask about our Christian faith.'' An urban city pastor put it this way: ''Before the shepherds sought the sheep. Today it is the sheep that seek the shepherd!''

Theological Thinking in Post-Mao China

What new expressions of the Christian faith have emerged within the Christian community in postrevolutionary China? This is a question of great interest for theologians in the West. What theological insights can Christians in China share with us out of their long experiences within a Marxist state?

Christian leaders in China are careful to say that for the most part they have been engaged more with tilling the Lord's vineyard than in plowing new theological ground. The immediate tasks of shepherding the flock, negotiating with the government, and providing resources for Christian nurture have left them little time for innovative reflection. That must come later.

There is also great diversity within the Christian community, and this diversity has been welcomed and celebrated in the postdenominational era. The preaching from the pulpits has been concerned with individual salvation, personal devotion and piety, and the practical matters of Christian life and witness in the community. After listening to Chinese preaching for some months, an American visitor to China commented that the sermons were not all that different from those he had heard in Hong Kong and in other cities of Asia. The good news of the gospel, the temptation to sin, the exhortations for the Christian life, are not all that different in a Marxist society from those in a capitalistic one! At this point prophetic preaching on social justice and political and economic themes would be considered inappropriate and un-welcomed. This is not to say that Chinese Christians are not involved in social issues and national reconstruction. They are. But their partici-pation in this is through the normal channels open to all Chinese citi-zens and not through membership in the Christian church.

Chinese theologians who are articulate in English are few in number. Western theologians who know Chinese are even fewer! A theological dialogue between East and West is just beginning. From addresses, sermons, and statements made by Chinese theologians in China and at international conferences abroad, we can hazard only a few observations about the direction some of their thinking is taking.

Most of this comes from the writings and addresses of Bishop K. H. Ting, the most articulate spokesperson for Three-Self churches. There is little information available about the theological thinking of the house congregations.

Traditional Theology.   First, many of the traditional doctrines of the church have been reaffirmed. K. H. Ting, in a sermon preached at Riverside Church in New York in September 1979, says it very clearly:

> I might as well begin by saying there is nothing strikingly new to tell you about man as sinner and about man standing in need of Christ's salvation. During the last 30 years, I've seen ample evidence to confirm this conception of man. I've met and have been moved by many revolutionaries, men and women of high moral calibre, who have for 30 or 40 or 50 years forsaken everything in dedicating themselves to the cause of making China a more livable place for their people. . . . Yet, it is these admirable souls, who would readily agree with Saint Paul that the good they want to do they somehow fall short of, and the evil they don't want to do they somehow do in spite of themselves. If people who set such high moral standards for themselves feel that way, then to us Christians it is clear there is no ground to suppose that the message of Christ's redemption and of the sanctification of the Holy Spirit has turned irrelevant or pointless.

In Bishop Ting's little book *How to Study the Bible* the ancient biblical doctrines are presented as timeless messages of truth and applied to everyday life. The one theme of the Bible is simply "how God loves human creation and has prepared in Christ the way of our salvation." God and humanity should be in harmony. But this harmony has been destroyed. Through the great sacrifice of Christ, this oneness of relationship has been restored.[11]

Liberation Theology.   Secondly, to the surprise of some, the reaction to liberation theology has been lukewarm. The Chinese are sympathetic with the emphasis on the necessity for a change in social systems, but they feel that liberation theology has "absolutized the relative" in equating the gospel with the liberation of the poor from social-political oppression. Bishop Ting, as spokesperson for the Chinese delegation at a Christian Conference of Asia consultation in Hong Kong, writes:

> But we feel that Christian theology must deal first of all with the relationship between human beings and God. That is a much more ultimate question which theology must not shy away from. We in China needed liberation. We do not want to return to our pre-liberation days. Yet we do not think that political liberation is a solution to that much more ultimate problem—the problem between human being and the ultimate ground on which the whole universe is structured. The question of life in Jesus Christ—that, somehow we feel that liberation theologians have not dealt with adequately. Maybe we need to read more of their books. New China has definitely produced better men and women, but these better men and better women are not the same as the "new man" that St. Paul speaks of.[12]

In a discussion of liberation theology at the Montreal Consultation, "God's Call to a New Beginning," in October 1981, the Rev. Zhou Fusan made a stirring appeal to keep the transcendental dimension in our thinking. Our daily relationship with God is primary, and liberation must always be more than deliverance from economic suppression. These theologians speak from a *postrevolutionary* situation. Their question is, "What shall one preach the morning after the revolution?" As one of the China delegation at Montreal put it, "If we preached liberation theology, it would empty our churches!"

The Revolution. Thirdly, Chinese Christians have come to stress the revolutionary nature of the times. It is here, they feel, the traditional theology failed them. In an address in Montreal, a Chinese pastor said that both the fundamentalists and the liberals in pre-1949 China were unaware of the revolutionary movement sweeping over the whole country. The fundamentalists preached the coming of Doomsday and the rescue of souls. The liberals were occupied with piecemeal social improvements which only retarded the collapse of the old order. Both failed to understand the radical nature of the changes that were taking place before their eyes.

To use again Bishop Ting's words, human beings are not only "sinners," they are "victims"—victims of oppressive systems, exploitation, and greed. In this discovery, the Christians of China have made common cause with the Chinese people. But the Christian faith, rightly understood, has much to contribute to these revolutionary aspirations. Christian love is more than pity, alms-giving, and being nice to people.

> It is to put ourselves in their position, to enter deeply into their feelings, to feel with them, to understand the justice of their cause, to be in a united front with them, to be fellow fighters with them, and to see how all their revolutionary strivings and all their industrial, agricultural, educational, artistic undertakings can get a deeper grounding and bear greater fruit if they can be made consciously to relate them to the purpose of God and the spiritual resources at the base of the whole universe. Love does mean all of this.[13]

While identifying with the causes of the Chinese people in the revolution, Christian theologians have been wary of engaging in Christian-Marxist dialogue. When asked about this, faculty members at the Nanjing Union Theological Seminary said that now was not the time. There are several reasons for this. There are few Marxist ideologists who are sufficiently knowledgeable about Christian theology. Relationship with Marxists has been a political, not an ideological one. Basic philosophical differences are acknowledged. There has been no attempt to accommodate the Christian faith to a Marxist world view as, for example, there has been in Cuba. A superb apologetic for the Christian position was made by Bishop Ting in his address to the students at the Nanjing Semimary back in 1957 and is summarized in Chapter 6.

Christian thinkers do believe that the Chinese position on Marxism is changing. There have been two schools of thought on this within the Chinese Communist party. The first of these has been called the "Whateverists"—whatever Marx or Lenin or Mao said must be correct. These are the fundamentalists who have insisted on the infallibility of the Marxist classics. The other school, which has gained the upper hand with the coming to power of Deng, has used the slogan, "Seek truth from facts." By this they mean that practice (praxis) is the sole criterion for the test of truth. The more pragmatic interpretation of Marxist doctrine may bring out additional changes and make it easier for a dialogue to commence.

Incarnation.   Chinese Christians have also gained a new appreciation for the doctrine of the incarnation. They have come to a deeper understanding of the necessity for Christ's identification with humanity and for his going through all the vicissitudes of human life. Christ "had to be made like his brethren in every respect, so that he might become a merciful and faithful high priest" (Heb. 2:17). In like manner, the church, which is the body of Christ and a continuation of the incarnation, must become identified with the people in whose midst they live and serve. The Chinese Church then must take part in the destiny of the Chinese people, share their joys and sorrows, their struggles and aspirations, their weal and woe.

They believe that in the past Christians were alienated from the Chinese people. This was one of the unfortunate consequences of Christianity being introduced as a foreign religion. Now they want to stress their identity with the Chinese people, of which Christians are such a very small part. They believe that in this way they can fulfill their role as priests and intercessors for all the Chinese people. This, for them, is the meaning of the "priesthood of all believers."

Community.   Another insight which they would share is an emphasis on community. Perhaps as a reaction to the excessive emphasis of the West on the individual, they are finding anew that there is much in the Chinese emphasis on life in community that is compatible with biblical teaching and experience. Both classical and contemporary China share this emphasis on the importance of the community over against the individual. Here is the sharpest difference between East and West. To cite one example: in the West human rights more likely mean individual rights, while in the East community rights are emphasized. Bishop Ting cites the value of what he calls "human collectives" for education, renewal, and correction:

> To me, an incompletely Christianized Chinese intellectual who has got a sprinkling of our Confucianist heritage of putting oneself over and above the masses of the people, it was quite a pilgrimage in the course of these years to be really sold to the educative and spiritual potentialities of human social organization. Individuals are weak in one way or another. But there is an inspiration in human fellowship which enables comrades to rise to levels unreachable to the mere individual. It is the common purpose and the common enthusiasm that inspires and transforms and uplifts.[14]

Unity.   Most Christians celebrate their newly found unity and the end of Western denominationalism. A spokesperson for Christian pastors in Beijing had this to say about their experience to a group from the U.S.:

Why should you be separated? The Church here in Beijing is united. This witness of the Christian Church in China is a special blessing and a grace from God. It is a result of the prayers of the worldwide Church. In the past, the light of the Gospel was shining, but it was hidden under a bushel basket. Today we are saying to put the light on the table. We have been through a very difficult period. But looking back, we can see it was God's way of preparing the Church for putting the light on the table. . . . We are forced to our knees. We gave up our divisions. We realized we had one Lord, one Faith, one Bible, one Baptism. We have lost our property, our buildings, our schools, and hospitals, and foreign connections. We realize our basic unity was in something else, not in the accumulation of resources. Jesus Christ is the real Cornerstone.[15]

Cosmic Christ. Christian friends in China have found new meaning in the New Testament concept of the Cosmic Christ. In recent years they have been caught up in revolutionary movements and earth-shaking changes. They have seen their churches broken up, their Bibles destroyed, their leaders scattered. They have experienced the birthpangs of a new nation coming into being. In all of these they have experienced the presence of the Christ who towers over history, who is the instrument and the goal of creation, who transcends all principalities and powers, who is the unifying force of the universe holding it all together. Again, to quote K. H. Ting:

> . . . you will find Chinese Christians not only talking about the Redeemer Christ, but more now about the Cosmic Christ, the Incarnational Christ, Christ as the crown and fulfillment of the whole creative process, the clue to the meaning of creation, the One whom we find very much talked about in the New Testament, especially in the Fourth Gospel, in Colossians and in Ephesians. And in this way we think that many contemporary thoughts and movements are not in contrast with the divine revelation or destructive of divine revelation, but rather means of illuminating that revelation. They are not adversaries to but glimpses and foreshadows of the way of Christ. In looking at reality this way, we think we are not diminishing the unique significance of the Christ, but are magnifying his glory and confirming his claims.[16]

The Catholic Church in Post-Mao China

Roman Catholic churches began to reopen in 1979, but they proceeded at a slower pace than did the Protestants. The two unresolved issues—Vatican recognition of Taiwan and the consecration of bishops—continued to complicate the issues facing the church.

In May 1980 the Chinese Catholic Patriotic Association was reconstituted but with probably less popular support than that enjoyed by the Protestant Three-Self Movement. Many priests and other Catholic leaders who were imprisoned have been released. But the cleavage between supporters of the association and those lukewarm or opposed to it is deep and continuing. In many rural and mountainous areas, the church appears to be carrying on clandestinely under lay leadership.

Michael Fu Tieshan was consecrated bishop of Beijing in December 1979 without Vatican concurrence. Roman Catholic liturgy and practice is pre-Vatican II. The Latin Mass is still used, which seems strange indeed for a church that is endeavoring to indigenize Catholicism and that emphasizes the independence of the Chinese Catholic Church. Bishop Fu and two associates attended the international conference on China held in Montreal, Canada, in November 1981. They were well received by their Roman Catholic colleagues from other parts of the world, who heard them present their case with sympathy and understanding. There is obviously much catching up to do as Chinese Catholics, long isolated from the rest of the world, reestablish contacts and explore the reestablishment of relationships with the Vatican which were broken in 1957.

In February 1981 Pope John Paul II seemed to take the first steps toward reconciliation when he issued a papal letter to Chinese Catholics while he was in Manila on his celebrated visit to Asia. The Pope had this to say about being patriotic Chinese:

> I am convinced that every Catholic within your frontiers will fully contribute to the building up of China, since a genuine and faithful Christian is also a genuine and good citizen. . . . There is therefore no opposition or incompatibility in being at the same time truly Christian and authentically Chinese.[17]

Unfortunately, however, later developments shattered the hopes for an early reconciliation.

In June 1981 the Pope appointed Bishop Dominic Deng Yiming of Guangzhou (Canton) to the new position of archbishop. Deng had recently been released from prison after serving twenty-two years and was in Hong Kong for medical treatment at the time of the announcement. Deng was one of the few bishops in China who was both recognized by the Vatican and was in the good graces of the Chinese government and church. From the point of view of the Vatican, the appointment was an act of reconciliation with the hope that Deng could aid in future mediation. However, since the appointment was apparently made without prior consultation with other Catholic leaders in China, it was viewed by them as political interference with their internal affairs. Deng has remained in Hong Kong. The Catholic Council of Bishops in China has countered by consecrating five more bishops in Beijing without papal approval.

More recently, on November 19, 1981, four Catholic priests were arrested by the security police in Shanghai. The charges were participating in an unauthorized religious pilgrimage, communicating Vatican directives to Catholics in China, and sending information about China abroad. When the Vatican issued a call for worldwide prayer for those suffering religious persecution in China, the Chinese bishops responded with an attack on the Vatican for false charges of religious persecution. Their position is that there is now no religious persecution, although there was during the time of the Cultural Revolution. Yet some priests and bishops, such as Gong Binmei, arrested in the mid-1950s, are still imprisoned.

Catholics have been coming in increasing numbers to the churches that are now open for mass and confession. It is estimated that in 1982 there were eighty such congregations which had been opened in the larger cities under the auspices of the Chinese Catholic Patriotic Association. Many more continue to practice their Catholic faith in their homes and in small gatherings led by laypersons and visiting priests as opportunity arises. There are some villages where the majority of the people have belonged to the Catholic faith for generations. They make up close-knit, self-sufficient communities and continue, as best they can, in celebrating the mass and going to confession. The total number of Roman Catholics today is variously estimated at between 1.5 million and 5 million members.

It must be remembered that Christians in China make up a very small part of the population. Neither Christianity nor any other religion is a factor in the lives of the great majority of the people. In the words of a guide to a group of American visitors at the Catholic Cathedral in Beijing, ''My friends, religion is no big thing in China today.''[18]

Yet the seed of faith has been sown. It has fallen into the ground and died. Today there is unmistakable evidence that through the dry, parched ground new sprouts have appeared which are very much alive and which are bearing fruit.

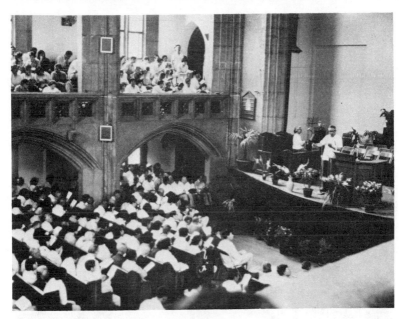

Two thousand people crowd into the sanctuary and adjoining rooms of the Mo En Protestant Church in Shanghai, having arrived early to obtain seats

Sunday service, 9:30 A.M., July 4, 1982 at Mo En Protestant Church service in Shanghai

Nanjing Union Theological Seminary

First seminary class of 47 selected from over 300 candidates, March 1981

10
The Meaning of the China Experience

He who has an ear, let him hear what the Spirit says to
the churches.

(Revelation 2:29)

The church of Jesus Christ has now emerged from the
shadows of the Cultural Revolution. It has confounded its critics and
surprised its supporters. But the church that has emerged is not the
same church as that of the missionary era. There is continuity with the
past. The same Lord is worshiped. The same gospel is affirmed. The
same liturgical forms are used. But there is also discontinuity. This
church has been profoundly changed by the experiences through which
it has passed. It has been tested in the fires of revolution. It has been
cleansed of the stains of foreignness. It has been freed from the burden
of denominationalism. To use the words of the delegates assembled to
reconstitute the National Christian Conference, they have been "bathed
in the grace of God." The Spirit has been moving in their midst.

The church is even now being buffeted by new pressures and facing
new dangers. Undoubtedly more challenges and struggles lie ahead.
But today they celebrate a time of awakening, new growth, and
renewal.

The first impulse of American Christians is to rush in with our aid,
our wealth, and our wisdom. With the best of intentions, we want to
pick up where we left off, to renew the missionary activity that was
interrupted. To check this impulse, many caution signals must be
raised.

Stop! Look! Listen!

This is not to say that all Christian witness and service among and
with the Chinese people is to be paralyzed. But first we must stop and
listen.

We must stop because even if we tried to rush in, it would not be permitted. The state has no love for any religion, much less that brought in by Christians from abroad. Residence and travel permits for foreigners are limited. Hospitals and schools are under direct government management. There is no opportunity for public preaching outside of the churches, for this is not included in the constitutional provisions for freedom of worship. Christian activity on the part of foreigners, even with the best of intentions, would undoubtedly be perceived quite differently by Christian groups. Some would probably be enthusiastic. Others would be fearful. Some would be antagonistic. A foreign Christian presence might drive a wedge into the newly found unity of the Christian community.

Some have suggested ways by which Christian witness and service might be infiltrated into China. This would mean covert activities, the smuggling of Bibles and literature, and the support of Chinese dissidents with foreign money. One would want to think very carefully about what kind of Christianity this would portray. There is also the very real possibility that such activities would lead to a harsher, more restrictive attitude on the part of the government. Some have cited examples in the past when Christianity successfully used clandestine methods to enter regions that were closed to them. But here there is a difference. In China there is now a live, vital growing *Chinese* church. This church needs growing room. It needs to be left to itself—at least for a while until it has had time for its own self-development.

We must listen. This is not easy to do, for there are many voices from China to be heard. Which are authentic? Which speak for the Christian community? Our knowledge of China today is so limited, so fragmentary, so tentative! There are many unanswered questions. What is the relationship between the church and the state? What forms and structures will the Christian community take? Will the church have a prophetic voice in addressing issues of society? Will there be a way in which Christian humanitarian service can be expressed?

We must listen in order to learn. Perhaps the first lesson is one of patience. One of the qualities of life displayed by individual Chinese Christians that has been most moving for Westerners has been their patience and endurance during these times of adversity. Chinese culture is impregnated with the concept of ''wu-wei''—an idea taken from the

Taoist sages often translated "doing nothing" and suggesting resignation. Perhaps our Christian brothers and sisters have added to this the Christian virtue of hopeful, expectant waiting: "If we hope for what we do not see, we wait for it with patience" (Rom. 8:25).

There are many other things we could learn from Christians in China out of their recent experiences: how to live simply without the accumulation of excess material goods; how to be the church of the poor; how to balance our individualism with a loving, caring community; how to engage in mission from the standpoint of weakness rather than that of strength. W. Stanley Mooneyham of World Vision has written that when the churches of China are open to us, "It might be more appropriate to respectfully ask to sit at their feet than to stand in their pulpits."[1]

Above all, we must listen to the Spirit. What is the Spirit saying to the churches out of this China experience?

The Meaning of the Communist Revolution

How shall Christians view the Communist Revolution in China? Such a radical upheaval involving one-fourth the population of the earth simply cannot be ignored. The difficulty of understanding this event is that we must try to come to terms with three generally recognized facts about the revolution: (1) many very positive things were accomplished, (2) these accomplishments were accompanied by an enormous cost in human life and suffering, and (3) these accomplishments were made by a party that is not only avowedly atheistic but has been actively involved in the suppression of a theistic faith and all religion.

No one denies these three facts. But the relative importance one places on each largely determines one's view of the revolution. These widely divergent views have been proposed over the years since the Communist party came to power.

The Anti-Christ. Some Christians in the West have instinctively placed any Communist state in the category of the anti-Christ, as totally evil. Because of its anti-God philosophy, its suppression of human rights and freedom, its persecution of the Christian church, this is the only possible position for Christians to take, they say. Communism is the personification of forces and influences which are diametrically opposed to the reign of God and should be identified with one or more of the images of the beasts or the dragon of the book of Revelation. This view would see communism as a monolithic power intent upon world conquest. The Christian answer must be to mount a crusade to destroy it. This view was widely held by American Christians in the early 1950s.

There are two problems with this view. First, it does not adequately consider the positive gains which have been achieved by the Communists in China. Many of these gains—literacy, emancipation of women, elimination of superstitious practices, a better life for the peasants— were those which missionaries worked toward but were unable to bring about. Today in the People's Republic many qualities of life are being emphasized that have traditionally been associated with the Protestant work ethic: honesty, frugality, hard work, and a strict moral code. A second problem with this view is its assumption of the monolithic nature of communism. Today, communism exists in too many conflicting, divergent, changing, sometimes mutually hostile patterns to be lumped together into one piece.

A Church Surrogate. At the other extreme is the position taken by some theologians and China watchers in the 1970s that communism is, in some sense, a replacement of the church as a means of grace. The visible church, in such a society, becomes almost irrelevant and is no longer needed. Attributes and qualities of the kingdom of God are assigned to the Communist Revolution. This view was expressed in some of the Båstad and Louvain papers referred to earlier in Chapter 7. Often quoted as an extreme statement of this position is this quotation from Joseph Needham who declared that the Chinese society of the present day

> is, I think, nearer to, further on the way to, the true society of mankind, the Kingdom of God if you like, than our own. . . . I think China is the only truly Christian country in the world at the present day, in spite of its absolute rejection of all religion. . . . "Where is Christ to be found?" . . . "where the good are, and where good things are being done." . . . That means appreciating what is happening in China at the present day.[2]

These words were written in 1974. Probably few would hold this view today, for what we now know of the Cultural Revolution has made this kind of identification of the new social order in China and the reign of God all but impossible.

Assyria—Rod of God's Anger. Two biblical images have been used which may help put the Communist Revolution into a clearer and fairer third perspective. The first of these is that of Assyria of whom the prophet Isaiah speaks in these terms:

> Ah, Assyria, the rod of my anger,
>   the staff of my fury!
> Against a godless nation I send him,
>   and against the people of my wrath, I command him,
> to take spoil and seize plunder,
>   and to tread them down like the mire of the streets.
>   (Isa. 10:5–6).

Assyria was a rod—an instrument of discipline, chastisement, and correction—in the hands of God. God used Assyria, a cruel despotic nation, to destroy many of the kingdoms of the Middle East and to purge and purify God's beloved children of Israel. But when the time of discipline was over, the rod of chastisement was itself discarded, and a faithful remnant, purified and strengthened, was to be returned to God's grace and favor.

In this view the Communist rise to power in China was an indictment both of the old Chinese order and the Christian movement. The tyranny of feudal lords, the corruption and greed of the ruling classes, the exploitation of the peasants, superstitious practices, the lack of concern for justice—one could go on and on—all were a part of the old Chinese order. The Christian missionary movement and the Christian church had been either too unconcerned about these matters, or too closely allied with the oppressors, or too weak to do much about them. So when judgment fell, the blow came on both the Christian movement and the old order of which it had become a part. The old order was destroyed. The Communist Revolution might be seen as God's instrument for doing this. With the destruction of the old order, the ground has been prepared for a new and more receptive hearing of Christianity. A new church—the remnant—has emerged more humble, purer, more

closely allied with the common people, and a more perfect instrument
of God's grace. Leslie Lyall mentions the Confucian clan system,
which was associated with ancestor worship, as one example of the old
order destroyed by communism, which may make the reception of
Christianity easier. He quotes a Jesuit writer as saying:

> The Communist occupation of China will one day be seen to be a
> providential preparation for the Gospel. The Chinese culture was al-
> most impervious to the Christian Gospel. It had to be broken up and
> opened to new questions and new answers before the Christian
> message could be given a hearing. That is what Communism is
> doing.[3]

Cyrus—The Lord's Anointed.   The second biblical image is
that of Cyrus, the Persian ruler who was instrumental in permitting the
return of the exiles to Judea. In Isaiah 44:28 God speaks of Cyrus as
"my shepherd" and says that he will "fulfill all my purpose" in rebuilding Jerusalem and in laying again the foundations of the temple.
Again in Isaiah 45:1–4:

> Thus says the LORD to his annointed, to Cyrus,
>   whose right hand I have grasped,
> to subdue nations before him
>   and to ungrid the loins of kings,
> to open doors before him
>   that gates may not be closed:
> "I will go before you
>   and level the mountains,
> I will break in pieces the doors of bronze
>   and cut asunder the bars of iron . . .
> that you may know that it is I, the LORD,
>   the God of Israel, who call you by your name. . . .
> I call you by your name,
>   I surname you, though you do not know me.

It is significant that God calls Cyrus "my shepherd" and "my
anointed." Even though Cyrus never knew Yahweh or the faith of
Israel, these messianic terms are applied to him. God called him to
fulfill God's purposes, to permit the return of the exiles, the rebuilding
of Jerusalem, and the temple.

The application to China is obvious although it would be more appropriate for the post-Mao era of Deng Xiaoping than that of Mao. The Cyrus image goes beyond that of Assyria and recognizes not just the destructive force of the Communist revolution but its positive accomplishments. One could list many: the unification of the country, establishment of law and order, literacy, health care, emancipation of women, and a more equitable distribution of wealth. Even more specific application to the religious scene would be the restoration of freedom of worship, release of prisoners, and the return of the churches to the Christian communities.

While these biblical images of Assyria and Cyrus are certainly helpful in clarifying our thinking, we must be wary of pushing the analogies too far. We do not find it necessary to make such biblical identifications for capitalism. Why then is it necessary for the Communist system? Is there a subtle temptation for the American Christians to view our system as the Christian norm and all other systems as deviants, requiring special explanations? Today, both communism and capitalism are in ferment. There may well be demonic elements in *both* systems—as well as signs pointing to the coming reign of God. God's last word on communism—as on capitalism—has yet to be spoken.

Lessons from the Christian Community

More important to Christians than the revolution itself is the experience of our Chinese brothers and sisters in Christ. We have much to learn. Some of this is *affirming* and some *challenging*.

Affirmation. Many traditional theological concepts and values have been reaffirmed, and yet these affirmations have been full of surprises. Certainly we have received evidence which confirms our historical belief in the sovereignty of God. Yahweh is in control of history and is working God's purposes out through both judgment and restoration. The old order has been destroyed, and the community of faith has been restored, but this has been done in ways which the missionary community could never have anticipated or even imagined.

Also affirmed has been the sinfulness of men and women. Nothing that has happened in China has made it necessary to rewrite the paragraphs in the confession of faith on human depravity. But one must be careful to note that this depravity applies to *all* parties—both East and West—that have participated in what we have called the China experience.

Christians in China have demonstrated the strength and resiliency of the Christian community. The fact that Christianity is alive in China is not because of the superhuman efforts of a few individual saints. Rather it is because of the power of the Christian community to nourish, sustain, and equip ordinary Christians to be faithful. Yet again there is the surprise. This community has not been like anything the church in the West has known.

Priority on the family is certainly another strength which Christians in China would share with us. It was in the family that Christianity was kept alive in the dark days of the Cultural Revolution. In earlier years it was the ancestral rites—closely associated with the family—of which the missionaries despaired!

The sufficiency of Scripture has likewise been confirmed by the experiences of our Christian brothers and sisters in China. The Bible has been about the only Christian literature available to the Christian community—and that often in short supply and laboriously copied out by hand and shared with each other. It is the same Bible, but it is being read anew—in the light of their different experiences and as the Spirit leads them.

Challenge.   The experience of the church in China is also a challenge to much in our traditional modes of thinking. It should force us to rethink some assumptions that we have taken for granted. It may even threaten some positions we have long cherished and considered sacrosanct.

Certainly the China experience should be a challenge to our denominationalism. Chinese Protestant Christians have moved beyond our historical divisions into what they have called a "postdenominational era." It would seem that this unity has been achieved without a loss of diversity in doctrine and practice. Some issues which have divided Christians in the West have simply been ignored. Others have been postponed. Eventually the church will have to face some of these issues (ordination, baptism, creed, liturgy) and others peculiar to the Chinese situation. Whatever new alignments may eventually emerge, there seems little desire to return to the traditional denominations. We must remember that denominationalism as we have known it in the West is a fairly recent development in the long 2,000-year history of the church.

What has happened in China is also a challenge to our ecclesiastical structures. The church that has emerged from the Cultural Revolution seems to have developed a stripped-down model of Christianity that is in sharp contrast to the elaborate institutional structures of the West. Chinese churchmen have spoken of their "liberation" from the administration of schools and hospitals and other agencies which were taken over by the government. One thinks of David, refusing to put on Saul's armour, preferring his own simple weapons. How necessary is the ecclesiastical machinery we tend to take for granted?

Another challenge concerns our individualism. Certainly the Chinese emphasis on community seems a healthy corrective to the extreme emphasis on the individual in our society. Chinese have used peer respect and peer disapproval effectively in influencing behavior. With some qualifications, could such an emphasis balance the insistence in our society that everyone is free to "do their own thing"? Chinese find our society preoccupied with social deviation—the delinquent, the homosexual, the drug addict, the criminally insane. They find this strange and distasteful, just as we find enforced uniformity in their society unacceptable. Maybe each can learn from the other.

The experience of Chinese Christians is a challenge to our wealth. The church there has learned to be the church of the poor. Its needs are simple, and it has refrained from embarking on ambitious programs which would require more resources than are available. Its leaders have steadfastly refused offers of aid from abroad. The church has not found its lack of wealth a liability but rather a point of contact with its people. Its experience forces us to ask the question, "What does it mean to engage in mission from the standpoint of weakness and poverty, rather than from the point of power and wealth?"

The church in China is a profound challenge to our worldliness. This comment was graciously shared by Charles West, when he read the first draft of this manuscript:

> Here are Christians who do not test their God by his historical successes, but who cling to him and count on him for life. That every human support and every earthly hope can be buried in a revolution-

ary avalanche, and yet that a community that lives in Christ can
emerge and bear its witness: this is the miracle that shames our
worldly calculations about the life and future of the Christian church!

The existence of any church in a social structure so different from
ours inevitably presents a challenge to our culture. In China the state is
avowedly hostile to a Christian theistic philosophy of life. The church
there, while affirming its love and loyalty to its country, has no illusions as to where the state stands. In our culture this may not be so
clearly perceived. There may be elements in our culture—its commer-
cialism, consumerism, greed, and hedonistic values—that are also
alien to Christianity, but the threat is more subtle and difficult to handle. In our interpretation of Christianity it is so terribly important to
make the distinction between what is "Christian" and what is "culture." This may not always be possible, but the attempt must be made.
Christianity must not be made a captive to any culture—East or West,
capitalist or Communist.

International Relations—Chinese Church Leaders

The churches of the West have much to learn from the experiences
of Chinese Christians. Only after listening to them have we the right to
raise the question, "What have we to offer?" What are the next steps
in establishing partnership relationships? Christian leaders in China
have spoken out forthrightly on this question, and it is well to listen
carefully to what they have said. The clearest exposition of their position is found in K. H. Ting's "A Call for Clarity: Fourteen Points from
Christians in the People's Republic of China to Christians Abroad."[4]
The statement was originally prepared as a response to some Chinese
Christian pastors in Hong Kong in December 1980. Since then it has
been widely reported and represents a clearly defined policy statement
about future relationships. The critical points of the statement are summarized below.

(1) Affirmation of the New China.   Chinese Christians take a
positive attitude to the New China. They point with pride to the material accomplishments and the high level of morality. Their patriotism is
"not without a prophetic and critical character." It does not mean
"blind praise" for everything that is done. They regard the policy of

religious freedom to be "a reasonable one" but have no illusions about the Communist party's atheistic point of view. Christians can cooperate in areas of "common ground" while "preserving differences" that exist between believers and nonbelievers.

(2) The Three-Self Principles. Chinese Christians are resolved to uphold the Three-Self Principles of self-government, self-support, and self-propagation. This is fundamental and must be recognized in any relationships with churches or councils outside of China. They cannot permit a return to the pre-1949 period when they felt that Christianity was represented as a "foreign religion." The Three-Self Principles mean that the church is not only independent of foreign churches but also of the government or party within China. It is wrong to speak of the Three-Self Movement as an "official church." China has no "official church." The Chinese church is run by Chinese Christians.

(3) The Unity of the Chinese Church. The present unity of Chinese Christians is unprecedented. Deep denominational divisions have been healed. Christians who previously would not even pray with one another now worship and share the sacraments together. This unity also exists between those who worship in open congregations and those who worship in homes. Chinese Christians deeply resent efforts made by some outsiders to split the church by dividing it into a "three-self church" and a "house church." Today the vast majority of Chinese Christians, no matter where they worship, are patriotic citizens and support the Three-Self Principles. Chinese Christians have been led along the road of postdenominational unity, not because they are better than anyone else but because of their "particular historical situation." They believe this has been a result of the "leading of the Holy Spirit" and that they have been allowed "to bathe in the ocean of God's grace."

(4) Evangelism—The Responsibility of the Chinese Church. No matter how large the population is and how small the church is, they feel that "the responsibility for spreading the gospel and building up the Church in China is the mission of Chinese Christians." They "wish to declare that no group or individual overseas should engage in evangelistic activity in China without the expressed consent of Chinese

Church authorities, who retain responsibility and jurisdiction in this area.'' Incidents have occurred where Americans have engaged in public evangelistic activity that resulted in hostility and the intervention of the police. This created a most unfortunate image of Christianity in China. Chinese church leaders do not wish to close the door of the gospel in China. But they are upholding the Three-Self Principles in order to guarantee that the door of the gospel may be open and remain open. To return to a ''colonial status'' would be ''self-destructive'' and in the long run this would really shut the door to the gospel.

(5) Activities in Non-Christian Enterprises.   A number of institutions and groups from abroad have been engaged in negotiations with Chinese schools, hospitals, communes, and other enterprises. Church leaders have no opinion on these exchanges except where church-related groups are involved. Then they fear that these activities might be a front for evangelism or for reestablishing mission work. If the relationship with the Chinese institution is being used as a cover to hide the true purpose of the mission, then a matter of ethics is involved. It is also a matter of undermining the Three-Self Principles of the Chinese church. When such negotiations are undertaken by Christian groups, the true nature of the enterprise should not be concealed, and there should be consultation with the Chinese church.

(6) International Relationships.   Because of limited resources of time and personnel, church leaders in China must give their first priority to domestic responsibilities. At this stage of history their international commitments and relationships must be limited and selective. They do wish to have contacts and exchanges with those churches and groups who respect the Three-Self Principles and who are friendly to the New China. They do not mean to suggest that they regard ''only those who approve of everything that New China does as friendly.'' But they are interested in basic attitudes. They will differentiate between those programs and groups which they feel are hostile and those groups with which they can engage in exchanges of mutual learning and true Christian fellowship.

(7) Material or Financial Contributions from Abroad.   The church in China is very small with limited financial resources, but

they are able to support themselves. They will not do anything beyond their means and become "parasitic." Since they are already self-supporting and independent, "there is probably no longer the need to maintain a simple 'closed-door policy' on the question of receiving contributions." Church leaders are considering the possibility of accepting contributions from friendly churches and groups abroad "with no strings attached and with due respect for the independent stance of our church, simply as an expression of the universality of our Christian fellowship." Possibly contributions could be made to local churches. Large amounts would be handled by the Council, perhaps for its pastoral work fund. This tentative idea will be discussed by the Three-Self Committee and the China Christian Council. It would have to be worked out with great care. To date we do not know of any definite decision which has been made on this important issue.

International Relations—Response from the West

As the dialogue between Christians in China and Christians in the West continues, Bishop Ting's "Fourteen Points" might well be used as a point of reference. What has been the response to this clear and forthright statement? Some have asked the question: "Who speaks for the Chinese Church? Bishop Ting has given one point of view. There are other silent voices which cannot be heard." This may or may not be true. Obviously no one person or group speaks for all Christians in any church—East or West. But the possibility of there being other silent voices does not invalidate the voice that is heard. Certainly this voice does represent the position of many Christians. If relationships are to be established with the Christian community in China at this juncture, then it is with this voice that one must deal.

Many churches in the West have received the statement with sympathy and understanding. Some questions have been raised. To some the statement has come across as a bit too defensive and too protective of the Chinese church. Does any church—East or West—have the right to stake out its claim to a piece of geography and say to outsiders, "No trespassing?" Probably not. But the *primary* responsibility for the evangelization of any land certainly does rest with the Christian community in that land. This is certainly a valid principle of Christian mission elsewhere in the world. And both the pre-1949 history of Christianity in China and the present state of church-government relationships makes it even more applicable there.

Another, more basic question relates to the nature of the church of Jesus Christ. Certainly the Three-Self Principle, however it is expressed, is basic and needs again and again to be affirmed and respected. On this there is no question. But the church is not only local and indigenous, it is also ecumenical and catholic. Not only must it relate to a particular nation and culture, it is transnational and transcultural. Not only is it independent, it is interdependent with every other part of the Body of Christ.

This is true of churches—East or West. We would confess that a temptation of the churches in the United States is to overdo our own Three-Self Principle and become too self-reliant, too nationalistic, too rooted and grounded in our own culture. At a time of racial crisis in the southern United States, the church there was helpfully reminded again and again by other churches, North and South, East and West, that loyalty to one's own culture might become a denial of the universality of the gospel. The same could be true for the church in China.

Bishop Ting has used the analogy of a "protective tariff" to describe the necessity for the Three-Self Principle in China. This is very helpful. At this stage of history, to open the floodgates for the importation of every religious commodity into China might well overwhelm the Christian community that is just now emerging from thirty years of isolation. This could stifle the growth and self-expression of the churches there and become destructive. A "protective tariff" may be necessary, but it should be used as a temporary expediency—not as a permanent principle for the advancement of Christianity on earth.

Toward a Responsible China Policy

Since the resumption of relationships with the Christians of China, the churches in the West have been engaged in study, theological reflection, and the formulation of an appropriate China policy. American Presbyterians (United and Presbyterian Church, U.S.) met in Richmond, Virginia, in May 1980 to formulate some theological foundations and principles later adopted by both denominations.[5] In August

1979 Maryknoll Fathers and Brothers adopted the *Society Response to China* with challenges, objectives, goals, and targets.[6] In June 1980 the United Board for Christian Higher Education in Asia formulated some specific objectives for their China Program and sent a delegation to China to begin its implementation. The Lausanne Committee for World Evangelization included in their Pattaya, Thailand, Conference of June 1980 a mini-consultation on reaching Chinese.[7] The Canadian China Programme sponsored an international conference in Montreal in October 1981 entitled "God's Call to a New Beginning." The Christian Conference of Asia held a consultation with church leaders from China in Hong Kong in March 1981.[8] The China Program of the National Council of Churches, U.S.A., prepared a policy statement on China for the May 1982 meeting of its governing board.

One could go on. All of these consultations and documents have been involved in the formulation of policy guidelines for post-Mao China. While there is much diversity in what is recommended, there is also much agreement. What is a responsible China policy for the church?

Thanksgiving. To begin with Christians should give thanks, thanksgiving for the unexpected, for open churches, for saints and martyrs of old, for freedom of worship today, for those who kept Christianity alive in their homes. Our churches in the West should be called upon to join with brothers and sisters in China to rejoice that contacts have been renewed and fellowship restored. Thanksgiving to Almighty God should be the first thing on the agenda.

Confession. Before we can look ahead and plan for the future, we must also seek forgiveness for what was done and what was not done in the past. This is not to discredit the sacrifices and accomplishments of the missionary enterprise in China. But it does mean to examine the record, learn from mistakes that were made, and seek forgiveness for our sense of cultural superiority and pride, our obscuring the power of the gospel through our reliance upon wealth and technology, our divisions, and our lack of faith.

A Sense of History. The God whom we know in Jesus Christ is Lord of history. God's power is the ultimate reality with which we have to deal. God's love gives life to us all. Nations and people, religions and societies find their meaning and destiny in the context of this power and love.

The Role of the Church.   God has called the church to be the community of those who confess God's name, respond to God's call, and bear witness to God in the world. It is the world to which Christ comes and which God reconciles to God's self, but it is the church where God is openly acknowledged and where divine witnesses are found.

Communicating the Gospel.   The task of communicating the gospel to the people of China is being carried out by the Christians of China. In this we rejoice and give thanks. Our ministry is to share our experience in evangelism in our own society with our Chinese brothers and sisters in faith and to support their work of making the reality of Christ known in any way they find helpful.

Unity.   We affirm the degree of unity which Chinese Christians have found amid the variety of their church life. In seeking relationship with them, this unity must be respected. In our eagerness to be helpful, we must do nothing that might hinder the visible unity of the Chinese Christian community. This unity is a challenge to us as we struggle with the diversities of our own church life and witness.

Self-Reliance.   Likewise, it is of crucial importance for the church in China to be truly Chinese in identity, culture, and loyalty. Chinese Christians have said that self-hood and self-reliance are among their highest priorities. This we affirm even though it means for the present maintaining a certain distance from them.

Mutual Ministry.   We welcome the ministry of the Chinese Christian community to our people, and in all humility and sensitivity to the realities of their situation, seek opportunity to minister to them. We need to listen, learn, and understand China and the experiences and insights of Christians there. Constituency education must be a major part of any responsible China program. As specific projects and proposals are considered, it must be clear that our programs will be developed in response to requests which we have received rather than upon ideas which we have initiated.

Ecumenical Endeavor. Programs should be carried out as part of an ecumenical endeavor rather than reestablishing denominational loyalties. This should not stifle opportunities for individual communions or agencies to respond to needs.

People-to-People Exchanges. At the present time specific programs of witness and service for denominations or councils are limited and in many cases may be unwise. At such a time churches can call upon their members to engage in and support people-to-people contacts and exchanges. These might include a wide variety of relationships such as association with students and visitors from the PRC in the U.S., tour groups to China, institutional exchanges, and the offering of individual service in educational and technical fields in China.

Honest and Open Relationships. We must, however, be honest and open in all relationships with the People's Republic of China, seeking to avoid any pretense or suggestions of surreptitious dealings.

Political and Economic Power. God is the judge of all nations and systems, the master of all forms of political and economic power. We are called to bear witness to this Lord in our nation and to support our Chinese fellow-believers in theirs.

A Practical Guide for Christian Action

Christians concerned about their own individual responsibility are asking questions about what specifically can be done to express their friendship with Chinese Christians and to engage in mission. What is now going on? What can individuals do? What should they not do? The most helpful way to deal with this is simply to list some of the questions that are being asked and give the best answers available at the time of this writing.

(1) *Can one serve in China today in some capacity? If so, how does one go about it?* Yes, the People's Republic of China is engaged in the appointment of English teachers and specialists to serve on contract in key universities. Salaries are paid by the PRC or the university involved and are adequate, but no one gets rich. Contracts are usually for one year and can be renewed. Foreign experts live in special dormitories. Applicants should be technically qualified, and English teachers

should have had training in teaching English as a second language. Positions are not always readily available, and sometimes there are long lapses between the time the application is made to the agency in China and when a reply is received. It helps to know someone or to have a contact with an institution in China.

Organizations which may be able to provide information about such positions and educational exchanges are: United Board for Christian Higher Education in Asia (Room 1221, 475 Riverside Drive, New York, N.Y. 10115), Committee on Scholarly Communication with the People's Republic of China, National Academy of Science (2101 Constitution Avenue, Washington, D.C. 20418), Council on International Educational Exchange (205 East 42nd Street, New York, N.Y. 10017) and the U.S.–China Education Clearinghouse (1860 19th Street, Washington, D.C. 20009).

(2) *If on such a contract, can the foreign expert engage in Christian activity*? Christian leaders in China have said that there is nothing to keep Christians, including foreigners, from bearing witness to their faith in personal conversations and relationships. They can attend and take part in the public worship services held in their city. They should be open about this and not try to hide or disguise the fact that they are Christians. They should not seek such appointments unless they are prepared to conscientiously apply themselves to the work for which they have been contracted. The appointment should not be a cover for any other kind of activity.

(3) *What about smuggling Bibles into China*? Most denominational boards and agencies, including the American Bible Society, would strongly advise against this for reasons given in earlier chapters.

(4) *Is it illegal to mail copies of the Bible into China*? The sending of one or two copies through the mails is not considered illegal. Sometimes such copies get through. Sometimes they do not. When traveling to China, one can take a few copies of English or Chinese Bibles or Testaments to use as gifts. These should be declared to the custom's inspector if one is asked about them. In most cases nothing is said. In China it is probably not wise to give away Bibles to anyone unless the person has requested one, or is a Christian, or there is reason to think they would appreciate one. Bibles, when so given, should be unmarked.

(5) *Where can Chinese Bibles be obtained?* The American Bible Society (1865 Broadway, New York, N.Y. 10023) has a wide range of selections, and these can be ordered by mail.

(6) *Is there any way I can help to provide Bibles for China legally?* Yes. Write the American Bible Society in New York and ask about their program. They are involved in the translation, printing, and distribution of the Bible in Chinese and have helped sponsor radio broadcasts of the Bible in the Chinese language.

(7) *Can one go to China as a student?* Yes. There are a number of such programs and opportunities each year. It is best to go with a group. Some colleges and universities are now providing such exchanges. Goshen College (Goshen, Ind. 46526) is one of these. The U.S.–China Education Foundation (1156 15th Street, N.W., Suite 1022, Washington, D.C. 20005, with a branch office at 3507 Ridge Road, Durham, N.C. 27705) arranges a number of such opportunities each year. For example, a spring semester of seventeen weeks in 1982 cost $3,295, including travel, tuition, board, and room. All levels of Mandarin Chinese are taught and several weeks of the program are spent in travel to Chinese cities.

(8) *When visiting China as a tourist, can I worship in Chinese churches and visit with Chinese Christians?* Protestant and Roman Catholic churches are open in practically all the cities visited by tourists. They would all welcome visitors from abroad. Sometimes the travel guides do not know about the existence or the location of these churches, and this has been a problem. Try to be gently insistent. Better yet, obtain addresses and telephone numbers before you leave. Services are not always at eleven o'clock!

In Beijing there are two Protestant churches with regular services: one at 21 Meizha Hutong, Dongdan Bei Dajie (phone 55-5086) and one at Xisi Nan Dajie at Gangwashi (phone 66-4027). The Roman Catholic Nantang Cathedral is at 141 Qianmen Xi Dajie at Xuanwumen Ne Corner (phone 33-6470).

In Shanghai the three Protestant churches that are most convenient for foreign visitors are the Mo En Church in downtown Shanghai, the International Church, and the Pure Heart Church. Addresses and times of services can be obtained from the Christian Three-Self Movement

Committee at 169 Yuan Ming Yuan Road, which is very near the Peace Hotel.

(9) *When in China, is it appropriate to give money to aid Christians or church work?* Definitely not. The money might not be accepted, and this would be embarrassing. Offerings can be put in the offering box, or the collection plate if it is passed, just as other worshipers do. It is appropriate to give some small gift of remembrance to those one meets.

(10) *Has it been possible for international Christian organizations to provide assistance in cases of floods or droughts?* Yes. For example, Church World Service and the Maryknoll Fathers donated $71,500 for relief work in China in response to requests which were made after floods devastated parts of Sichuan Province. The aid was routed through the World Council of Churches Commission on Inter-Church Aid and the International Red Cross. In August 1982 church donations were raised for flood relief in Guangdong Province and routed through the Hong Kong Christian Council.

(11) *Have there been examples of other contributions being made to specific programs in China by Christian organizations?* Yes. The United Board for Christian Higher Education in Asia is presently involved in supporting two library development projects at Sichuan University (Chengdu) and Shaanxi University (Xian).

(12) *Is it possible to provide scholarships for students from the PRC to study in the United States?* Yes. Many of the 10,000 students from the PRC who studied in the United States last year were here under private sponsorship. The United Board for Christian Higher Education in Asia has a faculty development program under which university faculty members are provided scholarships for study in the United States. A number of universities and church-related colleges are providing scholarships and assistance for PRC students. A number of denominations have provided funds for this purpose in a number of different ways. This is an excellent way to help cement relationships between our two countries and to train leadership for key institutions in China. Students from the PRC also make a real contribution to college life here in the United States. But there are some cautions. Emotional maturity, language aptitude, and intellectual ability are very important and sometimes difficult to determine before the student arrives. They are under great pressure to succeed in their study.

(13) *How can one be of help to Chinese students in the United States?* One major difficulty they face is that of language. Help might be provided in tutoring. Many would love to get away from institutional life and enjoy visiting in a home. Christmas vacations and summer holidays may provide special problems when dormitories are closed and other students go home. PRC students should not be singled out or treated as curiosities. Their presence should not be exploited by putting them "on show." We must learn to be helpful without being aggressive and friendly without being possessive. Christian hospitality can be shown without being rude or insensitive to the beliefs of others.

(14) *How can I keep informed of the latest developments about service in China and the Christian movement there?* A number of China newsletters are published regularly by Christian groups. See the appendix. The following handbooks, all published by the United States–China Education Clearinghouse (1960 19th Street, N.W., Washington, D.C. 20009) will also be helpful for those interested in China service: *China Bound: A Handbook for American Students, Researchers and Teachers* by Karen Turner Gottschang; *American Study Programs in China: An Interim Report Card* by Peggy Blumenthal; *An Introduction to Education in the People's Republic of China* and *U.S.–China Educational Exchanges* by Thomas Fingar and Linda A. Reed.

(15) *Is there anything else I can do?* Yes. Perhaps the most important thing of all: you can pray. This is the single most often repeated request heard by Christian groups visiting China. They have not asked for our money. They have not asked for our missionaries or our programs. They have asked that we join with them in prayer. This request challenges the churches of the West at a point of our weakness. We do other things better than praying. Perhaps it would have been easier if they had wanted our material wealth. But they have asked only for our prayers.

How does one pray for China? Several guides for prayer have been prepared which may help. *A Call for Prayer from China* has been prepared by this author and his wife, Mardia Hopper Brown. It may be ordered from the same address as the *China News* (General Assembly Mission Board, Presbyterian Church, U.S., 341 Ponce de Leon, N.E., Atlanta, Ga. 30365). Another such guide is *The People and Church in*

China, prepared by the Division of Overseas Ministries, NCC/USA (write Friendship Press, P.O. Box 37844, Cincinnati, Ohio 45237).

Looking to the Future

We live in precarious times. China, Asia, and the world have passed through many unpredictable twists and turns in the last thirty years—some of which have been traced in this book. We have no assurance as to what the future will hold.

It must be emphasized that our knowledge of China even today is fragmentary, incomplete, and inconclusive. There are limits to the free and open access to information. Discussion and debate of ideas is often made difficult by the political, cultural, and ideological differences. Considerable disagreement exists even among the experts as to what is actually taking place in China today. There is much more disagreement as to how to interpret the facts we know.

This much is clear. The church of Jesus Christ in China has emerged from the shadows of the Cultural Revolution. It is alive. Its life and witness are meaningful and vital. It is growing. It enjoys a degree of limited but genuine religious freedom. It is demonstrating a unity that transcends the denominationalism of the past, but this unity is fragile and easily damaged. Because of the ambiguities of its past history, it believes its first priority is self-reliance. Yet it is eager to establish relationships with the worldwide Christian community along principles of mutual confidence and respect.

Enormous problems and dangers lie ahead for China, Asia, the United States, and the world: the seemingly insurmountable problem of Taiwan, the future of Hong Kong, peace along China's long borders with the Soviet Union, North Korea, India, Afghanistan, and Vietnam. Natural calamities or increase in population could wipe out gains which China has made in the feeding of her millions. Sudden changes in government policy could alter relations with the West and with religious groups.

There is also great hope. No one in their right mind would have dared to predict the turn of events which these last few years have brought: the renewal of friendly relations between our two countries, the restoration of religious freedom, the opening of the churches, the vitality and growth of the Christian movement. But this is only a beginning. In God's own time China will make its full contribution to the welfare of nations, and our incomplete understanding of the nature of the Christian faith will be perfected by Chinese insights and values. In God's own time the people of China will become a part of that great multitude which no one can number, from every nation, tribe, people, and tongue saying,

> "Amen!
>> Blessing and glory
>> and wisdom and thanksgiving
>> and honor and power and might
>> be to our God for ever and ever!
> Amen."

(Revelation 7:12)

NOTES

CHAPTER 1: Who Would Have Believed It?

1. Roy Branson, "Chinese Protestantism," *The Kennedy Institute Quarterly Report*, 5 (Fall 1979):45–46, used by permission.
2. Orville Schell, *Watch Out for the Foreign Guests!* (New York: Pantheon Books, a Division of Random House, Inc., 1980), p. 5. For the fascinating story of Western advisers in China 1620–1960, see Jonathan Spence, *To Change China* (Boston: Little, Brown and Company, 1969).
3. P. Frank Price, *Our China Investment* (Nashville: Executive Committee of Foreign Missions, 1927), pp. 176ff.
4. Presbyterian Church in the U.S., *Minutes of the 119th General Assembly* (May 1979), p. 231.

CHAPTER 2: Wise Men from the West

1. Kenneth Scott Latourette, *A History of Christian Missions in China* (New York: The Macmillan Company, 1929), pp. 58–59, used by permission.
2. Ibid., pp. 91–130.
3. Ibid., p. 154.
4. Marshall Broomhall, *Robert Morrison: A Master-Builder* (London: Student Christian Movement, 1924). Latourette, *Missions in China*, p. 212–13.
5. Spence, *To Change China*, pp. 34–56.
6. Latourette, *Missions in China*, pp. 228–33. John K. Fairbank and Edwin O. Reischauer, *China: Tradition and Transformation* (Boston: Houghton Mifflin Company, 1978), pp. 276–89. John King Fairbank, *The United States and China*, 4th ed. (Cambridge, Mass.: Harvard University Press, 1979), pp. 158–71.
7. Latourette, *Missions in China*, pp. 271–75.
8. Zhao Fusan, "The Chinese Revolution and Foreign Missions Seen Through the May Fourth Movement," *China Notes 18* (Summer 1979):75, used by permission.
9. K. H. Ting, "Facing the Future or Restoring the Past?" an address given in Toronto in November 1979, p. 3, mimeographed.
10. J. H. Morrison, *William Carey, Cobbler and Pioneer* (London: Hodder and Stoughton, 1924), p. 53.
11. Stephen Neill, *Colonialism and Christian Missions* (New York: McGraw-Hill Book Company, 1966), p. 134.
12. Fairbank, *U.S. and China*, p. 162.
13. Latourette, *Missions in China*, p. 276.
14. Kenneth Scott Latourette, *The Chinese, Their History and Culture*, 3rd ed. (New York: The Macmillan Company, 1946), p. 354.
15. See next chapter for a fuller discussion of the Taipings.

16. Fairbank, *U.S. and China*, p. 196.
17. "People's Livelihood" meant a vaguely defined form of socialism and land reform. Both Chiang Kai-shek and Mao Zedong traced the legitimacy of their respective parties to Sun and his "Three Principles."
18. The celebration of this event on the tenth day of the tenth month has become known as the "double tenth" and is the birthday of the Chinese Republic. It is celebrated in Taiwan and to a lesser degree in the People's Republic of China.
19. James E. Bear, "The Mission Work of the Presbyterian Church in the United States in China, 1867–1952," unpublished papers in the Union Theological Seminary (Richmond, Va.) Library, vol. 1, p. 26.
20. Latourette, *Missions in China*, p. 680.
21. Of the 445 delegates who attended the 1900 conference, all but two were missionaries, ibid. p. 414.
22. Ibid., p. 623.
23. Ibid., p. 635.
24. Ibid., pp. 452, 652–55.
25. Ibid., pp. 656–62.
26. Fairbank, *U.S. and China*, p. 202.
27. Latourette, *Missions in China*, p. 506.
28. Ibid., pp. 512–13, 517.
29. John K. Fairbank, "The Chinese Revolution and American Missions," *China Notes*, 11 (Autumn 1973):41, used by permission.
30. Kenneth Scott Latourette, *A History of the Expansion of Christianity*, vol. 7, *Advance Through Storm* (New York: Harper & Brothers, Publishers, Inc., 1945), p. 362, used by permission.
31. Latourette, *Missions in China*, pp. 780–81.
32. Mary Brown Bullock, *An American Transplant* (Berkeley and Los Angeles: University of California Press, 1980).
33. Latourette, *Advance Through Storm*, p. 348.
34. Ibid., pp. 346–47, 349.
35. Wallace C. Merwin, *Adventure in Unity: The Church of Christ in China* (Grand Rapids, Mich.: William B. Eerdmans Publishing Company, 1974), pp. 32–33, 54.
36. Francis Price Jones, *The Church in Communist China* (New York: Friendship Press, 1962), pp. 16–18, used by permission; Merwin, *Adventure*, p. 49.
37. Frank A. Brown, *Charlotte Brown: A Mother in China* (Nashville: privately printed, 1953), p. 68.

CHAPTER 3: Red Star in the East

1. Visitors to Nanjing today will be interested in visiting the Taiping Museum which gives a Communist interpretation to this historic episode.
2. Later the Russians failed to deliver on these promises.

3. Two members betrayed China and became ministers in the pro-Japanese Nanjing government. One died in prison. One was shot by the KMT. The first chairman was expelled from the party. The others vanished into obscurity.

4. Edgar Snow, *Red Star Over China*, revised and enlarged ed. (New York: Grove Press, Inc. 1968), p. 158.

5. Vera Simone, *China in Revolution* (Greenwich, Conn.: Fawcett Publications, Inc., 1968), p. 170.

6. Harry Schwartz, *China* (New York: Times Books, 1965), p. 57.

7. Theodore H. White, *In Search of History* (New York: Harper & Row, Publishers, 1978), p. 195; cf. Ross Terrill, *Mao* (New York: Harper Colophon Books, 1980), pp. 159ff.

8. Frank A. Brown, *The Last Hundred Days* (Shanghai: pamphlet privately printed, 1949), pp. 8–9, 10.

9. The following sources have been used in this chapter. Fairbank, *U.S. and China*; White, *In Search of History*; John Leighton Stuart, *Fifty Years in China* (New York: Random House, Inc., 1954); Snow, *Red Star Over China*; James C. Thomson, Jr., *While China Faced West: American Reformers in Nationalist China 1928–1937* (Cambridge, Mass.: Harvard University Press, 1969); Harry Schwartz, *China*; Simone, *China in Revolution*; Lucien Bianco, *Origins of the Chinese Revolution, 1915–1949* (Stanford, Calif.: Stanford University Press, 1971); Fairbank and Reischauer, *China*.

CHAPTER 4: A Revolution Is No Dinner Party

1. Simone, *China in Revolution*, p. 174.

2. Jean Chesneaux, *China: The People's Republic, 1949–1976* (New York: Pantheon Books, a Division of Random House, Inc., 1979), p. 9.

3. See K. H. Ting, "A Call for Clarity: Fourteen Points from Christians in the People's Republic of China to Christians Abroad," *China Notes* 19 (Winter 1980–81):146–47, used by permission.

4. The following sources have been used in this analysis: Chesneaux, *China*, pp. 3–35, 173; Fairbank, *U.S. and China*, pp. 358–69; Leslie T. Lyall, *New Spring in China* (Grand Rapids, Mich.: Zondervan Publishing House, 1980), pp. 63–73.

5. Mao Zedong, *Selected Works*, vol. 3 (Beijing: Foreign Language Press, 1967):120.

6. Fairbank, *U.S. and China*, pp. 366–68.

7. Ibid., p. 369.

8. Ibid., pp. 381–83.

9. Chesneaux, *China*, p. 51.

10. Edgar Snow, *The Other Side of the River* (New York: Random House, Inc., 1962), p. 70.

11. Chow Ching-wen, *Ten Years of Storm* (New York: Holt, Rinehart & Winston, 1960), p. 97
12. Fairbank, *U.S. and China*, p. 373–74.
13. Snow, *Other Side of the River*, p. 425.
14. Fairbank, *U.S. and China*, p. 375.
15. Ibid., pp. 377–79. Chesneaux, *China*, pp. 45–50.
16. In the summer and fall of 1949 U.S. policy seemed to be leaning toward recognition of the People's Republic of China. The U.S. left all embassy and consular officials in place after the withdrawal of the KMT to Formosa. A White Paper was published, extremely critical of the Nationalist (KMT) government, and all aid to the Formosa regime was ended. Dr. J. Leighton Stuart, ambassador to China at the time, writes in his memoirs (*Fifty Years in China*, p. 270):

    > Without admitting any mistakes in United States policy, it [the White Paper] tried to place all the blame upon the National Government of China. . . . By implication it announced that the United States support of the National Government and the efforts of the United States toward survival of that government were at an end.
    >
    > Such was the officially declared position of my government in the summer of 1949.

    There is evidence that at an earlier stage in the civil war, the CCP would have been eager to reach a *rapprochement* with the United States. Whether this would have been the case with the war won is an open question.
17. Chesneaux, *China*, p. 65ff.; Fairbank, *U.S. and China*, pp. 399–401.

CHAPTER 5: Christianity and the New China

1. K. H. Ting, "Religious Policy and Theological Reorientation in China," an address delivered to faculty and students of Emmanuel College, University of Toronto, October 1979, p. 4, mimeographed. Published in *China and Ourselves* (Spring 1980), p. 15, used by permission.
2. Mao Tse-tung, *Report of an Investigation into the Peasant Movement in Hunan*, [made in 1927] (Beijing: Foreign Language Press, 1953), p. 45, as quoted in Richard C. Bush, Jr., *Religion in Communist China* (Nashville: Abingdon Press, 1970), p. 30.
3. Mao Tse-tung, "On the Correct Handling of Contradiction Among the People, January 1940," quoted in Simone, *China in Revolution*, p. 472.
4. Roman Catholic statistics are taken from *China and the Churches* (Brussels: Pro Mundi Vita, 1975), p. 39. Protestant statistics are from Kenneth G. Grubb, ed., *World Christian Handbook* (London: World Dominion Press, 1949), p. 249, and (1952), p. 141. *China and the Churches* source was used for Protestant institutions. The baptized Protestant membership is taken from the 1952 edition of the *Handbook* which is said to come from a National Christian Council of China survey conducted in 1950, the latest statistics available.

5. Francis P. Jones, ed., *Documents of the Three-Self Movement* (New York: Division of Foreign Missions, National Council of the Churches of Christ in the U.S.A., 1963), pp. 9–11.
6. Ibid., pp. 15, 15–16, 17–18.
7. ''Y. T. Wu (1893–1979): A Christian of Revolutionary China,'' *China Notes*, 17 (Autumn-Winter 1979–80): 85, used by permission.
8. Jones, *Documents*, p. 4.
9. Ibid., pp. 5, 4, 5.
10. Donald E. MacInnis, *Religious Policy and Practice in Communist China* (New York: The Macmillan Company, 1972), p. 24.
11. Jones, *Documents*, pp. 19, 20; *Church in Communist China*, pp. 51–55; Bush, *Religion in Communist China*, pp. 177, 186.
12. MacInnis, *Religious Policy*, p. 99.
13. Jones, *Documents*, p. 50.
14. Amnesty International, *Political Imprisonment in the People's Republic of China* (1978), p. 153; Jones, *Documents*, p. 99ff.
15. Louis Wei Tsing-sing, ''The Vatican and China: 1949–1974,'' *Christianity and the New China* (South Pasadena, Calif.: William Carey Library, 1976) 2:150. Used by permission.
16. Bush, *Religion in Communist China*, p. 111, used by permission.
17. Ibid., pp. 113–14.
18. *Fides* (September 5, 1964), p. 525, as quoted in ibid., p. 145.
19. Ibid., p. 39.
20. E. H. Hamilton, March 28, 1948, from Suchow; F. A. Brown, July 26, 1948, from Suchow; E. H. Hamilton, March 28, 1949, from Suchow; E. H. Hamilton, July 22, 1948, from Suchow; F. A. Brown, October 25, 1948, from Suchow.
21. Presbyterian Church in the U.S. Board of World Missions, ''A Statement on Policy in relation to Governments, particularly in China today,'' early 1950, p. 2, mimeographed.
22. Creighton Lacy, *Coming Home—to China* (Philadelphia: The Westminster Press, 1978), pp. 32–33.
23. Bush, *Religion in Communist China*, pp. 43–54.
24. *Tian Feng* (May 8, 1951), quoted in Leonard M. Outerbridge, *The Lost Churches of China* (Philadelphia: Westminster Press, 1952), pp. 221–23, as found in Bush, *Religion in Communist China*, p. 45.
25. Louis Wei Tsing-sing, in *Christianity and the New China*, 2:152.
26. Bush, *Religion in Communist China*, p. 47. Frank A. Brown, ''The Last of the Eight Thousand'' (privately printed, 1962), pp. 1, 2.
27. Frank W. Price, ''End of an Era in China Missions,'' *Presbyterian Outlook*, December 8, 1952, p. 5. Used by permission of the publisher, 512 E. Main St., Richmond, Va. 23219.
28. Jones, *Church in Communist China*, p. 107, used by permission; Jones, *Documents*, p. 73.

29. Harold S. Matthews, compiler, "Lessons for the Church from Christian Experience in China," Division of Foreign Missions, National Council of the Churches of Christ in the United States of America, 1951, pp. 15–18, 21–22, mimeographed.

30. Donald MacInnis, "The North American Churches and China, 1949–1981," *International Bulletin of Missionary Research* 5 (April 1981):50.

31. Price, "End of an Era," *Presbyterian Outlook*, p. 5.

CHAPTER 6: The Great Leap Forward

1. Chesneaux, *China*, pp. 72, 73.

2. Ibid., pp. 77–78.

3. Snow, *Other Side of the River*, pp. 418–19.

4. Ibid.

5. Fairbank and Reischauer, *China*, pp. 497–99; Chesneaux, *China*, pp. 99–100.

6. Ibid., p. 111–12.

7. Francis Jones, "Church Life in China Today," *Social Action* 26 (March 1960):24, as quoted in Bush, *Religion in Communist China*, p. 242.

8. Ibid., p. 220.

9. Jones, *Documents*, p. 152.

10. Ibid., pp. 156–67.

11. Bush, *Religion in Communist China*, p. 243.

12. Jones, *Documents*, pp. 183, 184.

13. Jones, *The Church in Communist China*, pp. 153–61.

CHAPTER 7: The Great Proletarian Cultural Revolution

1. Henry Kissinger, "Repartee with Mao," *Time*, March 15, 1982, p. 31, used by permission.

2. "The Gang of Four": *Jiang Qing*, Mao's third wife and former actress; *Wang Hongwen*, a young political leader in Shanghai and former cotton mill worker who became number three in the party hierarchy; *Zhang Chunqiao*, head of the political department of the army; *Yao Wenyuan*, another Shanghai journalist and later editor of the *People's Daily*, in charge of ideology and information.

3. Chesneaux, *China*, p. 157.

4. Song Yu, "A Scene From the Past Yields Hope for China," *New York Times*, August 8, 1981. (c) 1981 by The New York Times Company. Reprinted by permission.

5. Robert G. Orr, *Religion in China* (New York: Friendship Press, 1980), p. 132.

6. George N. Patterson, *Christianity in Communist China* (Waco, Texas: Word Books, 1969), p. 139.

7. "The Handwriting on the Wall," *Current Scene*, May 31, 1967, p. 2, as quoted in Bush, *Religion in Communist China*, p. 257.

8. John Fleming, "Some Glimpses of the Church," *Life and Work*, October 1980, p. 22, used by permission.

9. Bush, *Religion in Communist China*, pp. 343, 344. The New China News Agency bulletin appeared in *China Notes* 5 (April 1967):4.

10. Orr, *Religion in China*, pp. 123, 124.

11. Raymond Fung, "Case Studies from China," *International Review of Mission* 70 (April 1981):16–17, 12, used by permission. Fourteen of these case studies are included in *Households of God on China's Soil* (Geneva: World Council of Churches, 1982).

12. "Peking Indictment Accuses Radicals of Killing 34,000," *New York Times*, November 17, 1980, p. 3.

13. Xi Xuan, "Why Should a Theory Be Discarded?" *Beijing Review* 24 (November 2, 1981):21, used by permission.

14. Xi Xuan, "Had 'Cultural Revolution' Mass Support?" *Beijing Review* 24 (November 23, 1981):20, used by permission.

15. Zhu Yuanshi, "The Causes of the 'Cultural Revolution,'" *Beijing Review* 24 (September 14, 1981):15–18, used by permission.

16. Donald E. MacInnis, "New Man and New Society in People's China," *Christianity and the New China* (South Pasadena, Calif.: William Carey Library, 1976), 1:135–54.

17. Richard Madsen, "The New China and the New Self-Understanding of the Church," ibid., 1:175.

18. "China and the History of Salvation," Report of Workshop IV, ibid., vol. 2, appendix, p. 20.

19. " 'New Man' in China: Myth or Reality?" ibid., 2:45.

20. Ibid., p. 46.

21. Charles West, "Some Theological Reflections on China," *China Notes* 14 (Fall 1976):39, used by permission.

22. *Mao Zedong: Selected Works*, vol. 3, pp. 90ff.

23. Andrew K. H. Hsiao, "The Reawakening of the Church in China," *Ching Feng* 22 (1979):141–42, used by permission.

CHAPTER 8: The Post-Mao Era

1. Terrill, *Mao*, pp. 405–07.

2. Ibid., pp. 414–15, Ross Terrill, ed., *The China Difference* (New York: Harper Colophon Books, Harper & Row, Publishers, Inc., 1979), p. 74, used by permission.

3. Ibid., p. 71.

4. *New York Times*, September 10, 1976. (c) 1976 by The New York Times Company. Reprinted by permission.

5. *Beijing Review* 24 (March 9, 1981).

6. U.S. Department of State, *U.S. Policy Toward China*, July 15, 1971–January 15, 1979 (Washington, D.C.: Office of Public Communication, 1979), p. 45.

7. (c) 1980, 1981 by The New York Times Company. Reprinted by permission.
8. Terrill, *China Difference*, p. 46.
9. "China's Criminal Law and Law of Criminal Procedure," *Beijing Review 23*, (June 9, 1980):17–26.
10. Jerome A. Cohen, "Due Process?" in Terrill, *China Difference*, pp. 242–49.
11. John Fraser, *The Chinese: Portrait of a People* (New York: Summit Books, 1980), pp. 199–271.
12. Harriet Mills, "Literature in Fetters" in Terrill, *China Difference*, pp. 287–304.
13. See Leo A. Orleans, *China's Population Policies and Population Data: Review and Update* (prepared for the Committee on Foreign Affairs, U.S. House of Representatives, by the Library of Congress, 1981).
14. Christopher S. Wren, "China, to Relieve Unemployment, Gives Private Sector More Leeway," *The New York Times*, November 23, 1981, pp. 1, 34. (c) 1981 by The New York Times Company. Reprinted by permission.
15. Fox Butterfield, "Apathy Replaces Marxist Idealism Among Chinese," *The New York Times*, December 30, 1980, p. 1. (c) 1980 by The New York Times Company. Reprinted by permission.
16. Fairbank, *U.S. and China*, p. 415.
17. Butterfield, "Apathy," p. 6.
18. Deng Zhaoming, "The Youth of China Today: An Inquiring Generation," *Information Letter* (The Lutheran World Federation, November 1980, reprinted from *Ching Feng*, 1980, no. 3), used by permission. Also in *China Notes* 19 (Winter 1980–81), p. 154, used by permission.

CHAPTER 9: The Church Alive and Well!

1. Tracy K. Jones, *Occasional Bulletin of Missionary Research*, July 1979, p. 90, as quoted in "Reopening Church Doors in China," *The Christian Century*, January 30, 1980, p. 105.
2. Bulletin of the China Program Committee (NCC/USA) dated May 17, 1982.
3. A translation of the "Open Letter" appears in *China Talk*, 5 (April 1980), supplement.
4. A translation of the Resolution appears in *China Notes* 18 (Fall 1980):141.
5. Hu Liang, "Old Pastor Sun," *China News* 20 (April 1982).
6. National Council of Churches in the U.S.A. Delegation to the People's Republic of China (November 12–30, 1981), report issued Feb. 19, 1982, p. 4, mimeographed. See *China Notes* 20 (Winter 1981–82):193–98.
7. "Problems in Henan: Reports from Itinerant Preachers," *China and the Church Today*, 4:2 (1982), p. 2, used by permission.

8. National Council of Churches in the U.S.A. Delegation to the People's Republic of China (November 12–30, 1981), pp. 5–6.
9. Fox Butterfield, *China: Alive in the Bitter Sea* (New York: Times Books, 1982), pp. 7, 8.
10. Robert Lee and Frank Mar, "Reopening Church Doors in China," *The Christian Century*, January 30, 1980, p. 107.
11. K. H. Ting, *How to Study the Bible* (New York: Friendship Press, 1981).
12. K. H. Ting, "Theological Education in China," *C.C.A. Consultation with Church Leaders from China* (Hong Kong, March 23–26, 1981: Christian Conference of Asia), p. 55.
13. K. H. Ting, "Victims and Sinners," a sermon preached at Riverside Church, New York, New York, September 9, 1979, p. 3, mimeographed.
14. Ibid.
15. "A Message from Chinese Christians," *China News*, October 1981, p. 4.
16. Ting, "Religious Policy and Theological Reorientation in China," *China and Ourselves*, pp. 16–17.
17. *Religion in the People's Republic of China, Documentation* 5 (May 1981): 11.
18. Orr, *Religion in China*, p. 1.

CHAPTER 10: The Meaning of the China Experience

1. W. Stanley Mooneyham, *China: A New Day* (Plainfield, N. J.: Logos International, 1979), p. 187.
2. *China Notes* 12 (Spring 1974):15, 19, 20. A response to Needham and Båstad and Louvain is given by Charles C. West in *China Notes* 14 (Fall 1976) and 15 (Spring 1977).
3. Lyall, *New Spring in China*, p. 244.
4. The statement is printed in *China Notes* 19 (Winter 1980–81): 145–49, and in *Ching Feng*, March 1981.
5. "Joint Presbyterian Statement: Theological Foundations for Ecumenical Cooperation," adopted at Joint Conference, Richmond, Virginia. Approved by Program Agency, UPCUSA, and 121st General Assembly (PCUS). See also "Principles for China Program," adopted by the Division of International Mission, General Assembly Mission Board, PCUS, October 1980. These statements have been used throughout the following discussion on policy.
6. Maryknoll Fathers and Brothers, "The Third Year: A Report on Maryknoll's Response to China" 1982.
7. Lausanne Committee for World Evangelization, *Christian Witness to the Chinese People*, no. 6 in series, Lausanne Occasional Papers, 1980.
8. Christian Conference of Asia, *CCA Consultation with Church Leaders from China* (Hong Kong, 1981).

SELECTED
BIBLIOGRAPHY

BOOKS

Amnesty International. *Political Imprisonment in the People's Republic of China*. 1978.

Bianco, Lucien. *Origins of the Chinese Revolution, 1915–1949*. Stanford, Calif.: Stanford University Press, 1967.

Brown, Frank A. *The Last Hundred Days*. Shanghai: Privately printed, 1949.

_____. *Charlotte Brown: A Mother in China*. Nashville: Privately printed, 1953.

Bullock, Mary Brown. *An American Transplant: The Rockefeller Foundation and Peking Union Medical College*. Berkeley and Los Angeles: University of California Press, 1980.

Bush, Richard C., Jr. *Religion in Communist China*. Nashville: Abingdon Press, 1970.

Butterfield, Fox. *China: Alive in the Bitter Sea*. New York: Times Books, 1982.

Chesneaux, Jean. *China: The People's Republic, 1949–1976*. New York: Pantheon Books, a Division of Random House, Inc., 1979.

Fairbank, John King. *The United States and China*. 4th ed. Cambridge, Mass.: Harvard University Press, 1979.

_____, ed. *The Missionary Enterprise in China and America*. Cambridge, Mass.: Harvard University Press, 1974.

Fairbank, John K. and Reischauer, Edwin O. *China: Tradition and Transformation*. Boston: Houghton Mifflin Company, 1978.

Fraser, John. *The Chinese: Portrait of a People*. New York: Summit Books, 1980.

Hamilton, E. H. *China Diary*. Atlanta: Cross Roads Publications, 1976.

Jones, Francis Price. *The Church in Communist China*. New York: Friendship Press, 1962.

_____, ed. *Documents of the Three-Self Movement*. New York: National Council of Churches of Christ in the U.S.A. Division of Foreign Missions, 1963.

Kauffman, Paul E. *China, The Emerging Challenge: A Christian Perspective*. Grand Rapids, Mich.: Baker Book House, 1982.

Lacy, Creighton. *Coming Home—to China*. Philadelphia: Westminster Press, 1978.

Latourette, Kenneth Scott. *A History of Christian Missions in China*. New York: The Macmillan Company, 1929.

_____ . *A History of the Expansion of Christianity*, Vol. 7, *Advance Through Storm*. New York: Harper & Brothers, Publishers, 1945.

_____ . *The Chinese, Their History and Culture*. 3rd ed. New York: The Macmillan Company, 1961.

Lutheran World Federation/Pro Mundi Vita. *Christianity and the New China*. South Pasadena, Calif.: William Carey Library, 1976.

Lutz, Jessie G. *China and the Christian Colleges, 1850–1950*. Ithaca, N.Y.: Cornell University Press, 1971.

Lyall, Leslie T. *New Spring in China*. Grand Rapids, Mich.: Zondervan Publishing House, 1980.

MacInnis, Donald. *Religious Policy and Practice in Communist China: A Documentary History*. New York: The Macmillan Company, 1972.

Merwin, Wallace C. *Adventure in Unity: The Church of Christ in China*. Grand Rapids, Mich.: William B. Eerdmans Publishing Company, 1974.

Mooneyham, W. Stanley. *China: A New Day*. Plainfield, N.J.: Logos International, 1979.

Neill, Stephen. *Colonialism and Christian Missions*. New York: McGraw-Hill Book Company, 1966.

Orleans, Leo A. *China's Population Policies and Population Data: Review and Update*. Washington, D.C.: Library of Congress, 1981.

Orr, Robert G. *Religion in China*. New York: Friendship Press, 1980.

Pollock, John C. *A Foreign Devil in China: The Story of Dr. L. Nelson Bell*. Grand Rapids/Minneapolis: Zondervan/World Wide Publications, 1971/1972.

Price, P. Frank. *Our China Investment*. Nashville: Executive Committee of Foreign Missions, 1927.

Simone, Vera. *China in Revolution: History, Documents and Analyses*. Greenwich, Conn.: Fawcett Publications, Inc., 1968.

Snow, Edgar. *The Other Side of the River*. New York: Random House Inc., 1961.

_____ . *Red Star Over China*. Rev. and enlarged ed. New York: Grove Press Inc., 1968.

Spence, Jonathan. *To Change China*. Boston: Little, Brown and Company, 1969.

Stuart, John Leighton. *Fifty Years in China*. New York: Random House Inc., 1954.

Terrill, Ross, ed. *The China Difference: A Portrait of Life Today Inside the Country of One Billion*. New York: Harper Colophon Books, 1979.

_____ . *Mao*. New York: Harper Colophon Books, 1980.

Thomson, James C., Jr. *While China Faced West*. Cambridge, Mass.: Harvard University Press, 1969.

PERIODICALS AND NEWSLETTERS

Beijing Review. China Publications Centre, P.O. Box 399, Beijing, China. (Weekly. General news and comments, published by an agency of the People's Republic of China).

China and the Church Today. Chinese Church Research Center, Hong Kong. Distributed in U.S. by Christian National, 1470 N. Fourth St., San Jose, Calif. 95112. (Bimonthly publication edited by Jonathan Chao).

China and Ourselves. Canada China Programme, Canadian Council of Churches, Suite 201, 40 St. Clair Ave. East, Toronto, Canada M4T 1M9. (Newsletter published quarterly).

China Bulletin. Centre for Chinese Studies, Pontifical Urban University, Via Urbano, VIII, 16, Rome 00165, Italy. (News of the Roman Catholic Church in China).

China News. General Assembly Mission Board, Presbyterian Church in the U.S., 341 Ponce de Leon Ave., N.E., Atlanta, Ga. 30365. (Newsletter published quarterly).

China Notes. Division of Overseas Ministries, NCC/USA, Room 616, 475 Riverside Dr., New York, N.Y. 10115. (Scholarly articles, news reports. Published quarterly).

China Update. Program Agency, United Presbyterian Church, Room 1144, 475 Riverside Dr., New York, N.Y. 10115. (Occasional newsletter).

China Talk. China Liaison Office, World Division, Board of Global Ministries, The United Methodist Church, 2 Man Wan Road, C-17, Kowloon, Hong Kong. (Newsletter, published quarterly).

Ching Feng. Christian Study Center, Tao Fong Shan Ecumenical Centre, Tao Fong Shan Rd., P.O. Box 33, Shatin, N.T. Hong Kong. (Scholarly quarterly journal on religion in China).

Information Letter. Marxism and China Study Project, Lutheran World Federation, P.O. Box 66, 150 Rte. de Ferney, 1211 Geneva 20, Switzerland. (Quarterly journal).

Religion in the People's Republic of China. China Study Project, 6, Ashley Gardens, Rusthall, Tunbridge Wells, Kent TN4 8TY, England. (Documentation, translation of significant articles and news accounts, published quarterly).

Tripod. Holy Spirit Study Centre, 6 Welfare Road, Aberdeen, Hong Kong. (Bimonthly publication in English and Chinese by Roman Catholic society).

INDEX